P9-CQF-436

THE COMPLETE IDIOT'S GUIDE® TO

Managing Your Money

Fourth Edition

*by Robert K. Heady and Christy Heady
with Hugo Ottolenghi*

ALPHA

A member of Penguin Group (USA) Inc.

ALPHA BOOKS

Published by the Penguin Group

Penguin Group (USA) Inc., 375 Hudson Street, New York, New York 10014, U.S.A.

Penguin Group (Canada), 10 Alcorn Avenue, Toronto, Ontario, Canada M4V 3B2 (a division of Pearson Penguin Canada Inc.)

Penguin Books Ltd, 80 Strand, London WC2R 0RL, England

Penguin Ireland, 25 St Stephen's Green, Dublin 2, Ireland (a division of Penguin Books Ltd)

Penguin Group (Australia), 250 Camberwell Road, Camberwell, Victoria 3124, Australia (a division of Pearson Australia Group Pty Ltd)

Penguin Books India Pvt Ltd, 11 Community Centre, Panchsheel Park, New Delhi—110 017, India

Penguin Group (NZ), cnr Airborne and Rosedale Roads, Albany, Auckland 1310, New Zealand (a division of Pearson New Zealand Ltd)

Penguin Books (South Africa) (Pty) Ltd, 24 Sturdee Avenue, Rosebank, Johannesburg 2196, South Africa

Penguin Books Ltd, Registered Offices: 80 Strand, London WC2R 0RL, England

International Standard Book Number: 1-59257-298-7
Library of Congress Catalog Card Number: 2004115918

07 06 05   8 7 6 5 4 3 2 1

Interpretation of the printing code: The rightmost number of the first series of numbers is the year of the book's printing; the rightmost number of the second series of numbers is the number of the book's printing. For example, a printing code of 05-1 shows that the first printing occurred in 2005.

Printed in the United States of America

Note: This publication contains the opinions and ideas of its authors. It is intended to provide helpful and informative material on the subject matter covered. It is sold with the understanding that the authors and publisher are not engaged in rendering professional services in the book. If the reader requires personal assistance or advice, a competent professional should be consulted.

The authors and publisher specifically disclaim any responsibility for any liability, loss, or risk, personal or otherwise, which is incurred as a consequence, directly or indirectly, of the use and application of any of the contents of this book.

Most Alpha books are available at special quantity discounts for bulk purchases for sales promotions, premiums, fundraising, or educational use. Special books, or book excerpts, can also be created to fit specific needs.

For details, write: Special Markets, Alpha Books, 375 Hudson Street, New York, NY 10014.

Publisher: *Marie Butler-Knight*
Product Manager: *Phil Kitchel*
Senior Managing Editor: *Jennifer Bowles*
Senior Acquisitions Editor: *Renee Wilmeth*
Development Editor: *Ginny Bess Munroe*
Senior Production Editor: *Billy Fields*

Copy Editor: *Tiffany Almond*
Cartoonist: *Richard King*
Cover/Book Designer: *Trina Wurst*
Indexer: *Angie Bess*
Layout: *Angela Calvert*
Proofreading: *Mary Hunt*

This book is forever dedicated to Robyn-Jo Brooke Heady, beloved sister of Christy Heady and daughter of Robert K. Heady, who died December 12, 1997 at age 28.

Christy shared her first lessons in reading and writing with Robyn-Jo when they were little girls and loves and misses her more than any words she reads or writes can ever express. Through her spirit, Robyn-Jo's grace continues to show the true meaning of life, education, and purpose.

Her father especially remembers Robyn-Jo's positive-spirit, personality, wonderful sense of humor, the laughter, her deep artistic perception, a devotion to healthy mind, body and soul, her love of little children, and a spiritual evolution and understanding that eventually eclipsed us all. You shall always and forever be our blessed angel in our hearts, our souls, and our minds.

We also invite our readers to remember Robyn-Jo through a nonprofit charity near where she lived, the Children's Health Program, Inc., PO Box 30, Great Barrington, MA 01230. CHP's program helps low-income families by providing transportation to doctors, nursing and pediatrics aid, food baskets, a clothing exchange, children's health insurance, and even collecting needed items through church groups.

3575

Contents at a Glance

Contents

Foreword

To hear some people tell it, managing your personal finances is like performing your own brain transplant.

Of course, the people who say this are brokers and financial planners, and they make their living handling other people's finances. Handling your money takes some brains, but it isn't brain surgery. Most people can handle their own affairs.

Unfortunately, the best salesmen on the planet dwell on Wall Street. They could sell flea condominiums to dogs. And if you want to figure out whether you're being served or sold, you need to supplement your own good sense with knowledge. This doesn't mean that you have to spend the next 10 weekends memorizing the Securities Act of 1933. But it does mean that you should know where to look up questions like:

- Why would anyone put an Individual Retirement Account in a variable annuity? Answer: To get a big, fat commission. Annuities and IRAs are both tax-deferred. Putting an IRA in an annuity doesn't make your account any less taxable. It's only a smart move for a shady broker.

- Will my nice banker give me free checking? Sure. And your statements will be delivered by Leprechaun Express, too. Seriously, if you look hard enough, there will be a string attached to your free checking account, and the other end will be tied to your wallet.

- Is $1 million in life insurance enough for a 20-year-old male nonsmoker? Unless he has small children and a big mortgage, the 20-year-old probably shouldn't have any life insurance at all. Insurance protects your dependents— and if you don't have dependents, you don't need much life insurance.

- Is there any way to slice half a point or more from my mortgage rate? Sure. Make sure your credit is solid, look for special offers from the bank that has your checking account—and shop around.

This is where *The Complete Idiot's Guide to Managing Your Money, Fourth Edition*, comes in. Sooner or later, you'll need to know which to believe: Your own common sense or those folks in suits who try to sell you things. This book can help you figure out what to look for in a checking account, a mortgage, or your own 401(k).

Even better, you'll get up-to-date information on new tax breaks and pitfalls. Thinking of donating your old car to charity? You might be better off selling it yourself and donating the proceeds. Saving to send Junior to Juliard? Save yourself some taxes with a state-sponsored 529 college savings plan.

A guide, of course, is only as good as the people who write it. You're in good hands here. Robert Heady has spanked three generations of bankers for excessive fees and bogus advertising claims. And he's showed thousands of consumers how to shop for the highest-yielding bank CDs and lowest-rate loans.

Christy Heady is the best-selling author of *The Complete Idiot's Guide to Making Money on Wall Street*.

And Hugo Ottolenghi is the executive editor for the *Daily Business Review* in West Palm Beach, Florida.

With this team at your side, you won't have to worry about getting sold a bunch of investments and services you don't need. You might feel a little sorry for those poor salesmen, though.

John Waggoner
USA Today
McLean, VA

Introduction

No matter who you are—an ordinary family that's head-over-heels in debt, a senior citizen confused by investment choices, or a college freshman starting to build your credit—there's something valuable here for you. You need practical, down-to-earth help written in plain English.

So we're putting the language of money into basic, everyday street language instead of the commonly seen financial mumbo-jumbo that only a Wharton School graduate can figure out. We want *you* to understand it and to make heads or tails of your personal financial situation.

This is a book written from the trenches, not from an ivory tower. We don't live there, and neither do you. The world of personal finance has become too darn complicated for the average Joe and Jane to understand. The proliferation of high-rate, big-fee credit cards has shoved millions of consumers into horrible debt, teetering on bankruptcy. Scams have taken over where only legitimate credit counseling used to help. The country has been invaded by thieves and crooks who rip off your Social Security number and other personal identification, and run up huge bills in your name. Meanwhile, the glut of financial information keeps growing faster than a barrel full of sea monkeys.

So we are doing this for *you*. We have been inside banks and brokerage firms, insurance companies, mortgage companies, car dealerships, and the credit bureaus. We've answered thousands of questions from consumers who desperately needed help. We'll show you, chapter by chapter, the most important basics you should know. And, we'll arm you with tips that will immediately strengthen your personal money situation.

Sure the cards are stacked against you because of the complex way the money world works. But by learning the inside tricks that you'll never read in a newspaper or magazine article (or hear in a 20-second sound bite on TV), you're going to come out dollars ahead. And what else? We're going to take the "I" out of "Idiot" for you by telling it like it is. Just the bare facts, and some tips and tricks to help you along the way.

This book will help you …

- Avoid costly mistakes and save a bundle when shopping.

- Know the key questions to ask before signing up for anything—credit cards, mortgages, auto loans, checking, savings accounts, you name it.

- Earn more money when you invest and understand how to handle market fluctuations.

- Save more money when you borrow, whether it's for a car, a house, or school tuition.

- Cut through the muck before you get trapped in the wrong financial deal.

- Find your way out of debt before creditors ruin your life for years.

- Rebuild your credit if it's been injured.

- Protect your personal financial privacy.

- Find online resources to help you get the information you need *quicker*.

But most important, this book will help you *relax* with better financial peace of mind.

If you are looking for a no-nonsense book that will finally help you manage your hard-earned cash, you've come to the right place. Here's how it works:

Part 1, "Getting the Most Bang For Your Buck," establishes some basic information about getting started in managing your money. This section will help you learn how to make that first big decision—getting started! Plus you'll learn insider secrets about getting out of debt—and staying out. You will also learn how to make effective personal financial planning decisions by learning what to read, what to watch, and who to believe. And get secrets to simple investment strategies and learn how to ride out market fluctuations from the investment pros.

Part 2, "The ABCs of Really Smart Banking," is a section that will surprise many of you with its revealing banking information on how banks make tons of money from your accounts, whether you have $25 or $2,500 sitting in them. But it doesn't stop there. You'll learn why credit unions may be the best place to park your cash, find out the secrets of CD shopping (and who pays the top rate), and how to spot the key warning signals when it's time to move your account.

Part 3, "Maximizing Your Dollar Whether You Borrow or Save It," is for everyone who has ever tried to get credit (and didn't), or attempted to cut credit card costs but didn't know how. Additionally you'll learn how to protect your credit record and find secrets to car shopping and mortgage shopping. Plus the biggest tip of all in the credit world—how credit agencies really "score" your application—and what you can do to make the grade.

Part 4, " Taking Care of You and Your Financial Future," provides specific information to help you get the most from your paycheck. And in the event of a layoff, strategies are given to help you protect yourself financially. You'll learn how to get the most from your 401(k) and how governmental changes and market fluctuations have affected this retirement vehicle. You'll also get helpful and motivating insurance, tax, and retirement strategies to secure a path to financial freedom.

Extras

We know you don't own a secret decoder ring to help you in the confusing world of financial planning—and you shouldn't have to. This book has a few easy-to-recognize signposts that offer tips, tricks, and tidbits to help you along the way. Look for these elements in this book that will point you in the right direction.

Watch Your Wallet
Sometimes making the wrong decision when you manage your money can add up to trouble—and a lot of bucks. Take heed of these warnings to help save yourself some dough.

Fiscal Facts
The world of financial planning is often confusing, mysterious, and just plain puzzling. Not anymore. These boxes will put you in the know, by deciphering in plain English what financial buzzwords mean.

The Money Line
These boxes provide relevant information so you know what you're doing as you trek further on your path in the money world.

The Road to Riches
There's a lot of bad advice being offered in the financial world. In these boxes we'll offer you tried and true tips for making the most of your assets.

Acknowledgments

We sincerely acknowledge the following people, companies, and organizations who provided research and assistance for this book: Dan Pederson, of Savings Bond Informer; National Foundation for Consumer Credit; National Association of Automobile Dealers; bankrate.com; American Bankruptcy Institute; Mortgage Bankers Association; Veribanc, Inc. and its founder and research director, Warren Heller; Department of the Treasury, the Federal Reserve, and Federal Trade Commission; American Bankers Association; and Privacy Rights Clearinghouse.

Robert K. Heady also acknowledges his research assistant, Linda J. Anderson; John Lee, former finance editor of *The New York Times*, who discovered Bank Rate Monitor's value and put its interest rates on the map for millions of readers; Mark Mathes, former editor of Tribune Media Services who marketed Mr. Heady's personal finance column to U.S. newspapers; and, above all, the memory of the late James Vincent O'Gara, executive editor of *Advertising Age*. In the beginning, long ago, Mr. O'Gara and his editor, the late John Crichton, the father of author and director Michael Crichton, made this book possible by taking a chance on a wet-behind-the-ears reporter and teaching him, by example, the meaning of accuracy, integrity, independence, and objectivity that make for good journalism. Lastly, we acknowledge that special, rare breed of print and broadcast journalist across America—the reporter who digs for and delivers the kind of urgent, current information that the little guy can use to really help improve himself or herself in his or her personal finances in life.

Christy Heady has been honored to spend time with so many brilliant and creative minds in her career and would like to acknowledge the companies of Morningstar, Bloomberg, the American Bankers Association, AARP, the Congressional Budget Office, Edelman Public Relations, the Consumer Bankers Association, Bankrate.com, Hewitt & Associates, Hulbert Financial Digest, AOL, Microsoft, Consumers Digest, Chicago Tribune and CNN.

Trademarks

Part 1

Getting the Most Bang for Your Buck

Consumers face more complex and intimidating financial issues than ever before. There is a record increase in the number of get-out-of-debt scams, and identity thieves prey upon the innocent. Congress has enacted several laws that affect 401(k) accounts and your income and estate taxes. Events on Wall Street have impacted investors to often question whether or not they should even be in or out of the market.

This section reveals how to arm yourself with the right information, a disciplined perspective, and keen observation skills, so that the language of money and investing *can* be simple in creating a solid financial future.

Chapter 1

Financial Planning Made Simple

In This Chapter

♦ Discovering how everything in your life revolves around the mighty dollar and what you can do to benefit from it

♦ Why sweating the small stuff may foil your financial plan

♦ Learning the simple ways to motivate yourself to wealth

Put away your wallets because getting started in financial planning has nothing to do with money.

Life, and especially your financial one, boils down to one simple thing: making decisions. Take a moment and think about all the choices you make on a daily basis: what to wear to work, which project to work on, whether or not to put in overtime, what to make for dinner, or what to read the kids before bedtime. Now think about all the "money" decisions you make. Don't think you have many? Guess again.

Everything you do in life involves your wallet—from taking family vacations to bringing your lunch to work to seeing a new movie to getting married or having a baby. There's a cost to living, and that's why we're here to help. This chapter introduces you to basic money management principles and gets you started on your own personal financial path.

Time Is Money

A lot of people spend a whole lot of time worrying about the small stuff—a little extra yield on their savings, a few dollars less in mortgage payments, slightly higher returns, and slightly lower commissions.

While these actions may line your pockets with a few more dollars, managing your money does not have to be this complicated, worrisome, or tedious. If you spend all your time focusing on fractions of a point, you may lose sight of the big picture.

Instead, make the right financial choices in life on a handful of major decisions rather than focus on the little details. Over the long haul, this will help alleviate any stresses about future financial security. After all, time and money are both precious commodities—why wrap yourself up in minutiae?

Achieving success is really the result of making good decisions, and making good financial decisions is based on a long-term focus. That's all. But don't let fear of making mistakes intimidate you. Even a bad decision results in a learning experience.

Even if you decide not to make a decision, you are making a decision to remain stuck; or, even worse, someone else will make it for you. Do you really want someone else making the decisions about building your financial security?

If you find yourself in a financial limbo, ask yourself the following questions:

- ◆ Why am I putting it off?

- ◆ What do I have to fear by not doing it?

- ◆ What type of pleasure do I receive by indulging in procrastination?

- ◆ What will it cost me if I don't do it now?

Take this information and apply it to the following simple steps toward getting started in financial planning:

- ◆ **Make the decision to *make a decision*.** Sounds silly,? Making a decision is often the hardest step. But if you break it up into simple little steps, you'll find decision-making easy and far from intimidating. Just say "okay," and you've done it.

◆ **Make decisions often.** Let's use an analogy. Every year without fail, during the first week of January, memberships and the line for the treadmill at your local health club increase. The New Year's diet is in full swing, and every gym rat in the nation has made the decision to do something about his or her health, image, and weight. But this doesn't last very long because these people only make a decision once; they don't decide on a daily basis "I'm going to go to the gym today." If these people made decisions often, perhaps they would reach their fitness goals. If you make the decision to create a personal financial plan, are you going to stick with it just once?

◆ **Be flexible.** You don't live in just a black-and-white environment. You need to allow for some gray areas, which often disguise themselves as mistakes. Although mistakes come from making the wrong decision, they create experiences you can learn from, and that might help you make the *right* decision next time!

◆ **Enjoy making decisions.** Making decisions can be a blast! For example, if your mistakes help you learn to make better decisions, and your next decision turns out to be a great opportunity, wouldn't you have enjoyed making that decision? You'll enjoy it more when you create more great opportunities!

◆ **Create short-term and long-term goals.** Many people plan for their financial futures by working so hard today that by the time they reach their long-term goals, they're exhausted and have forgotten why they worked so hard to get there. Long-term goals are important, but so are short-term goals. Creating short-term goals will give you a sense of accomplishment or satisfaction.

◆ **Do your homework.** It'll be more fun than studying for that geometry test you prepared so hard for in high school! Doing your homework in the money world will allow you to make your money work as hard for you as you do for it.

Begin shaping your financial destiny today by making simple decisions such as setting goals and doing your homework.

The Money Line

In 2003, just 71 percent of people polled said they saved for retirement, down from 75 percent in 2000, according to a report from the Employee Benefit Research Institute, the American Savings Education Council and Matthew Greenwald & Associates. Even when the economy is weak, it's important to keep your financial goals in mind—and invest for your future!

Procrastination Does Not Pay Off

Now that you've made the decision to create a plan, your next step is to understand why getting (and staying) in control of your finances is imperative for you and your family. Scare tactics do not work. Better-informed decisions come from knowledge that we intend to give you in this book. For example, did you know that most high school seniors do not have access to basic personal finance classes? According to a 2002 national survey by the JumpStart Coalition for Personal Financial Literacy, most high school seniors do not have basic personal finance knowledge. Handling credit cards, paying taxes, and even saving for the future are concepts that our future generation in the United States cannot grasp and will, therefore, have trouble managing all of their lives.

But this financial illiteracy doesn't stop at high school students. The Coalition also suggests that many adults lack the skills and knowledge to make sound financial decisions, too.

We've seen it happen with the 1.6 million bankruptcies filed in 2003 and filings in the first quarter of 2004 were higher than in any first quarter since the U.S. Bankruptcy Courts started keeping statistics. The increase in bounced check fees bank account holders are paying each year for not having sufficient funds in their checking accounts are also ghastly.

But there is a bigger problem. We are living in a society of information overload. Where do you go to get good reliable advice? How can you determine which professional to use—your Aunt Marge's broker, your cousin the life insurance agent, the Internet, the bookstore, or free seminars sponsored by a local brokerage firm? We cannot tell you exactly what to do, but we can help by sharing our knowledge and insight of the world of personal finance.

Ignore the Statistics and Stick to Your Plan

The next time you're in a bookstore, look at the first chapter of five other financial planning books. Statistics abound, such as:

♦ The average life expectancy at birth today is 80 years for women and 75 years for men, according to the U.S. Administration on Aging.

♦ The average American spends 18 years in retirement, notes the U.S. Department of Labor.

♦ Less than 40 percent of the U.S. workforce has no company pension plan; only 11 percent of workers in small companies with less than 25 employees are offered one.

♦ By the year 2010 it will cost more than $120,000 to get a four-year education at a public university.

Although this information is correct, are these scare tactics working? Do they make you get off your duff and start managing your finances? After hearing from thousands of Americans who still have money problems, we didn't think so.

Me, Retire? Never!

We all make excuses to get out of managing our money: no time, not enough extra cash, or retirement is far, far away. One big reason we avoid planning is because of fear. Many people think that if they take a bare-bones look at their finances, they'll have to accept that they're in debt or don't have enough money to pay for their child's college education. Next they may think that they'll wind up old and impoverished. Goodness, why worry about that now? Others simply think managing their money is B-O-R-I-N-G. Save for the future? D-U-L-L. No instant gratification. Why put that extra $100 bucks in a savings account to earn about fifteen cents?

Why have we developed such a nonchalant attitude toward the future, anyway? During our childhood, many of our parents gave us a piggy bank and a few pennies and taught us to "save for a rainy day." However, few explained *why* we were supposed to do it.

Planning for your future doesn't mean you're expecting something terrible to happen. Buying a life insurance policy doesn't mean you're going to die, does it? Much of your fear will quickly disappear once you realize how easy it is to make your savings grow for retirement. It's never too early to learn—or to start. The whole idea of managing your money is to save a dollar here and there, and then take that dollar and build it into two.

Setting Goals to Help Get You There

It's time to take the next step in the lessons of financial planning by setting some goals.

If your goal is to win $100 million in the lottery you can forget it. The odds are something like 80-million-to-1 to collect all that dough. And while Las Vegas is a destination hot spot of choice for Americans, don't bet the family farm on those one-arm-bandits for the quickest way to wealth. Cha-ching, it ain't gonna happen.

Winning the lottery or collecting thousands of quarters on a lucky slot machine are possible ways to create instant wealth, but *playing* these games is not. And even if you *do* win the lottery, you'll have enough financial planning burdens to make you go berserk. The tax bite alone is enough to give you a migraine. So let's talk about setting some more practical goals.

Setting goals isn't difficult. It's figuring out how to reach them that gives you a run for your money (no pun intended). You know that you need short-term and long-term goals, so take out two pieces of paper and let's get started. On the first piece of paper, write down any short-term goals you want to accomplish. Short-term goals usually have a time frame of three years or less. These may include, but are not limited to, creating an emergency fund and paying off your credit cards and student loans.

The Money Line

Do you understand the key elements of investing? According to the Investment Company Institute (ICI), approximately 53 million U.S. households own mutual funds. ICI states that mutual fund owners are seasoned investors with long-term investment goals.

Divide the next piece of paper into four time frames: 5 years, 10 years, 20 years, and 30 years. Write down what you want to accomplish in each. For example, in 5 years you may want to buy a house. Ten years from now you may want to take a vacation to Europe. Twenty years from now you'll have to send the kids to college. And 30 years from now you plan to retire.

On both pieces of paper, write down how much money each goal is going to require. Be honest with yourself; the amount of money you'll need to meet each goal may surprise you. You may have already allocated some of the money that you'll need; if so, good for you. Whether you have or not, most of you are going to have to learn how to manage your money to be able to achieve your goals.

Now total up how much money you're going to need to meet all of your goals. The numbers are astounding, aren't they? But that doesn't mean you have to change your goals. In fact, you can keep those goals and accomplish many of them by following the concepts in this book! This book is designed specifically to help you meet the short-term and long-term goals that you have set for yourself and for your family—and save money in the process.

All it takes is a little knowledge and self-discipline. Most folks say that knowledge is power, but we disagree. Knowledge is power if—and only if—you put it to use!

The Least You Need to Know

- ◆ The first step toward managing your money is making the decision to start planning for your financial future.

- ◆ Fear of making mistakes shouldn't keep you from making more decisions. Think of a mistake as something that will help you make a better decision next time.

- ◆ It's also important to write down your short-term and long-term financial goals and how much money you need to achieve them. Then, read the rest of this book for information on how to reach those goals.

- ◆ Good financial planning requires you to do your homework, and you've already learned the first part of homework and research: you are studying this book!

2

Managing the Debt Monster

In This Chapter

- ◆ Deciding whether or not you really need a credit card
- ◆ Understanding credit card terms
- ◆ Tips on getting—and remaining—out of debt
- ◆ Filing for bankruptcy the last resort

You're not alone. The average American is carrying more debt than ever and is in trouble. Little wonder: He or she has 6.5 credit cards on average, while the average household carries a total of 14.3 cards. That translates to severe financial pain for families that are overextended, and it even breaks up families. Bankruptcies are on their way to a new record, as the national balance on credit cards, auto loans, and other consumer loans tops $1.8 trillion. Plus, mortgage debt is another $6.7 trillion.

Bill collectors are having a field day, trying to collect more than $2 billion of overdue debts this year, vs. only $73 billion in 1990.

Chances are you carry a credit card. From Platinum to Gold to plain vanilla plastic, consumers are having a love affair with credit cards. It's powerful, but like Marvel Comics superheroes, you must decide whether to use your plastic for good or evil.

Knowing your credit limit is the key to staying out of financial trouble and filing for bankruptcy, as 1.6 million Americans did in 2003. Well, superhero, your mission, should you choose to accept it, is to decide how much debt you can afford simply by *creating a spending plan and sticking with it.* Remember, in order to save for the future, you must pay for the past. This chapter will help you discover top-notch tips for reducing your debt, ways to measure your financial health, and strategies to reduce your expenses.

Determining If You Are in Debt Trouble

To determine whether you are having problems managing your debts, indicate whether the following statements are true or false:

_____ You use credit cards where you used to pay cash, such as at the grocery store and restaurants.

_____ You have depleted your savings—or worse, used cash advances from credit cards—to pay old, past-due bills.

_____ You have lost track of how much you owe.

_____ You put off paying your telephone and utility bills in order to pay high credit card bills and other debts.

_____ You regularly receive letters from collection agencies.

If most of your answers are true, you have a debt problem. Read on to find out what you can do about it.

Fiscal Facts _____

About 40 percent of credit card holders pay off their balances each month, but the folks with balances are letting them pile up more and more. The average credit card debt per household was $9,205 in 2003, up about $1,400 from 2000 and more than double the $3,646 figure in 1993. The figure for those who revolve their balances has shot up from $4,230 in 1995 to $5,610 in 2000, according to the Credit Research Center at Georgetown University.

Measuring Your Financial Health

Checking in with a financial doctor rates right up there with having your teeth cleaned. It's painful (and the taste of rubber gloves is not pleasant), but if you want pearly whites, you've got to go through the torture.

In managing your money, your goal is to get out of debt, right? Once you meet that goal, what do you want to accomplish financially? Do you want to:

Buy a car? (See Chapter 14)

Buy a house? (See Chapter 15)

Insure your health and wealth? (See Chapter 20)

Retire comfortably … or even rich? (See Chapter 22)

Before you reach those goals, you must figure out how bad the problem is. To do that, you must do three things to measure your financial health. First, compare your assets to your liabilities by completing the worksheets in this chapter. Second, determine what your expenses are. Third, create a budget and trim the financial fat.

Developing a Budget

Unless we light a firecracker and place it under your chair, the only way we can motivate you to keep track of where your money goes is to scare you. So here goes.

If you don't track where all your money goes, what will happen over time? You'll wind up in the cold month of January wondering how the heck you spent $2,769 on Christmas presents for the family, you'll know your banker better than you'd like because you'll probably bounce checks all over town as a result of mismanaging your finances, and someday you'll live on a monthly Social Security benefit check of $455 (that's it!) because you piddled all your money down the drain when you were young. Does that scare you? It should!

"Budget" is a scary word; it's too constrictive for some folks. What you need to understand, however, is that everybody needs to have a daily record of where all his or her money goes. Accept it and motivate yourself toward the feeling of accomplishment. The true reward of having a budget is something all Americans want: control. Imagine having control over *all* of your finances. Once you do, you can reach your dreams and financial goals even faster!

What Do You Spend Money On?

First, you need to figure out where your money goes. Create your expense categories and fill in the amount you spend on a monthly basis for each category. To get a more accurate picture, you may want to check all your receipts from the past several months. Your categories can include, but are not limited to …

- **Auto expenses.** Car payments, auto insurance, maintenance, gas (save your receipts!)

- **Clothing expenses.** Overgarments, undergarments (all your garments), shoes, and socks

- **Dental expenses.** Periodic cleaning, dental work, oral surgery, and so on (whatever isn't covered by insurance)

- **Dining expenses.** Restaurant expenses, even if it's for fast food

- **Entertainment.** Movies, plays, concerts, the zoo, whatever

- **Education.** School supplies, tuition bills, and so on

- **Gifts.** Birthdays, holidays, weddings, Bar Mitzvahs

- **Groceries.** Separate into two categories—food and drugstore items—if possible

- **Home-based business.** This should be broken down into smaller categories, including equipment, supplies, taxes, and so on

- **Household expenses.** Items necessary for the upkeep of the house (paint, lawn maintenance, and so on)

- **Household items.** Plants, furniture, dog (just kidding)

- **Insurance.** Separate your policies into categories, such as life, health, and homeowner's

- **Rent or Mortgage.** Your biggest expense (probably); important for tax return purposes

- **Taxes.** Real estate and income taxes paid (don't forget income tax refunds as a source of income)

- **Utilities.** Phone, electric, gas, water

- **Vacations.** Hotel stays, airplane tickets, new luggage, meals, sightseeing tours, souvenirs

There's probably more, but this list gets you started on the right foot.

How Do You Trim the Fat?

From the expense categories you create, pick a few expenses you can live without … for good. If the children are stuck on seeing a movie every Friday night, rent a video instead of going to the show.

As another example, set yourself a limit, such as to eat out only twice a month. After your rent or mortgage, the largest component of "where your money goes" is probably dining out. That nasty habit costs the average American around $5,000 a year. You could pay for Junior's tuition at some state universities with that dough. Keep the following tips in mind to help reduce some of your expenses and save money in the long run:

- ◆ Establish an emergency fund that equals about three month's worth of basic expenses. Then you won't have to turn to plastic for every unexpected bill.

- ◆ Lower your tax withholding. Why give the IRS a free loan while you're paying an average of 16 percent interest on your debts?

- ◆ Increase the deductibles on your automobile insurance. Even bumping up a $100 deductible to a $500 deductible could lower your premiums on comprehensive insurance by 25 or 30 percent a year.

Adding Up the Pluses and Minuses

There's no greater mess to clean up than unorganized, mismanaged financial affairs, which is why so many people stick to organizing their financial records about as long as they do a New Year's diet. Determining your assets (what you own) and liabilities (what you owe) gives you a clear picture of what you're worth.

Begin with organized records. These may include, but are not limited to, checkbook registers, recent bank and brokerage statements, copies of your income tax returns (keep these for at least three years), and paycheck stubs. Forget the shoebox theory; keep these and all of your financial records in a well-organized file cabinet for your personal finances.

Once you have all of your information intact, you can fill in the first of three worksheets (taken from *The Complete Idiot's Guide to Making Money on Wall Street, Third Edition*), which is a financial property assets worksheet that includes all the money in your bank accounts, brokerage accounts, and other investments.

Financial Property	Date Purchased	How Much Did You Pay?	Today's Date	What's It Worth Today?
Bonds (type)				
Bond mutual funds (type)				
Certificate of deposit				
Checking accounts				
Coin collections				
Money market accounts				
Pensions & profit sharing plans				
Savings accounts				
Savings bonds				
Stocks				
Stock mutual funds				
Treasury securities				
Other				
Total Financial Property				

A financial property assets worksheet.

Next, by completing your personal property worksheet—which is also an asset—you'll assess how much your physical property is worth. For example, your home is probably the largest (in physical size and financial size) asset you own. Write in when you bought your home, what the price was, and how much it's worth today. If you're not sure—and want to make more than an educated guess—contact an appraiser to be certain.

Personal Property	Date Purchased	How Much Did You Pay?	What's It Worth Today?
Appliances (washer & dryer, etc.)			
Automobiles			
Boats, campers			
Computers			
Furniture			
Fur coats			
Home			
Home furnishings			
—curtains			
—rugs			
—tableware (glasses, dishes)			
—blankets			
—lamps			
—silverware			
Jewelry			
Paintings			
Stereos			
Televisions			
Miscellaneous			
Total Personal Property			

A personal property assets worksheet.

Finally, calculate your liabilities—all the things you owe. The main thrust of this worksheet deals with loans, such as auto loans, student loans, and your mortgage, but remember to put down ALL of your outstanding credit card balances. Your liabilities show how much debt you carry.

What You Owe	To Whom	Interest Rate %	When Is It Due?	How Much Do You Owe?
Bills, bills, bills				
—electric				
—gas				
—retail stores				
—telephone				
—other				
Loans to family				
Loans to friends				
Automobile loans				
Bank loans				
Credit cards				
—credit card #1				
—credit card #2				
—credit card #3				
Furniture loans				
Student loans				
Mortgage				
Home equity loans				
Miscellaneous				
Total Liabilities				

A liabilities worksheet.

Two kinds of debt traditionally exist, although we're going to add a third: good debt, bad debt, and you-just-have-to-pay-it-to-live debt. This last type of debt would include electric bills, gas bills, and telephone bills. More often, they're referred to as expenses, although they are "owed" debts.

The single largest component of good debt would be your mortgage loan because your mortgage is for your house, which is an asset. You must report your mortgage loan on your liabilities worksheet.

Watch Your Wallet _____

Stay away from anyone who promises to help you with your debt trouble for a "small fee." These people work for places known as *recovery houses,* and they're preying on everyone—especially the elderly. Contact the Federal Trade Commission (FTC), 202-326-3650, to report any wrongdoing. One of the best organizations to help you manage your debt is your local Consumer Credit Counseling Service office. But, the only person who can get you *out* of debt is *you!*

Bad debt makes up the bulk of the liabilities worksheet. It is what siphons most consumers' paychecks.

Americans have long been battling a war to reduce bad debt. Bad debt is what you still owe on your car, your credit cards, your unsecured personal loans, and even your student loans. Obviously, the name of the game is to have as few "bad-debt" liabilities as possible and to increase your wealth substantially.

Understanding Why Sticking to the Minimum Can Hurt

Paying only your minimum card balance will result in a much larger debt than your original purchases were worth. Let's say your balance on an 18 percent credit card is $3,000 and that each month you make the minimum payment of 2 percent on the balance, with a $10 minimum. It will take you 36 years and two months to pay off the card. The total interest you'll pay on the $3,000 will be a staggering $7,587.

Here's another example. Suppose you buy a leather couch for $1,500 and put it on your MasterCard. You can't pay the entire bill this month, but that's no problem! You only have to make a minimum payment to remain in the issuer's good graces. However, as other debts start adding up, you only meet the minimum payment for the next year or so, or at least until you get out of the hole with your other bills.

Then, one year later, a friend drops her cigarette on the couch. Now it's torched, and you need a new couch. You get rid of the couch, but you're still paying for it on your credit card. "Surely I've paid it off by now," you think. Well, think again.

How long does it take to pay off such a debt? If you *only* meet the minimum monthly payments, and your credit card has an average annual percentage rate (APR) of, let's say, 19.8 percent interest, it will take you more than 22 years to pay off that $1,500 couch. This is a classic example of how bad debt can work against you. The more debt you are burdened with, the longer it will take to dig yourself out of a hole. Therefore, your first priority should be to eliminate nonproductive debt.

Controlling Your Debt Once and for All

Instead of screaming "Arrrrgh!" and thinking about putting your head in an oven, start planning now to wipe out the debt monster as quickly and painlessly as possible. You can do it. It'll just take a little patience, gumption, and discipline on your part.

The alternative is worse, we assure you.

Don't feel guilty—you're not alone. Consumers charged more than $100 billion on their credit cards during the last holiday season, or 23 percent more than the year before. They used their major cards—Visa, MasterCard, and American Express—more than 1.5 billion times, or *two million times per hour*, according to CardWeb.com.

Right now 78 percent of Americans are in debt. They owe an average of $8,500 on their credit cards, and pay a typical interest rate of 18 percent, which works out to a nontax-deductible cost of $1,530 a year. Total credit card debt outstanding in 2003 was $683.4 billion, up from $568.5 billion in 2000, and nearly triple the $232 billion in 1993. So much for how you got into this mess. How are you going to get out of it? Follow these steps:

Step 1   Take control of your personal finances instead of letting them control you. The biggest mistake people make is that they wait too long to act, according to CCCS in Atlanta. Total up your bills so you can realize the scope of the problem and work through it quickly. As the problem gets larger, the steps become more difficult. Just trying to reshuffle your debts and saying to yourself, "I'll do better next year," won't do it.

Step 2   Track expenditures. The average Joe hasn't the foggiest notion of how much he spends each month and where it goes. At the beginning of the month, track your family's spending for 30 days. Note how everything from coffee and cigarettes to meals out drain your cash flow.

Step 3 Trim spending. Credit cards are the most critical place to start. Consumers carry as many as nine credit cards, so you should review them all—one by one—and write down the amount owed and the interest rate. Cut up all but one or two cards with the lowest rate and switch the other balances to them. Contact your creditors for reduced rates and lower fees. (You'll be surprised at how many will agree. Even if they say no, you've lost nothing.)

Step 4 Because your debt, especially those rip-off credit card finance charges. NEVER pay those robber barons only the monthly minimum amount due. Increase your monthly payment to get out of debt faster—by adding even only $10 or $20 more each month to each credit card. It'll make a sizeable dent in what you owe. If you don't do that, it could add years to the time it'll take to pay off the cards.

Step 5 Mark your calendar for recurring expenses such as auto tags and insurance, phone, Internet, birthdays, and anniversaries.

Step 6 Don't borrow any more money, period. Debt consolidation hustlers tempt you with home equity loans and lines of credit to pay your bills, but although your monthly payments will decrease, chances are that in two years you'll be more deeply in hock. History shows that most people return to their bad credit card habits after getting such loans. Also, suppose you wind up losing your home because of a home equity loan?

Step 7 Hands off your 401(k). You'll be paying penalties to steal from your future and end up paying taxes on your retirement money twice instead of once.

Step 8 Steer clear of fly-by-night "debt counselors" working out of their basement, who may charge you $500 or $600 up front for what you can get for free, or as little as $10, from Consumer Credit Counseling Services at 1-800-388-CCCS.

Step 9 Be patient. You can't get out of debt overnight, and a casual approach to the problem won't work. We're told that it may take a person 20 repetitions to change a habit, starting with the way they think and then the way they act.

It's worth it.

Using Your Savings

Before you use your savings to pay off the budgetary fat, determine your debt-to-equity ratio. It's simple. Answer this: How much of your paycheck goes to pay your debts? The smaller the percent of your monthly pay allocated to credit cards (as well as other loans and debt), the better.

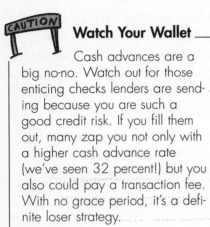

Watch Your Wallet

Cash advances are a big no-no. Watch out for those enticing checks lenders are sending because you are such a good credit risk. If you fill them out, many zap you not only with a higher cash advance rate (we've seen 32 percent!) but you also could pay a transaction fee. With no grace period, it's a definite loser strategy.

The rule of thumb is this: *Current assets should be approximately two times greater than current liabilities.* Keep in mind, then, that your monthly debt should not exceed 36 percent of your monthly income.

So lump together all of your assets (what you own) and your liabilities (what you owe). If you have socked away a ton of cash in your bank account and you have revolving debt on your credit cards, it's time to pay those off. Why not use your savings? It'll be in your best interest because you won't be paying any more than you have to!

Getting Outside Help

If you're having trouble implementing these strategies to resolve your debt crisis, it may be time to seek outside help. Obtain your local Consumer Credit Counseling Services office number at 1-800-388-CCCS. Another available resource is the National Center for Financial Education, P.O. Box 34070, San Diego, CA 92163, which provides support services for cardholders who need assistance managing credit.

To prevent getting scammed by any fly-by-night outfit, ask the company these questions up front:

♦ Are they a member of either the National Foundation for Credit Counseling (301-589-5600), or the Association of Consumer Credit Counseling Agencies (703-934-6118)? If they are, you've probably eliminated 90 percent of the scams.

♦ Do they belong to the local Chamber of Commerce? If not, watch out.

♦ Is the agency a nonprofit corporation? The best ones are. Call your state's department of corporations.

♦ Does it have a listed phone number? Can you visit their offices? If not, stay away.

♦ Will they provide you with a complete list of fees and charges in black and white, including initial fee, plus fees for application, processing, and maintenance? If they won't give you one, walk!

Battling Debt's Biggest Culprit

Americans have been able to *buy now and pay later* since the evolution of the plastic credit card. But this plastic has caused millions of Americans a problem: With enticing credit card offers promising generous credit lines, it has become impossible to climb out of debt.

That's why you should treat your credit card as a tool, not a cure-all. The rule of thumb: If you don't have the cash, don't use the card!

A credit card should be used as a convenience for emergencies; it is nothing more than a tool. Having a credit card or two is a necessity, but becoming laden with $20,000 in credit card debt is a burden and a very common one. Typical clients of Credit Counseling Centers of America are dual-income families with high incomes. However, they have fallen into the habit of overspending; they have no savings and up to $20,000 in credit card debt.

Becoming a Debt-Buster

If there's one rule you remember from this chapter, let it be this one: *Pay your bills on time.* Almost all lenders will look at whether you're current or late with your bills. Most lenders are lenient, and will tolerate a maximum of 30 days late. If you are currently behind on your accounts, catch up before you apply. This is how you can make the grade to get credit. You have to fit the profile of the people who pay their bills on time.

Filing for B-A-N-K-R-U-P-T-C-Y

Financial troubles have led millions of Americans to file for bankruptcy, often using the process as an "alternative." How wrong. Filing for bankruptcy is the *last resort* to your financial woes, not a choice. If you are in debt and *need* to file, however, there are pitfalls you can avoid.

Most often, you don't have to file unless it's necessary; declaring yourself bankrupt is not an alternative, it's a necessary solution. One bankruptcy attorney in Chicago claims that he has yet to see a situation where the filing was not required.

If you are having difficulty meeting your rent or mortgage payments, you're completely extended beyond your credit limit, the collection agencies are uncooperative, and you need more than a credit counselor, you may need to file *Chapter 7* or a *Chapter 13*.

The first thing you should do is seek the advice of an attorney, who will guide you into which bankruptcy proceeding you should file, according to your personal debt situation.

Here's how they work. When you file either Chapter 7 or Chapter 13, you are issued a restraining order by the court, which will protect you from all further proceedings against you until all previous debts are cleared. The restraining order includes protection against wage garnishing, creditor harassment, and foreclosures without a court order.

Fiscal Facts

There are two basic ways of filing for personal bankruptcy. **Chapter 7** gets rid of all debts (except some taxes and maybe alimony payments). **Chapter 13** allows people with steady income to pay off bills over a 36-to-60-month period.

Chapter 7 is used mainly if you have unsecured debts. For example, if you have furniture or appliances as unpaid collateral, you can return these without paying for them. But, if you want to keep these things, you might be allowed a reaffirmation agreement with your creditors. Also, attorneys' fees are set so you can establish an installment plan.

Chapter 13, a wage-earner plan, brings immediate relief by letting you pay your bills rather than letting them go (unlike Chapter 7). You are eligible for an extension plan that allows you to pay back all your bills within a certain period of time, usually 36 to 60 months. Costs incurred by the attorney are added to the total of your other debts and are paid through your payments to the court trustee.

But be warned: in 2001, Congress passed a tough, new bankruptcy law that makes it harder to file a Chapter 7 to wipe out all debts. In effect, it submits consumers to credit counseling and a "means test," where a judge decides whether he or she can afford to pay off up to 25 percent of their debts. If they can, they must file a Chapter 13 instead. The bright side to filing for bankruptcy is immediate relief, particularly with a Chapter 7. The dark side is a black mark that remains on your credit record to haunt you for 10 years.

But all is not lost. It is still possible to potentially establish a "new" credit record and obtain a secured credit card, by depositing some funds up front. Some companies that offer secured credit cards have guidelines that are a bit more flexible. If you've filed for bankruptcy and need information about applying for a secured credit card, turn to Chapter 13, for details on how to do it.

Filing bankruptcy does not have to be a cataclysmic event in your life. You do have options, and depending on your circumstances, you can rebuild your financial future!

The Least You Need to Know

◆ Credit cards are the biggest reason people fall deeply into debt and can even lead to bankruptcy.

◆ To measure your financial health, add up the worth of everything you own and compare it to the cost of everything you owe. A financially healthy person should have twice as much in assets as he or she has in liabilities.

◆ To reduce debt, use some of your assets (such as your savings) and reduce expenses so that you can pay more toward the debt.

◆ For help dealing with your debt problems, contact your local credit counseling office through the national number, 1-800-388-CCCS. But, be careful who you do business with.

◆ To keep your spending on track, you need to establish a budget.

◆ Filing for bankruptcy is not an "alternative" or a "choice." It should be looked on as a last resort.

Chapter 3

Everyday Money Language You Should Know

In This Chapter

- ◆ Why you can't believe "interest rate experts"
- ◆ Which key interest rates and market indicators give you a clue to the future
- ◆ What you should read and watch to keep up in the money world
- ◆ How to map your personal finance game plan
- ◆ Which investments are safe and which ones are not

It's the toughest question: How in heck can you make your money grow in such a complicated environment? Who can possibly understand all the investment gibberish and advice that comes sailing your way from banks, brokers, financial planners, the government, and news media? It's enough to drive you bonkers. The stock markets and the world economy are all over page one, but millions of average people are just as baffled, mixed up, and frustrated by the money world as you are. They're panicked about Social Security one day going down the drain, and are afraid they'll have to work well into their seventies just to survive.

The person with $10,000 in cash to stash somewhere doesn't have a guaranteed clue of where to put it, or for how long, or at what interest rate, or at what annual return to expect. There are enough confusing options to make his or her head spin. Yet he or she doesn't know whom to trust, whether his or her broker is talking straight, or how safe their bank is versus parking their money in a mutual fund. Expert advice is hard to come by, and even top economic gurus goof when they predict whether mortgage rates are going up or down. This chapter is the first step toward carving your way through the money world without going out of your gourd.

Your first lesson is to realize that economic "experts" have a lousy batting average when it comes to reading a crystal ball. On the same day, one oracle swears that the Dow Jones average will go through the roof in the next couple of years, while another pundit across town warns you to dump all your stocks now because the world is teetering on the edge of a depression. Hey, they both can't be right—in fact, they can both be wrong! Instead of listening to all their malarkey—that's mostly what it is—you've got to do some common-sense thinking on your own.

Most people try to keep up by scanning the newspaper business pages, watching money shows on TV, subscribing to a financial newsletter or two, or chatting with their banker, broker, or financial planner. They perk up when a neighbor tells them she has a friend who has a friend who knows somebody named Marvin the Broker who's been helping all the wealthy widows in town make a bundle on their investments. Well, guess how smart Marvin is at giving advice when the economy crashes in Bangladesh? Not very smart, we assure you. Plus people are finally learning that when some brokers or analysts tout a stock, they're doing it for their *commission*, not because they really believe in their own advice.

On your own, you have to sponge up every tip you can, sort through whatever vital information you come across, and research the heck out of whatever you're considering investing your money in. But, there are a few factors you can watch (featured later in this chapter) that will gain you an edge, starting now. Just remember that things are changing faster and faster. The knowledge you go to bed with tonight may be outdated by the time you wake up tomorrow.

Watch the Rates: They're the Big Clue!

More than anything, follow the market indicators and key interest rates. They're the main clue to how the economy is performing and where the markets are going. Here's what to keep your eye on:

◆ **Leading economic indicators.** Issued monthly, these appear in stories in newspapers and on TV. They are a composite index of 10 economic indicators designed to predict economic activity six to nine months in advance. They include things like jobless claims, manufacturers' new orders for consumer goods and materials, housing starts, the level of the Standard & Poor's Index, and consumer confidence reports. The key is to track the trends over six months or more to get a feel for where the economy is heading.

◆ **U.S. interest rates.** Especially the Federal Reserve's "discount rate" and "federal funds rate." The Fed is the master controller of all rates. It can raise rates to cool off the economy by making borrowing more expensive, which, in turn, cuts into corporate profits and reduces stock prices.

◆ **The health—or weakness—of foreign economies.** These economies have a direct influence on your investments, and maybe even your job. It used to be that this country's stock market only reacted to domestic indicators such as jobs, incomes, prices, retail sales, and the gross national product. Now it's a whole new ball game. When a foreign economy plunges, like what happened with the Asian tech wreck of third quarter 2000, the U.S. stock market takes a dive and vice-versa.

Typically when the value of foreign countries' currencies tumble, many U.S. investors pull their money out of those regions. From there on, it has a domino effect. Because U.S. companies can no longer sell as many goods in those lands, it hurts the companies' profits—and drives down their stock prices. Wall Street isn't dumb. When it sees such a scenario shaping up, possibly even affecting Europe and Latin America as well, it starts selling off those stocks and the Dow falls like a rock.

◆ **The banks' "prime rate."** When the Fed changes its rates, the banks immediately chime in by raising or lowering their prime rate by the same margin. The prime affects what banks charge their corporate customers to borrow money, thus affecting their profits. The prime also influences the rates you earn on bank CDs, and what you pay on most credit cards, home equity loans and lines of credit, and auto loans. If the prime goes up by $1/2$ percent, so will the cost of your variable-rate credit card. The Fed's action also affects Treasury bill rates that can determine the interest you pay on an adjustable-rate mortgage.

◆ **The U.S. inflation rate.** This is the most critical thing the Fed pays attention to. If it suspects consumer prices and other inflationary signals are in the wind, it will hike its key rates by $1/4$ or $1/2$ percent to stave off the threat. Conversely, the Fed may try to stimulate the economy by lowering rates if it believes the economy is weak.

◆ **Banks' long-term CD yields.** This is the most unscientific indicator of all, but we've used it to accurately predict a general U.S. rate rise, or drop, in advance. Keep your eye on big banks' five-year CDs. If the institution believes rates will be higher in the months ahead, it may increase long-term CD yields faster than those on short-term accounts, such as six months or one year. The reason is that it's cheaper for them to capture five-year CD business by paying an above-market rate now, than by paying an even higher rate down the road.

Do these tips carry over to your stock and mutual fund investing? Yes, indeed. The stock market is super-sensitive to interest rates for the reasons we have just given. Historically, when rates have gone down, stock prices have generally gone up; when rates have risen, stock prices have dropped. But not always. When interest rates and the rate of inflation remained extremely low between 2001 and 2004, many Wall Street investors saw their investments tank. Why? The economy was officially in a recession from March to November 2001, and in the dumps much longer than that. The Fed was cutting rates while companies were cutting jobs, all in an effort to avoid severe financial troubles. Everyone suffered—CD and stock market investors. In 2004, it looked like both rates and the stock market were headed up as the economy's prospects improved.

Watch Your Wallet

If you think an expert who puts out a newsletter has inside knowledge of a major rate move, forget it. The highway is littered with their bad guesses, and the real problem is, no one keeps track of how awfully wrong those guys have been with their predictions. The honest truth is that some so-called economic wizards and gurus who report on the financial world have had a terrible batting average when it comes to predicting anything. To find out which ones do, consult *Hulbert Financial Digest*, the definitive guide to financial newsletters, which is offered through CBS MarketWatch.com.

And the problem can get huge. News reporters often pick up wrong predictions from the "experts," then pass them along to you. For example, a TV financial reporter may warn that "higher rates are around the corner, according to Baxter Busterman at XYZ Financial Corporation, and this will affect your mortgage payments and what you pay on credit cards." Busterman may be all wet. You're better off checking out and comparing several different news sources—especially the in-depth business pages of leading newspapers. These will give you a better, more balanced view of what's happening.

Know Where to Go for All the Good Stuff

You've already learned that the "experts," who try to guide you through the money world, don't carry a crystal ball. Some people in the media don't really know their way, either. Even if some of them did, you couldn't learn everything you need to know from a 20-second sound bite, could you?

So where can you go? Here's a rundown of just a few of the different sources of information available to you—and what you should be looking for from each one when you do your homework.

Newsworthy Newsletters

There are hundreds and hundreds of newsletters around, eagerly gobbled up by millions of novices and professional investors. *All* those little journals can't be right, can they?

No, not all of them can. Many simply give their opinions and theories without backing them up with good, solid data. Others make a killing by preaching gloom and doom, scaring the pants off readers in hopes they'll want to be better prepared before the world ends. All too often, the publishers who create these newsletters are self-serving—churning out their publications with one hand, and taking your money to manage your investment portfolio with the other. That is downright unethical and deceptive. You want to get your information only from people who do not have a hand in your pocket. It's called independent journalism, and it's the best kind.

Don't waste your time or money on every single newsletter out there. Your subscription bill alone could be thousands of dollars, even before you invested one red cent. And who says the information is any good? Instead zero in on respected sources who know what they're talking about and have the best track record of picking good investments, giving good advice, and providing the facts and figures to back it all up.

One way to cut through the muck is to follow *The Hulbert Financial Digest*, 1-888-485-2378. This is the newsletter of newsletters! For a special rate of $59, you can get 12 monthly issues of the *Digest* (regular price $135), an introductory booklet (regularly $15), a newsletter directory (regularly $20), and long-term performance ratings back 20 years (regularly $30). The *Digest* covers newsletter recommendations and performance based on the following time periods: 1 year, 3 years, 5 years, 8 years, 10 years, and 15 years.

Trying to track down the latest information in the banking industry? Need help locating an out-of-state bank that pays the highest interest rates on its CDs? Log on to www.bankrate.com to learn the highest CD rates in the country. You will also get all the latest national and local rates and averages on CDs, Money Market Accounts, mortgages, credit cards, and auto and home equity loans.

If you want thorough updates about the mutual fund industry, look into Sheldon Jacobs' *No-Load Fund Investor* or *Morningstar Fund Investor*. Both publications focus on performance information and highlight current events in the mutual fund industry. The *No-Load Fund Investor*, (1-800-252-2042), which tracks 996 no-load funds, is published 12 times a year (regular subscription $139, $129 on the web) and comes with *The Fund Family Directory* (regularly $10). Sheldon Jacobs' website is www. sheldonjacobs.com. *Morningstar Fund Investor*, (1-800-735-0700), is $89 for a one-year subscription.

There's been an explosion of helpful personal finance information on the Internet in the past couple of years. These sites will definitely help you manage your money in every way, from a dinky checking account to cutting your credit card debt and planning for retirement:

- **www.msn.com** (and then click on "money") has all the latest personal finance information.

- **www.CNN.com** keeps you posted on everything from Dow Jones averages to clearly-written articles on all phases of personal finance.

- **www.bankrate.com** is an information-loaded website filled with the latest bank savings and loan rates, plus helpful, up-to-the-minute articles on personal finance.

- **www.Bloomberg.com** is the Internet presence for *Bloomberg Personal Finance* magazine, one of America's best-known providers of electronic market data and business news.

- **www.smartmoney.com** is the site for the personal finance magazine of the same name.

- **www.Cardtrak.com** is where to find the best low-rate credit cards of all types—Standard, Gold, you-name-it—including cards with no annual fee.

Fast *Internet* Calculators That Do Your Figuring for You

Want to know whether you should refinance your mortgage now, and how much you'll save? Whether you should lease or buy your next car? Or how long it will take you to pay off your credit card or home equity loan?

Run, do not walk, to use the fantastic (and easy) financial calculators on the Internet. Several website operators offer these super-simple calculators that enable you to figure anything in a jiffy. All you do, on a mortgage loan, for example, is go to www.interest.com and punch in your interest rates and points from different lenders, the amount you're borrowing, and how often you'll be making payments—and bingo—you get all your answers! This is a great way to try several "what-if" scenarios to learn which deal is best for your pocketbook. You'll see it all, including full amortization schedules on your loans; your costs month by month; and over all the years of your loans, how much you've paid against the principal and interest, and how much you still owe. Check out these online financial calculators:

- **http://mortgage.interest.com/content/calculators/index.asp** is the website for Mortgage Market Information Services, is a great tool for new home buyers and refinancers.

- **http://www.bloomberg.com/analysis/calculators/mortgage.html**. Bloomberg's mortgage calculators will tell you how much you can afford to borrow, your monthly payment, the benefits of prepaying your loan, and more.

- **http://www.fmcalcs.com/tools-tcc/fanniemae/calculator** tells you how much house you can afford, whether now's a good time to refinance, the net cost, the amount you'll save.

The Boob Tube

Here's a quick rundown of the financial programs on television that report the latest financial market news and business industry changes. By learning the information provided in this book, you'll be able to determine how the stories and reports on these TV programs affect your wallet.

- **CNN's *Moneyline*,** which airs Monday through Friday at 7:00 P.M. EST, is packed with nationwide and worldwide coverage of breaking business news, financial market stories, and straightforward economic reports.

- ***Nightly Business Report*** is a daily TV program that airs on PBS stations at 6:30 P.M. EST. Veteran financial journalist Paul Kangas covers the action in the stock market and interviews many investment experts. A sister program of *NBR*, called *Morning Business Report*, airs daily at 6:00 A.M. EST.

- ***CNBC*** is angled more toward the sophisticated investor. It covers the financial markets and business news round-the-clock. During the trading day, several stock market tickers crawl at the bottom of the screen. The channel offers many half-hour programs that deal with specific investments, such as mutual funds, real estate, and technology stocks.

◆ *Wall Street Journal Report* airs every Sunday morning (viewing times and channels vary nationwide). This program—considered the television version of the daily newspaper, *The Wall Street Journal*—covers the key financial events of the week and interviews experts in the financial and business fields.

Reading All the Fine Print

One of the most consumer-friendly newspapers is *USA Today*, which offers a "Money" section. This section not only covers the most urgent stories of the day about the financial markets, but also gives information about the nation's top business happenings—and many personal finance stories that affect *you*.

Here's a list of others you may want to take a look at:

◆ *Money Magazine,* (1-800-633-9970), is a monthly publication that broadly covers areas of personal finance and money management, ranging from investment articles to feature stories. This long-established magazine also carries a special section on where to find high-yield CDs and good deals on credit cards.

◆ *Smart Money,* (1-800-444-4204), is a monthly magazine that also reports on a wide scope of personal finance matters. Its investigative articles show which investments will earn the reader top interest, which ones won't, and why. www.smartmoney.com.

◆ **Kiplinger's** *Personal Finance,* (1-800-544-0155), is also a monthly publication geared to the individual's personal financial needs. Articles have an educational tone and cover everything from financial planning to stocks and bonds and other investments. www.kiplinger.com.

◆ *The Wall Street Journal,* (1-800-568-7625), is one of the most powerful daily business newspapers available. You learn about "Who's Who" and "What's What" in Wall Street. It covers virtually every type of financial market—nationwide and worldwide—and reports world events that have an impact on your money. It's most famous for its "C-section," which lists the critically acclaimed column "Heard on the Street," a great place to find out today what's going on tomorrow. Also, if there's a new trend in CDs, stocks, or bond investing, odds are that *Journal's* ace reporters will cover it. www.wsj.com.

◆ *Business Week,* (1-800-635-1200, magazine; 1-888-878-5151, website), gives readers no-holds-barred articles and reports about companies and specific company profiles. Additional stories include performance information, business strategies, personal investing, economic reports, and Wall Street's latest news. www.businessweek.com.

◆ *Investor's Business Daily* is a daily financial newspaper that has become another relevant source for the inside scoop on national and worldwide business and financial matters. www.investors.com. You can e-mail them directly at custcare@investors.com with any customer-related service questions.

Learn How to Understand the Mumbo Jumbo

If someone were to pull you off the street and ask you to explain the difference between *rate* and *yield*, what would you say? No need to feel at a loss for words anymore. After you learn what these terms mean, not only will you be able to tell what the difference is between rate and yield, but you could probably educate your banker or broker about the methods of compounding, too.

A rate is what you earn on a CD or savings account before compounding (don't worry—that's defined here, too), or the interest you are charged on a loan.

A yield is the interest you earn after the savings rate has been compounded.

Compounding simply means more interest being added to the interest you've already earned.

APY stands for Annual Percentage Yield. It's the total amount of interest you earn on an account in exactly one year.

APR stands for Annual Percentage Rate. Usually associated with loans, the APR is a complex mathematical formula that includes other charges on the loan, in addition to the interest rate.

An index is a well-known benchmark, such as the prime rate used by a financial institution to set its interest rates. The rate you earn or pay will move up or down according to changes in the index.

> **The Road to Riches**
>
> If you are a conservative investor, keep in mind that CD investments at credit unions pay more than CD accounts at banks or thrifts. Credit unions also charge a lot less on personal loans, such as new cars and credit cards.

After tracking interest rates and bank, stock, bond, and mutual fund accounts for years—and answering thousands of questions from troubled average Joes and Janes like yourself—we've uncovered some of the basic concepts you need to know to fight your way through the money world.

Determine What Kind of Investor You Are

You do have a personal financial game plan, don't you? You should have a fairly good idea of what your cash position and costs might be in the early and distant future. (If you need a good review, go back to Chapter 2.) Ask yourself this question: What does that picture look like today, next month, or next year? Get a pencil and jot it down. How much have you set aside for investing? What are your short-term and long-term debts? What is your likely income over the next couple of years? Your job position? Your age? Your health?

It doesn't stop there. How much will you need to live comfortably when you retire? Are you living off an inheritance left to you by a rich uncle, or are you scraping along with monthly checks from investments that are your lifeline? Are you saving for a little cottage by the sea? Will Junior need beaucoup extra bucks if he decides to go for his Master's degree? How much will you need beyond your Social Security and 401(k) plan? What are you going to do about unforeseen medical bills and other emergencies?

Estimate how much extra money you have to invest, how much more you're shooting for, and when you'll need it. This rule applies whether you're out to make just a few hundred bucks or are wheeling and dealing in the seven figures. Your number of investment choices is mind-boggling. So, before you set out on your safari with machete in hand, go into a quiet corner and have an honest little chat with yourself to determine what kind of investor you are.

The Money Line

During the Great Depression, when the banks closed, consider this fact:

No one ever lost a dime in a federally insured bank, thrift, or credit union for up to the $100,000 insurance limit.

Uncle Sam Offers the Best Safety Net

As you'll see in Chapter 9, deposits at banks, thrifts, and credit unions are backed by the full faith and credit of the federal government, up to $100,000 per person including principal and interest at the same institution. You can, however, achieve more than $100,000 in deposit coverage by having accounts at several financial institutions.

That also takes into account the late 1980s, when hundreds of sick outfits went belly-up. Today, institutions have rebounded like you wouldn't believe, and they're making record profits. So you can toss aside whatever outdated fears you might still hold. And if you're wondering just how safe Treasury securities are, they're also backed by the full faith and credit of the U.S. government.

How Long Can You Be Without the Money?

This is a critical decision lots of people skip over. If you're tempted to succumb to the razzle-dazzle of a stockbroker's pitch or some super-high rate in a bank ad, before you plunk down your cash, remember this: You might need the money sooner than you think.

If you need your cash six months or a year down the road for an emergency or something else you hadn't planned for, what are you going to do? What if the investment rate picture and other financial factors change and you want to move your money to a higher-earning instrument? What do you do then? If you withdraw your funds early, you'll probably be charged a stiff penalty.

Answering all of these questions helps you figure out what type of *liquidity* you are looking for in an investment. The following table shows how each investment product is ranked, not only by risk, but also by liquidity—and if there are any penalties for cashing in early!

Fiscal Facts

A **liquid** account means that you may withdraw your money from the account at any time without paying a penalty. For example, there's no penalty when you take any of your funds out of a bank Money Market Account, but there is a penalty if you withdraw money from a bank CD account (see Chapters 9 and 10). The CD account is not as liquid as the Money Market Account.

Liquidity in the Money Jungle

Investment Type	How Quickly Can I Get My Money?	Penalties?
Least Risky		
Federally insured:		
Savings accounts	Immediately	No
Checking accounts	Immediately	No
CDs	At maturity	*

continues

Liquidity in the Money Jungle   (continued)

Investment Type	How Quickly Can I Get My Money?	Penalties?
Treasury bills	Five days after selling or wait until maturity	No
U.S. Gov't. money funds	Next day	No

Small to Moderate Risk

Savings bonds	Six months	Loss of interest
Money Market mutual funds	Next day	No
U.S. Gov't. securities	Five days after selling or wait until maturity	No
U.S. Federal Agency bond funds	Next day	No

Moderate to Slightly Higher Risk

Mutual funds	Next day	No
Municipal bonds	Five days after selling or wait until maturity	No

Risky

Blue-chip stocks	Three days after selling	No
Closed-end mutual funds	Three days after selling	No
Small cap stock mutual funds	Next day	No
Small cap stocks	Three days after selling	No
Corporate bonds	Five days after selling or wait until maturity	No
Convertible bond funds	Next day	No

Very Risky

Futures/commodities	Depends on contract	Varies
Options	Next day	Varies
Gold	Varies	N/A
Sector funds	Next day	No
Junk bonds	Five days after selling	No

* If you liquidate your CD before maturity, you face an early withdrawal penalty of up to six months' worth of interest, and an IRS penalty.

Ask the Right Questions—Get the Right Answers!

Failing to ask the right questions is one of the biggest and most common mistakes. It often separates the winners from the losers in investing. The time to pin down your banker, broker, or even your financial planner, is *before* you sign on the dotted line, not afterward. That sounds simple enough, right? Of course. Except very few people know which questions to ask! It's an art in itself, but you can do it.

On bank accounts, study the key questions in the chapters in Part 3. These cover buying CDs and basic savings accounts, opening a checking account, and figuring out which fees to avoid.

Never—repeat, never—take the word of the average teller or account representative at a bank. They are honest and well-meaning folks, but often they haven't been informed about the bank's latest interest rates or other changes in bank policies. Always ask to speak to an officer.

How bad can it get? One day when we were surveying bank CD rates in a Florida city, 10 different employees at 5 different bank branches gave us 12 different interest rates on the same account! Believe us, checking and double-checking your information always pays off. As they taught us in journalism school, "If your mother tells you she loves you, check it out."

If you're still confused by all the rates, yields, and gibberish, use the best machete of all. Ask the bank one simple question: "If I give you my money today, how much will I have in my account at the end of one year—*in dollars and cents, not percent*—after subtracting all fees and charges?" It works like a charm, and you'll probably see the bank rep's face turn 12 shades of purple. But, don't stop there. Ask the same type of question when you borrow: "How much will my total cost of the loan be in dollars?"

If you're dealing with a full-service broker, tell him that you want discounts on your commissions. Ask him if he will meet with you every three months to review your account. Most brokers do business only by phone, rarely face-to-face.

Ask them the same question: "How many dollars will I have at the end of the year?" It may be difficult to pinpoint an answer because the financial markets fluctuate quite a bit, but if you can nail down the track record and performance history of this broker, you're ahead of the ballgame. Home run!

Lastly, make sure you watch those hidden fees. At first glance, it looks like there are only two big patches of trees in the jungle:

1. The money you put in

2. The money you take out

Not so. There's something else lurking out there. Hidden among the jungle's branches and vines are a million fees and charges that can whittle down your cash—without you even noticing it! The best way to protect yourself is to shop the fees at several outfits. You'll be amazed at the differences. For example, if you don't generate at least $100 in commissions at Smith Barney Shearson, your account will get slapped with a $50 inactivity fee.

Watch Your Wallet

Before you sign any document, ask for a copy of the bank's, or broker's, complete fee schedule. Take it home and study it. When you go back, ask for an explanation of every conceivable charge you could get hit with in the type of account you're opening. Just by following these tips alone, you'll probably get back many times your small investment in this book!

The Least You Need to Know

◆ Take any investment advice you get—whether it's from a neighbor, the paper, or a TV financial "expert"—with a grain of salt. Analysts and brokers do not have great track records in predicting where the market will go.

◆ Keep your eye on the Leading Economic Indicators and key interest rates. They're a big influence on the stock market, bank rates, and the general economy.

◆ Step one is to always know what your broad financial goals are, how much money you can play around with, and how much risk you can handle in case the market drops.

◆ Don't be afraid to ask your banker or broker questions, especially if you don't understand something. Make sure you're aware of all the fees that could be involved when you do business with them.

Chapter 4

Secrets to Simple Investment Strategies

In This Chapter

- ◆ Determining what type of investor you are
- ◆ Deciphering the pros and cons to investing in stocks, bonds, and mutual funds
- ◆ Learning how to harness the tremendous power of Wall Street to meet your needs

There is no doubt that a good, solid investment plan builds wealth. Yet the financial markets are often compared to a casino as billion-dollar fortunes have been created and lost overnight.

What's an investor to do?

If your goal is to become an instant millionaire, consider applying as a contestant for any of the latest reality TV shows. Making money the old-fashioned way—spending less and saving and investing more—works. Follow the annual returns of S&P 500, one of the financial markets major indices, over the past eighty years and you will find the trend is relentlessly upward. If in 1929 you'd invested $100 in these stocks, you'd be sitting on more than $175,000 today, assuming you reinvested all the dividends.

Investing in the financial markets all boils down to this. It's a bet that corporate profits will rise. Based on the historical evidence, it's a pretty good wager. This chapter explains the basic investment strategies and helps you learn what type of investor you are.

Creating Your Investment Profile

If you don't chart a clear course in your financial affairs, you'll face rough seas ahead. So ahoy mates—time to create your personal investment profile. Keeping it simple, you can figure out your profile based on your risk tolerance, your return needs, your time horizon, and your tax exposure.

To assess your risk tolerance, ask yourself how much you can afford to lose. This factor is extremely important because of the severe consequences of taking on too much risk. If you understand what your risk tolerance is, you won't have to press the panic button because you've got yourself covered. The rule of thumb: If your investments are keeping you up at night, then sell. No investment, especially a risky one, is worth losing sleep over.

To determine what kind of investor you are, picture the worst-case scenario. Ask yourself how much you can afford to lose in a one-year time frame, and then match it to one of the following profiles:

- ◆ You're a conservative investor if you can sustain losses of no more than 6 percent over a one-year period. That means if you have $1,000 invested and the markets take a tumble, you could withstand losing up to $60 without reaching for the Pepto-Bismol.

- ◆ You're a moderate risk investor if you can withstand losses in your investment portfolio of no more than 15 percent over a one-year time frame.

- ◆ You're a high-tolerance-for-risk investor if you can generally withstand losing between 15 percent to 25 percent of your portfolio in a span of one year.

Risk is a fact of life for any investor. Stock markets plunge. Companies go bankrupt. Greedy corporate bigwigs make mincemeat out of employee retirement accounts as was the case with Enron. And there are countless other little ways to lose money much less dramatically and less painfully. But the truth is, you can probably handle a lot more risk than you think. You simply have to recognize the dangers that exist and learn some easy exit strategies to protect yourself.

Your return needs make up the other half of the equation in the "risk-reward" profile. Once you determine your risk profile, you'll have a general idea of your reward, which is your return. Unfortunately, there is no investment that allows you to have your cake and eat it, too. You can't earn a high return and protect 100 percent of your initial investment (your principal) without exposing your cash to the ups and downs of the financial markets. That's where the trade-off comes in. If you want to protect your portfolio as much as possible, you won't earn as much in a reward, unless you implement some defensive money strategies. Socking away a few dollars in a safe-money account, such as a money market account, for emergencies is a good example of such a defensive strategy.

If you want to protect your initial investment, you'll typically receive a lower return, usually in the form of a lower annual income (such as interest payments you receive from a bond or CD investment). Second there is a trade-off between *income* and *growth*. The more certain you are about your annual payment, the less risky the investment is and the lower the potential return in the form of growth.

Your time horizon directly affects your ability to reduce risk. For example, volatile investments, such as *small cap stocks*, where prices fluctuate greatly over the short term, are considerably smoother over a longer time horizon. That's why diversification is so important; you're not putting all your eggs in one basket. If your time horizon is short, however, you can't be as effectively diversified across all the different types of markets.

Fiscal Facts

Investing for income is *not* the same as **investing for growth**. When you invest for income, you are seeking a steady stream of payments. On the other hand, when you invest for growth, your aim is to try to have your money grow (sometimes referred to as "appreciate") over a longer time frame.

Fiscal Facts

A **small cap stock** is a stock from a company whose market capitalization (the market price of the company) is $250 to $1 billion.

Your time horizon begins when you start investing that first buck in your portfolio. If you are investing to save for a child's education, for example, you have already dictated your time horizon. It ends when you withdraw the money. So what defines a short-term, intermediate-term, or long-term time horizon? Industry standards say that if you need the money within one to two years, you have a short-term time horizon. Two to five years constitutes an intermediate-term time horizon. And more than five years is long-term.

Finally, consider your tax exposure. It's hard to determine because the tax laws are constantly changing. The bottom line in investing is what Uncle Sam says you get as leftovers—or in some cases, what you owe *him*. If you are in a high-income tax bracket, you need to be concerned with tax implications that seem to appear magically when you invest—including some obligations you incur. That's where timing comes into play.

The Pros and Cons of Investing Your Money

You cannot get rich quick, no matter what anyone promises you. You can, however, get rich slowly. That's why making money on Wall Street is all about thinking long-term. You have the potential to reap great rewards. In exchange for these rewards, you do take on risk. The often-quoted legendary trader Bernard Baruch coined a phrase that we're sure is on every investor's mind: "I'm not so concerned about the return on my money as I am about the return *of* my money!"

Of course, every investor wants the highest, assured return possible. But returns aren't certain—and neither is the future. If you keep the following adage in mind, it will get you started in your investment course:

> **Seek out investments that pose the greatest amount of return with the least amount of risk.**

What you consider to be the greatest amount of return depends on your investment profile. For example, you may favor high-risk maneuvers to gain a quick buck and not care that you could lose all your money. On the flipside, your grandpa loses sleep every time there's an announcement that the Federal Reserve Board is meeting to discuss the country's state of the economy. Will they raise or lower short-term interest rates? No wonder Grandpa, who doesn't like to bear much risk, favors conservative money market accounts rather than whipsaw stock market swings.

Whatever kind of investor you are, one strategy rings true if you want to spread, and possibly reduce, your exposure to investment risk. It's called asset allocation.

Here's how asset allocation works. Your portfolio's risk can be moderated by mixing stocks and bonds. They are both very different animals. Stocks are actually "claims" against real assets. When you buy stock, you are actually buying a piece (a share) of a company. Bonds, on the other hand, are debt that typically promise fixed returns. Because of their differences, the return on each tends not to follow similar patterns. Consequently, combining stocks and bonds moderates your portfolio's risk.

Of course, stocks and bonds are not the only two financial vehicles that make up an investment portfolio. Adding mutual funds to your portfolio, for example, helps allocate a percentage of your portfolio to another asset class.

The following tips can help you tackle and reduce your exposure to risks that are associated with investing your money:

♦ **Keep an eye on reports of reduced purchasing-power risk.** Simply, this is how much bang you can get for your buck. For example, what you buy for a dollar today will not buy you the same product 10 years from now.

♦ **Keep your eye on market risk.** (Market risk is just being exposed to the ups and downs in the financial markets.) An increase in the amount of risk that the financial markets and our economy experience will cause any investment to decrease in value.

♦ **Keep enough cash or accounts that can easily be converted to cash in your investment portfolio.** If you don't have enough investments that are fairly *liquid* (they are *illiquid*), you run the risk of not being able to get at your money without a hassle, penalty, or loss. For example, if the market is topsy-turvy, you could be forced to sell your investment at a significant loss if you need the money immediately.

♦ **Monitor any type of inflation reports.** The uncertainty over future inflation rates, called inflation risk, can eat into your profit—and in some cases, your principal! An investment that can't keep up with inflation will not be able to grow, leaving you with little purchasing power. The best indicator of inflation is the Consumer Price Index (CPI). Check Chapter 3 for additional economic indicators.

Fiscal Facts

When an investment is **liquid**, you can easily sell it and get your money out of it.

If your investment is in real estate, it might be difficult to sell the property because there are no buyers. Therefore, you're stuck. Your investment is **illiquid**.

♦ **Watch for any changes in the business sector.** Industry risk is based on how the industry you've invested in is doing as a whole. The certainty of a business's ability to pay income, principal, and other returns due to investors may suffer if the company or the industry as a whole is not doing well. Some of the magazines, websites, and financial TV programs listed in Chapter 3 are good resources to monitor changes in the business sector.

Investing in Stocks: A Crash Course

Most people think of the stock market when it comes to investing. This is probably because it has been around the longest and is the most talked about, not only on Wall Street, but Main Street. It can also be extremely profitable—in 1999 you could throw darts at any tech stock and make money. Yet the markets can turn on you, as most major U.S. stock indices started falling in 2000 and were still well off their peaks in mid-2004.

Market events like this one have traditionally seduced investors to pull their money out of the market. The culprit? Fear. They became afraid to invest, and that is the biggest mistake to make, because if you don't invest in the market, you could be missing out on the opportunity of a lifetime.

Everyone should have some exposure to stocks, even a conservative 70-year-old couple. Historically, the returns on a portfolio of long-term Treasury bonds, those debt obligations issued by Uncle Sam, have been more volatile (that is, riskier) than a portfolio of 90 percent bonds and 10 percent common stocks. Stocks held alone are riskier than bonds held alone (remember the asset allocation, spread the risk around), but through the magic of diversification, you can add some stock to an all-bond portfolio and actually reduce the portfolio's risk.

Since 1926, the volatility of an 80 percent bond and 20 percent stock portfolio has been equal to that of a 100 percent bond portfolio. This helps explain why many investment advisers do not recommend a stock weight of less than 20 percent.

Of course, you cannot just throw caution to the wind and become greedy. That's mistake number two. If you're looking to sink your money into poor-quality stocks on dreams of getting rich overnight, you'll probably pay too much for them and lose your hard-earned savings. Greed is *not* good despite what was said in the '80s. It didn't work ten years ago and it won't now. What *is* good is *learning as much as you can about your stock investments*—and the best place to begin is right here.

And Now, the Basics

Fiscal Facts

A **security** is any type of investment product, including notes, stocks, and bonds.

The word stock is a shortened form of the phrase common stock. Common stock is a *security* that represents ownership in a company. When you buy stock, you buy shares, which represent a proportion of ownership in that company. In order for a company to offer common stock, it has to "go public," which happens when the company needs to raise money. This is known as an initial public offering (IPO). The next time the company wants to raise money, it conducts a secondary offering. After a company is publicly traded, its stock can be bought through most brokerage and discount brokerage firms.

The Money Line

Shares are usually sold in round lots, which are groups of 100. Less than that is an odd lot. To figure out how much ownership you have, simply take the amount of shares you own and divide it by the number of shares outstanding, which is the total amount of shares that the company has issued and is currently traded by the public. For example, if you own 100 shares of XYZ Company and there are 1,000,000 shares outstanding, then you own .0001 or 1/10,000th of the company. It won't get you the CEO's parking spot, but at least it gives you an idea of how common stock refers to ownership. To find out how many shares are outstanding, you can call a broker for a quote and ask for this information, or you can check the financial pages.

Why invest in stock? The stock market boasts the best returns you can get on your money, if you keep it invested over a long time frame. Remember, there are ups *and* downs! Many times, investors park their money in stocks to receive dividends. Investors who buy common stock are hoping the company will generate profits so these profits can be distributed to shareholders. These dividends are distributed on a quarterly basis. You should know the four dates in the dividend cycle to ensure what you're entitled to … and when you will get it.

For cash dividends, the process begins with the declaration date, which is the day the board of directors announces that the company will pay a dividend. On this date, the company also declares the amount of the dividend payment and the record date.

Next is the ex-dividend date, which comes four days before the record date. On the ex-dividend date, the investors who purchase the stock for regular way (three-day) settlement are no longer entitled to receive the dividend. If you bought the stock on the ex-dividend day, you will not show up on the company's books as a shareholder until the day *after* the record date. Instead, the dividend is mailed to the previous owner. Typically, the market value of the stock drops by the value of the dividend when it opens for trading on the ex-dividend date.

Then comes the record date, when the company asks the registrar to provide a list of current shareholders so that the company knows who is entitled to the dividend checks. To receive the dividend, you have to be on the company's books as a shareholder as of this date. If you are not, you do not receive the dividend.

It all ends on the payment date, when the company actually cuts the dividend checks. This date is usually about two weeks after the record date, so as to give the company time to generate all the dividend checks.

Enter the Tax Man

Not only can you receive dividends when you invest in stocks, but you have the potential to make a profit when you sell the stock. This profit is known as a capital gain. The difference between the price when you buy the stock and when you sell it is known as your return. How do you make a capital gain? Buy low and sell high! It's one of the investment industry's oldest and well-proven tricks of the trade.

Finally, a tax benefit comes into play when you invest in stocks. You do not incur a taxable event until you sell the stock. For example, even if you bought 100 shares of XYZ Company stock at $25 a share and it's currently trading at $100 a share, you don't have a profit until you sell it. That means you don't have a taxable situation to report to the IRS on your tax return (unless, of course, you receive dividends along the way). Until you do so, it is known as a paper profit.

When buying a stock, choose one that is consistent with your investment goals. The following list describes the three major types of stock:

◆ **Growth stocks.** Growth stocks are touted as one of the easiest ways to make money because the companies that issue them are built for growth. You can define a growth stock company as one that has maintained faster-than-average gains in earnings and profits over the last few years and its future looks similar. The only difference within this category is that there are large growth stocks, medium-size growth stocks, and small-size growth stocks. Each type depends on company sales. Some examples of growth stocks include Microsoft, Intel, McDonalds, and Eastman Kodak. Growth stocks tend to have higher *profit-earnings ratios* (p/e's) than other stocks!

Fiscal Facts

When searching for a growth stock to invest in, check out the company's **profit-earnings ratio** (the p/e). This tells you whether the stock is overvalued or over-priced. It's calculated by taking the price of the stock and dividing it by its earning per share. In summer 2004, the average p/e ratio was hovering around 30. The higher the p/e, the more the stock has a potential to be overpriced. *Value Line Investment Survey* is a great resource for this type of information.

Just as growth stocks can increase in value, they can also sink in value. To minimize the risk involved with these volatile stocks, invest in large growth stocks and hold them as part of the long-term section of your investment portfolio. Some growth stocks offer some pretty decent dividends, too.

◆ **Income stocks.** If making a steady income off your investments is more important to you than earning a large capital gain some time down the road, consider investing in income (dividend-paying) stocks. Examples of these stocks include electric, gas, and telephone companies. Although income stocks tend to be less volatile than growth stocks (and don't have as much price appreciation at times), a stock with solid dividend increases can pay more over time than bonds.

◆ **Growth and income stocks.** With these stocks, you can benefit from the price appreciation and also collect income through dividend payments.

  Some examples of growth and income stocks include DuPont, Emerson Electric, and Dun & Bradstreet. Growth and income stocks, at times, may not be able to capitulate on as much of a growth rate as some pure growth stocks.

Other types of stocks are available. These include cyclical stocks, which are considered to "ride the economic highway" because the companies involved depend on the state of the economy.

Initial public offerings (IPOs) are another opportunity, though they can often be a bit risky because the company is a new publicly traded stock. In an IPO, a new or old company publicly sells stock for the first time. The offering is made through a prospectus, which gives previously private information about the company and its key personnel along with an assessment of the company's finances and the risks of investing in the company. In an IPO, a certain percentage of stock is transferred to investors that held shares in the private company. The rest is sold to the public through brokerage firms. They, in turn, first offer the shares to their clients. After the stock begins trading on an exchange, anyone can buy the shares.

The ideal situation is to enter the stock market when it's rising and exit when it's falling, but it isn't that easy. All too often, small investors bail out after the market has started to fall and jump in after it has started to rise. Because the stock

Watch Your Wallet

To realize a profit from cyclical stocks, you must time your buys and sells carefully (or you can diversify your portfolio to help smooth out the ride). *Buy* cyclical stocks when their well has just about run dry but their situation can't get any worse (buy low), and *sell* cyclical stocks when they are enjoying record profits and everything seems hunky-dory (sell high).

market movements are jerky, investors, particularly new ones, should always plan on investing in stocks for the long-term—no jumping in and out. The bottom line? Unless you have a crystal ball and can predict the future of the market, investing in good, solid growth stocks typically wins hands-down over the long haul.

Making Money in the Bond Market

Just as companies issue stock to raise money, they can also issue bonds. Stock, as you know, represents ownership in a company. Bonds, on the other hand, represent an IOU from the company to you. As a bond investor, you are *lending* your money to the corporation or government. This "loan" requires the bond issuer to pay you the amount borrowed plus interest over a stated period of time. Bond investments are also known as fixed-income investments because they typically pay interest to bond-holders on a semi-annual basis. This interest is considered income, hence the name.

The following sections explain common bond jargon and the types of bonds available. Before you read on, however, learn the cardinal rule of investing in bonds:

Interest rates and bond prices move in opposite directions.

Understanding Bond Jargon

When you invest in bonds, make sure you know the following:

◆ The maturity date is a fixed date when the amount of money borrowed by the company must be paid back to you. Although there is a stated maturity date, you don't have to hold it until maturity. You have a right to sell it whenever you want. (Hint: What you want to do is sell it for a profit. Remember, "Buy low and sell high.")

◆ The amount of the original investment is the face value or the par value. This amount is equal to the amount of money you agreed to lend to the borrower or company. You can, however, buy bonds that are more than the face value, known as a premium, or less than a face value, known as a discount.

◆ In exchange for these companies borrowing your money, they promise to pay you back your principal plus interest. This interest is based on the bond's coupon rate, which is either a fixed rate that pays you the same amount of interest every year (typically every six months) or a floating rate, which fluctuates and is based on some predetermined index.

You can always buy a bond and wait until maturity to get your money back. Or you can buy a bond and hope to sell it at a price higher than the one at which you bought it, even *before* its maturity date. This is practicing the art of buying low and selling high.

You see, even though bonds have a face value, they also have a current market value, which fluctuates. The current level of interest rates determines what the current market value is. Suppose you owned tens of thousands of dollars' worth of 30-year government bonds that were issued in the early 1980s with coupon rates averaging 13 percent—some even as high as 15 percent that mature in 2010. These specific bonds are still earning that coupon rate or interest today, which makes them pretty attractive, considering the average market yield on a 10-year Treasury security was about 2 percent in mid-summer of 2004. Because you own these attractive bonds that pay high rates of interest, other investors (like us) would be willing to pay you a higher price for the bonds. Why? Well, as of this writing, the federal government was not offering 30-year bonds. Inflation-indexed bonds issued in 2002 were yielding just over 2 percent. We'll sacrifice our dollars now to get that higher coupon rate.

Whether you practice the strategy of waiting until maturity, or selling your bond out in the market before maturity, you should be aware of the current yield of a bond. The current yield is the return (expressed as a percentage) that the bond would earn in the current marketplace. To calculate this percentage, you divide the total market value of the bond by the annual interest payment, and multiply that total by 100.

Let's plug in some numbers. Suppose you bought a bond with a $1,000 face value and a 10 percent coupon rate at a price of 90. This means that you paid 90 percent of the face value of the bond. Because the bond has a face value of $1,000, the current market value is equal to $900 in this example. ($900 is the current market value. Depending on the direction of interest rates, this current value may be different *tomorrow*.) The annual interest paid on this bond is equal to the coupon rate multiplied by the face value, which would be $100 in this case (10 percent of $1,000). Your finished equation would be ($100 ÷ 900) × 100, which equals a current yield of 11.11 percent. The current market value depends on what interest rates are and the overall bond market.

If you decide to hold onto your bond until maturity, you should concern yourself with another type of yield: the yield to maturity (YTM). This is a measure of the total return you can expect to earn if you hold the bond until maturity. It's difficult to calculate, but you should ask your broker what it is before you invest your money. In a nutshell, it takes compound interest into account.

Knowing the Different Bond Types

The U.S. Government offers the safest kind of bonds—Treasury bills, notes and bonds—as they are backed by the full faith and credit of the U.S. government. No other bond investment (with the exception of Ginnie Mae securities, which are bonds issued by a government agency that pools mortgages together) can make this claim. In exchange for the degree of safety, Treasury investors receive lower interest rates than those on comparable bonds of different issuers.

U.S. Bonds and other U.S. debt instruments are discussed at length in Chapter 9. In this section we offer a rundown of the other types of bonds available:

- **Municipal bonds.** The interest payments you receive on these government bonds are exempt from federal taxes. In fact, in some states, they're also exempt from state and local taxes.

- **Government agency bonds.** Even though these bond securities are issued by a government agency, they are NOT backed by the full faith and credit of the U.S. Government—just the issuing agency—and carry a "moral obligation" (with the exception of Ginnie Mae, as noted previously). Depending on the agency, most minimum denominations are as high as $25,000 per bond. The three best-known agencies are Freddie Mac, Ginnie Mae, and Fannie Mae. Each was created to pool together a large quantity of mortgages and produce mortgage-backed securities. How do they do this? They purchase them from banks and savings and loans. These mortgage-backed securities offer higher yields (and thus more credit risk) than Treasuries. Even though these agencies are borrowing money from investors with the promise to pay them back on the maturity date plus interest, the interest income you receive can fluctuate.

- **Zero-coupon bonds.** This type of bond is named such because they are issued with no coupon rate at all. Zero-coupon bonds are issued by the Treasury Department (Treasury zeros), corporations, municipalities, and government agencies. You buy these bonds at a deep discount from their face value. You make money off the increase in the bond price as it approaches maturity. Keep in mind, however, that even though you don't receive any semi-annual interest payments, you *are* taxed on these interest payments at all levels.

- **Corporate bonds.** The biggest attraction of corporate bonds is the higher yields they offer. You may find that they offer two more percentage points than a Treasury security of the same term. Of course, more risk is involved because they are not backed by the full faith and credit of the U.S. government. Minimum denominations? $1,000 face value per bond and on up.

◆ **Junk bonds.** Also known as high-yield bonds, a junk bond is simply a corporate bond that offers a higher yield. Technically, junk bonds pay such high rates of interest that the corporation may not earn enough money—either through sales or bottom-line profits—to cover the interest payments investors should receive every six months. Note that you should be wary of credit risk. Follow the ratings given by S&P's and Moody's, often quoted in sources like *The Wall Street Journal* or online at www.standardandpoors.com or www.moodys.com. Junk bonds come from issuers who are less credit-worthy. There is a danger they could not repay the principal and interest during tough economic times.

Getting Started with Mutual Funds

Mutual funds allow investors to pool their money into a large fund organized by investment professionals. Investors own shares that represent stocks and bonds in several different companies. The number of shares you own depends on how much money you put in. The more you invest, the more shares you can buy. You don't need a trillion dollars to get started, either. Some mutual fund companies allow you to begin with as little as $50 a month. Plus, you can have access to your money all the time. And you can even invest in mutual funds that don't charge *any* sales charges. Mutual funds also tend to be less risky because they build on the idea of diversification.

Two types of mutual funds exist: load funds, which charges you a sales commission, and no-load funds, which do not charge their shareholders any sales commissions but often other expenses are assessed, such as management fees or advertising expenses. (Keep in mind, however, that just because a load is being charged does *not* mean you'll earn a better return.) The following table shows a payoff comparison on a $1,000 investment in a no-load vs. a load mutual fund. Assume a 12 percent return on a no-load fund vs. a fund with an 8.5 percent load. As the table demonstrates, no-loads are usually the best way to go.

Watch Your Wallet

If a mutual fund salesperson approaches you to invest in a company's mutual funds, ask what's in it for them. Does he or she receive a commission? Make sure you check out the company's performance history, going back 5 to 10 years if possible.

No-Load Versus Load

Timing	No-load	Load	Difference
Investment less load	$1,000	$915	$85
Value at one year	$1,120	$1,025	$95
Value at five years	$1,762	$1,613	$149
Value at ten years	$3,106	$2,842	$264
Value at twenty years	$9,646	$8,826	$820

Source: Taken from The Complete Idiot's Guide to Making Money on Wall Street, Third edition

How to Pick a True No-Load Fund

You know that if you buy a mutual fund through a broker, you will pay a commission—a load. You can buy a mutual fund directly from the company and not pay a load, which is a good, cost-effective move. But, some no-load mutual funds are not *pure* no-load funds; they can hit your pocketbook with some fees and charges. Some of these not-so-obvious fees include the following:

- **12b-1 fees.** Also known as 12b-1 plans, they are charges that cover marketing and promotional costs. These fees range anywhere from $1/4$ percent to 1 percent of the fund's total assets each year.

- **Expense ratios.** These are typically expressed as a percentage of total investment, which shareholders pay for mutual fund operating expenses.

- **Fees for reinvesting your dividends.** These fees can really wallop your wallet. Make sure you ask your shareholder rep if this type of fee is involved. You want to avoid funds that charge it.

- **Management fees.** This pays for the portfolio manager of the fund. Typical management fee expenses run about $1/2$ percent.

- **Back-end load funds.** These funds have been hyped as no-load funds, but they are *not*. Even though all your money goes to work for you in the beginning when you invest, you get nicked

> **CAUTION**
>
> **Watch Your Wallet**
>
> Because no-load doesn't always mean no-fee, you must be careful. The total cost of fees is deducted from the fund's earnings. One mutual fund company that touts its funds as no-load charges its shareholders up to 1.5 percent of their investments to open an account, stating it's a "portfolio reimbursement fee."

with a "penalty load" if you withdraw your money before a certain time. The longer you keep your money invested in the fund, the less of a back-end load is assessed.

One final note: All this talk about no-load fees may make you believe a broker who tries to tell you that the marketing costs and other expenses associated with the fund are *really* what keep no-loads from being no-loads. Teach the lug something new; explain that *no-load means there are no sales commissions*. And then steer clear of the sales pitch. You can do your own homework and save hundreds of dollars in commissions!

Mutual Fund Selection Secrets

Keep the following factors in mind when selecting a mutual fund:

- **Select no-load funds whose objectives coincide with your own.** Are you looking for growth? Income? Or both? You can narrow your mutual fund search by matching the investment objective of mutual funds available to your own investment objectives. For example, if you are a Nervous Nellie who can't sleep a wink because of the ups and downs in the stock market, don't plunk down all your money in an emerging market fund that invests solely in Third World countries.

- **Look for mutual funds that can provide at least a 3- to 5-year track record.** You should be able to select your mutual funds based on performance history. Five-year track records will tell you how well (or poorly) the fund did in a variety of environments—when interest rates were high or low, when the stock market was up or down, and when our economy was in an inflationary period or a recession. For a quick review of economic cycles, look at Chapter 7.

- **Don't limit yourself to just one type of mutual fund.** Even though a mutual fund offers diversification, you can invest in more than one. Fifty? Well, forget it. The experts would label that as mutual fund overkill. You can diversify your mutual fund portfolio by choosing a growth fund, an income fund, an international fund, and perhaps a bond fund. If you divide your money among three or four different types of stock funds, you'll always have some money invested in the most profitable sector of the market.

- **Buying last year's biggest winner is foolish.** Don't even think about it. Maybe the portfolio manager got lucky. Instead, stick with a fund that is a steady performer instead of moving in and out of funds trying to catch the waves.

◆ **Enroll in an automatic investment plan with at least one of your mutual funds.** This program's awareness is increasing in the world of the wee investor. As little as $50 a month can be electronically debited and transferred from your bank account to your mutual fund account. Because you are doing this on a regular basis, you can take advantage of any dips in the share price. This is known as dollar-cost averaging.

Where to Go for More Info

If you're in the market to invest in mutual funds, several sources of performance information are available. Only with more than four thousand mutual funds to choose from, how can you cut through the murk?

One option is to check out *Morningstar Mutual Funds*, a bimonthly newsletter published by Morningstar, Inc. It is considered to be the most informative and user-friendly survey of mutual fund performance, covering more than 11,000 funds total. Morningstar rates each fund with a star rating system on a scale of zero to five; five stars is the highest honor given to a mutual fund. Each fund receives a star (or no stars) depending on a combination of past performance and the risks involved. The newsletter is available on a three-month trial basis for $55—and it's free at your local library reference desk and on the Internet at www.morningstar.com. A dozen newsletters are published by Morningstar, so to find one that fits what you're looking for, visit www.morningstar.com, call 1-866-608-9750 or write to Morningstar, Inc., 225 W. Wacker Drive, Chicago, IL 60606.

CDA Weisenberger, a division of Thomson Financial, is a rating service that tracks the performance of almost 6,500 funds in its reports *The Mutual Fund Report* and *The Mutual Fund Update*. These reports are updated monthly and are available in a newsletter report format or in a software package. Call 1-800-232-2285 or write to CDA Weisenberger, 1355 Piccard Drive, Rockville, MD 20850 for more information.

The *Value Line Mutual Fund Investment Survey* also tracks performance information on 2,000 mutual funds, providing in-depth coverage and analysts' opinions on the equity of each and fixed-income mutual funds for subscribers. This report is also available in your local library, but if you would like more information about subscription rates, call 1-800-634-3583 or visit www.valueline.com.

One Last Word About Loads

Load funds typically charge an average 4 percent sales fee. But depending on what load fund it is, the 4 percent load may not be charged at the same time. Many times, when you buy a load fund—and we're not recommending that you necessarily do so—the fund company offers Class A, Class B, and Class C shares. As if the industry wasn't complicated enough!

Class A shares are front-end loads—meaning when you invest $1,000 in a 4 percent load fund, your $40 is automatically taken out before it's invested. The sales fee was charged at the beginning—the "front"—of your investment. Class B shares assess a 1 percent annual charge to your account—that's its sales fee. Class C shares are back-end loads, so the load is charged when you sell.

The bottom line? Stick with no-load funds for the least costly investment strategy.

Whether you are investing for the long haul or even on a short-term basis, mutual funds make sense for an investment portfolio. They offer professional management, no sales charges (in the case of no-load funds) and diversification.

The Least You Need to Know

- ◆ If you want to make money by investing, you have to know your investment profile. Take into consideration your risk tolerance, your financial goals (and dreams!), your time horizon (which is when you need the money), and your tax exposure.

- ◆ The way to make money in investing is to buy low and sell high.

- ◆ You can make a good return off growth stocks if you invest for the long term.

- ◆ Interest rates and bond prices move in opposite directions.

- ◆ Mutual funds usually involve less risk because your investments are diversified. Make sure you look for a no-load fund that doesn't involve a lot of extra fees.

Chapter 5

The Road to Becoming a Millionaire

In This Chapter

- Learning the secrets of all millionaires
- How to make money the old-fashioned way—and keep it
- Why it's important to know the personality traits of millionaires
- How millionaires diversify their wealth

So you want to be a millionaire. Spending less and saving more may seem like a simple, antiquated method to the road to riches, but it is actually one that does work.

Becoming a millionaire is not about instant riches, unless of course you have the final answer that garners you a million bucks. What is a millionaire? Basically, it is someone who is a person of means or resources. Nowhere in the definition does it say "get-rich-overnight."

The most famous wealth index is the Forbes 400, which surreptitiously is noted for the maximum number of people that could fit into the high-society ballroom of John Jacob Astor, America's richest man before the Civil War.

Inclusion on this list required personal wealth of $91 million just twenty years ago. By 1999, however, $625 million was required for inclusion on a list that included 268 billionaires.

And while this year's Forbes 400 richest in America touts that there's more money at the top than ever before, know that there can be, but does not definitely have to be— more anxiety and worry as you climb higher. The point? Live simply, take it one day at a time, and stick to your plan. This chapter will show you how simple living will yield simple millions in savings over the long haul.

Invest in Yourself

Spending money may seem like a pastime of the wealthy, but there are always sound financial decisions made prior to each purchase and, of course, a handsome investment portfolio doesn't hurt either.

By now, you have learned how to make the decision to manage your money more effectively, get out of debt and stay there, and set up a personal financial plan that will enable you to reach your financial goals. So what is the common denominator among the three?

You!

You are learning about personal financial planning and investing for yourself—not your neighbor, your Uncle Moe, or your neighbor with the latest model BMW. You are adapting new—and smart!—financial habits that will help you reach your financial goals. But, the most important habit is to pay yourself first.

> **The Road to Riches**
>
> The money you pay yourself doesn't have to be a lot. In fact, even if you sock away $10 a week for the next year, you'll have $520 by the end of the year. Over time, and depending on how you invest this money, it can grow into thousands of dollars. You have a number of financial products to invest in, as you learned in Chapter 4.

Treat yourself as if you were a monthly bill. Call it the "Pay Yourself First" category. By doing so, you begin to practice the art of self-discipline. By earmarking your personal "bill," you are creating your financial future without even realizing it.

There is one requirement: Do it before Friday night out with the boys, your daughter's Girl Scout dues, or monthly health club fees. Pay yourself every time you get paid. If you have direct deposit, many employers offer the feature of having a percentage of your paycheck directly deposited to a second bank account if you wish. By implementing this feature, you automatically pay yourself first.

The Millionaire Personality

Every year a survey of wealthy people is performed by the Phoenix Companies, which sells financial products, to see how these millionaires feel about the economy and their financial goals. The most common traits among these millionaires surveyed include:

♦ They work hard, are often self-employed, and consider work a joy.

♦ They are frugal and live below their means.

♦ They save and invest well.

♦ They are disciplined.

♦ They buy assets, not nonappreciating liabilities.

Understand that creating wealth initially has nothing to do with money but more to do with discipline and establishing (and following) good habits. By doing so, the odds are in your favor to create a future path to financial success.

Make Your Money Work For You

Many millionaires follow a written financial plan that includes many of the items that you learned about in Chapter 4—establishing financial goals, a time horizon, and risk tolerance, for example.

By creating a financial plan—with or without the help of a professional—you will be able to implement a disciplined routine, much like consistent weight training that makes lean muscles pop.

The Road to Riches

Part of your investment plan should include knowing when to sell. Typically, when you buy a stock, for example, you should have a target price in mind of when to sell it. After all, why are you buying it in the first place? The only way you can profit is if you sell it at a higher price than you bought it.

Wealthy investors know that they don't necessarily have to sell their stock if it doubles in price from where they bought it. If a stock doubles in price, who's to say it won't do it again? What you should do is continuously reevaluate your stock using the same reasons you bought it in the first place (good earnings, good management, competitive product, and so on).

One way is to execute one of the lowest-cost investment strategies around to build wealth. It's an old-fashioned method that wins hands down: dollar-cost averaging.

Dollar-cost averaging is a smart investment strategy. All you do is make fixed, regular investments in a stock or any type of mutual fund, even if the market is rising or falling. This strategy works in your favor, no matter what the market does.

When you dollar-cost average, you have a variety of choices including all different types of mutual funds and stocks, such as in a dividend reinvestment program. No matter which investments you choose to dollar-cost average your way into, make sure you choose your investment on the basis of your financial goals, your risk-comfort level, and your age.

For example, when you buy shares in an equity mutual fund and the price rises, you buy fewer shares. When the price falls, however, you buy *more* shares. Plus, over the long haul, the average cost of your share will be less than the average price or market price when you sell.

You can start with $100. One hundred dollars a month, invested over a 12-month period, is $1,200. Easy enough. But oh, how it can grow. You'll be amazed at how $200 a month can grow, too. If you want to see how dollar-cost averaging is practiced, look at the following table.

How to Get There from Here

Time	Amount of Investment	Price Per Share	How Much of Investment Do I Own?
January 15	$200	$10	20.00
February 15	$200	$12.50	36.00
March 15	$200	$14	50.29
April 15	$200	$13	65.67
May 15	$200	$13	81.05
June 15	$200	$9	103.27
July 15	$200	$10	123.27
August 15	$200	$11.25	141.05
September 15	$200	$13.50	155.86
October 15	$200	$15	169.19
November 15	$200	$14.50	182.98
December 15	$200	$14	197.27

Time	Amount of Investment	Price Per Share	How Much of Investment Do I Own?
Total number of shares:			197.27
Current price per share (on December 15th):		$14	
Total Investment:	$2,400.00		
Total Value of Portfolio:	$2,761.78		
Net Profit:	$361.78		

And that's just for one year! It's never too late to start an investment program by dollar-cost averaging. And, it works! If you dollar-cost averaged your way to wealth by investing in the Dow Jones Industrial Average beginning at its highest peak in 1929 (before the Crash) and purchased at the *highest* price every year until the mid-1960s, you would still be rewarded more than *300 percent* on your money.

Create a Cash Withdrawal Discipline

Banking is an integral part of your overall financial plan, but, unfortunately, as we consumers push for convenience, banks in turn charge higher fees. It's up to you to shop around for a bank that not only meets your financial needs, but also charges you less for doing so.

Monitor your ATM withdrawals. Decide how much you will take out each week and make it last. Make it a little tight. And try to decrease it over time if you can. If you have money left at the end of the week, put it into a type of savings account that earns interest. This is a rule of most everyday millionaires—they live well *below* their means. (For more information about the banking industry, have another look at Part 3.)

Build a Portfolio of Mutual Funds

Investing in more than one mutual fund is a great way to diversify your portfolio. But the question always remains: How many mutual funds are too many? Like a nervous five-year-old taking swimming lessons for the very first time, just getting your feet wet is a better beginning than jumping straight into the deep end.

Getting your feet wet doesn't necessarily mean putting all of your money in a conservative mutual fund. That strategy would not be practicing diversification, and you wouldn't be lowering your risk. Conservative funds may maintain a lot in cash periodically, which may not be what you want when you diversify. You lower your risk by mixing stock funds, bond funds, U.S. and overseas funds, and money market funds. Diversification offers the idea that a gain in one fund offsets losses in another. In financial mumbo jumbo, you should create a portfolio of funds that have a low "core correlation" with one another.

The first step is to look at your whole investment picture; decide what you're trying to achieve. Make these goals reachable, not astronomical. Next, set parameters to determine how much money you can afford to lose and how much money you plan on keeping "liquid" (safe). This will help you decide how risk-tolerant you are. Sorry, folks, but a lot of the players in the mutual fund industry don't do enough to inform or protect the investor against the risks associated with fund investing. Your goal is to look for the highest return with the lowest risk.

Of course, the higher the reward, the greater the risks. Experts tell us that people should be educated about risk. If you think you're going to lose 100 percent of your money and stick it in a money market fund that earns *less* than inflation, that's just as bad as investing in a fund with a 20 percent fluctuation rate!

Your age will also determine your selection of mutual funds. If you're fairly young, you can be more aggressive in your investment approach. Keep 70 to 80 percent in aggressive investments, such as growth and aggressive-growth mutual funds. Pre-retirees should still maintain a portion of their mutual fund portfolio in growth investments, though they should pull back to allocation percentages around 40 percent. Balance the remaining 60 percent between safer investments; for example, a small percent in money market and some in growth and income funds.

Don't Just Buy—Diversify

By allocating your money into several different investments, you reduce your risk. Think of it this way: If you put one dozen eggs into one basket, and a few in another, and so on, and then you drop one basket, only a few are cracked and the others are intact.

To see how this theory works with investing, let's say you have $10,000 to invest. You've done your homework and have come up with a beauty of an investment: a company stock that created the gadget that takes the salt out of the ocean. You found they have great management, their good-debt versus bad-debt ratio is healthy, and historical performance numbers are appealing. You sink all of your $10,000 into this stock and wait for it to take off.

> ### The Road to Riches
>
> Even if you are not investing or trading yet, consider paper trading as a way to exercise your millionaire muscle. By practice investing with pretend money, you can begin to improve your financial success. While it is true that the experience that you get from investing or trading with real money is much quicker and much more powerful than the experience you will get from paper trading, the emotional pain from making mistakes is a lot more manageable with paper trading, because there is no real loss of money.

And boy, does it! Two years later, the stock has increased by 50 percent. You have roughly $16,000 including reinvested dividends. And then, tragedy strikes. The company president jumps ship, the money they lent to that small country off the coast of Argentina *won't* be repaid, and earnings estimates are seven times below Wall Street's expectations. The stock drops 25 percent in value in one day, and another 25 percent the next. Your eggs are smashed to pieces!

This is an exaggerated example, but an excellent way to show the benefits of diversification. Financial research shows that if you own 20 to 25 stocks, you won't get burned by one bad investment.

Let's use another example. If you take that $10,000 and split it up among several types of equity mutual funds (growth or aggressive growth), an international equity mutual fund, and maybe a bond fund of some sort, you will reduce your risk, especially if one fund zigs while the others zag. This is practicing the art of diversification!

Curb Your Tax Exposure With Tax-Deferred Investing

This may be the biggest, most overlooked secret. Of all the retirement programs available to Americans, only 60 percent of Americans admit to contributing to some type of retirement savings program. Why?

Because they want instant gratification. Credit cards, however, have cured short-term boredom, enticing men and women to charge now and pay later. Unfortunately, this bad habit dissuades us from socking away any money for the future because we're trying to climb out of debt today.

But millionaires know differently. They lay off the plastic and instead take home more money from each paycheck (remember they work hard and enjoy it) and save for their futures at the same time with tax-deferred accounts. The most common kind are 401(k)s and IRAs. Retirement accounts are a great way to strengthen your future financial success.

With a tax-deferred account, the assets inside grow and compound without Uncle Sam getting his fair share until it's time. When you do pay taxes is when you take the money out, which is when you're typically in a lower income-tax bracket anyway.

The benefits? Let's say you save $2,000 a year at 4 percent for 30 years in a regular savings account, you'll have $96,000 after paying taxes. However, if you sheltered your $2,000 each year in your IRA at 4 percent, your savings increases to almost $117,000 because of the tax-deferred feature.

Another example that shows the benefits of tax-deferred investing is a comparison of a tax-deferred versus taxable investment strategy. Let's say you invest $2,400 a year in a tax-deferred account that earns 8 percent interest per year. Hypothetically speaking, after 30 years your account would be worth $271,880. If you invested the same $2,400 in a taxable account without sheltering your investment gains, you would have $169,671, assuming a 33 percent tax rate.

You can see why using a tax-deferred approach is a smart long-term money management strategy, and one long celebrated by the wealthy.

Expand Your Knowledge—and Dollars—Outside the United States

We live in a global economy. Many of the products we buy are imported. Many U.S. companies have more than half of their revenue generated from overseas sales. Socking away a portion of your investment dollars—no matter how old you are—to invest in world financial markets is a common investment strategy today, and it can be *very* rewarding. But, there are some short-term *and* long-term ups and downs.

Allocating a portion of your investment portfolio to international (non-U.S. companies) or global (both overseas and U.S. companies) investing is a smart move, as long as you do two things:

♦ Understand the biggest risk involved with international and global investing: currency risk. For example, if money must be converted into a different currency to make a certain investment, changes in the value of the currency relative to the American dollar will affect the total loss or gain on the investment when the money is converted back. This risk usually affects businesses, but it can also affect individual investors who make international investments. also called exchange rate risk.

♦ Maintain a long-term time frame for your international and global investments (at least five years).

It used to be that all the world's currency exchange rates were tied to the U.S. dollar. But, when the United States stopped pegging the value of its dollar to gold in the early 1970s, which created *currency risk* if you were to invest or exchange your money for local currency abroad. The reason this is risky is because the rate at which the currency is calculated (converted) is determined by the current state of world economies. If Europe is in a recession, its Euros may be worth more (or less) in U.S. dollars, depending on how our economy is doing and vice-versa.

Fiscal Facts

Currency risk is simply the risk involved when you convert foreign currency back into dollars or into other currencies.

For example, if you're an American tourist in Japan, you will quickly learn that the number of Japanese yen you get for $1,000 may be different tomorrow than it is today. That's because the currency fluctuates in value, and when put into the conversion process, your end result (how much yen you get for your American dollars) will change. To learn the value of the American dollar against other foreign currencies, Oanda. Com offers data on up to 164 currencies worldwide. Simply log onto www. oanda.com/convert/classic.

You don't need to keep all of your money in the good ol' USA to become a millionaire. It would be a mistake to avoid investing abroad because so many investments, such as mutual funds, have made it so easy to do so. You should, however, still monitor your international and global investments, and add international or global funds (because of the diversification) to a portfolio of U.S. stock and bond funds. This strategy helps reduce the amount of money the entire portfolio will lose in today's global economy. So before you park your pesos overseas, make sure you do your homework!

Also stashing your cash in foreign markets is a long-term process. That's why, if you want to iron out the volatility, you should plan for the long haul. Ask yourself how long you can leave that money there. If you need it right away, stick your money into a less aggressive investment. Unless they are highly skilled as day-traders in foreign currency markets, overseas investing is not for short-term investors.

Get Professional Advice, Just Don't Pay an Arm and a Leg for It

Full-service brokers will charge you up to $4 just for sending you a trade confirmation. This makes the increase in postal rates and tollway fees look miniscule by comparison, doesn't it? Like banks, full-service brokers may charge you an inactivity fee of close to $50 if you do not generate at least $100 in commissions in one year. And—get this—account holders can get penalized with a $50 maintenance fee just for having the account. That's like paying someone $50 a year just so they can hold onto *your* money. No way, José!

Unless you truly need a full-service broker, opt for a discount broker. You still get research reports, but no advice. And, no ghastly fees, either! The discount brokerage business has become even more competitive in recent years. The established firms are Quick & Reilly (1-800-793-8050), Charles Schwab & Company (1-866-855-9102), and Fidelity Investments (1-800-343-3548). But there are now deep discount brokers, such as Ameritrade (1-800-454-9272), E*Trade (1-800-387-2331), Scottrade (1-800-619-7283), and TD Waterhouse (1-800-934-4448). All have websites at which you can manage your account.

The Least You Need to Know

- *Pay yourself first!* Before any other financial obligation, allocate a small portion to an investment for yourself and your financial future.

- Invest in several different investment products to reduce your risk.

- Stay informed about your investments. This means doing your homework!

- Invest in retirement accounts to help plan for tomorrow and reduce your tax exposure.

Part 2

The ABCs of Really Smart Banking

Almost everybody has a bank account. But, just about everybody is also frustrated by how banks gouge their pocketbooks—low rates on savings, high rates on credit cards, and fees and more fees on everything from ATMs to talking to a live teller. While you're being nickel-and-dimed to the poorhouse, the banks make bucks deluxe off your accounts. Ironically it's the little guy who can't afford it who gets clobbered the hardest—not the well-heeled customer who maintains big account balances.

Meanwhile you need to know how to read the interest rate cycles—whether rates are going up or down, and how you should plan your investment strategies. This section teaches you how to find the highest yields, how to avoid outrageous bank fees, and when it's time to switch banks.

Chapter 6

What Bankers Won't Tell You

In This Chapter

- ◆ How banks cash in on customer fees and charges
- ◆ How bank mergers give your pocketbook the shaft
- ◆ Why banks sometimes drag their feet in raising or lowering rates
- ◆ Why average consumers and not wealthy folks pay the bills

Bank profits are rising—more than $50 billion a year at last count, including $2 billion in ATM fees alone. So how come they keep slapping you with higher fees and paying you next-to-nothing on your savings? Because the public knows zilch when it comes to understanding how and why banks operate the way they do. They don't know, they don't complain. It's all a person can do to balance a checkbook and hunt for high savings rates in a low interest rate environment. There's a method to the banks' madness when they lure you to automatic tellers and charge outrageous interest on credit cards and loans. And, they don't bother to tell you how all their big mergers are shorting you on the bottom line.

Granted, banks have to make money to stay alive. But you can keep more of that money in your pocket if you learn some of the banker's innermost secrets. This chapter explains some of the key secrets in simple English.

How Banks Profit

Banks come out ahead when they rent your money (savings accounts and CDs) at one price, and then peddle that same cash to someone else in the form of loans (credit cards, auto loans, and mortgages). Look at the bank as though it were a little one-room building with two doors—one in front, the other in the back. You deposit your savings at the front door, and then the bank marks it up and lends the money to folks lined up at the back door to borrow.

Consumers have witnessed many different banking cycles. More than 20 years ago, before deregulation hit, which allowed banks to pay whatever rate they wanted to on savings accounts, banks offered low rates on lending products. A typical 30-year mortgage rate ran an average six to seven percent.

But times changed after the federal government enacted deregulation. Banks were then allowed to offer rates on certificates of deposit up to 10 percent or more. The problem was the money they lent to borrowers at pre-deregulation rates did not help their bottom line since banks make their profit on the spread, which is the difference between what banks earn on the money they borrow and what they pay in interest on consumer savings products. Many banks went bust.

As the country rolled into the 1990s, and interest rates began to plunge, banks cut their savings rates faster than they cut loan rates. That's called managing the spread. The result was that their profits got bigger and bigger. In addition to financing the enormous banking bailout by paying more taxes, you picked up the tab by earning less on your savings and paying more when you borrowed.

But that's only half the story. Banks began going fee crazy. They raised virtually all their old fees on accounts and invented a slew of new fees, which have been driving up their profits even higher.

The Money Line

There are 500 million checking, savings, and other accounts at U.S. banks, thrifts, and credit unions.

Every $1 deposited in a bank generates $7 to $10 in loans.

The Road to Riches

Banks don't advertise this fact, but you *can* negotiate a better deal on fees, and sometimes on interest rates. The decision about which fees to waive may be up to the branch manager. Competition from mutual funds and brokerages has made this wheeling and dealing possible. Credit card fees and rates are a particularly good place to start bargaining; competition in this area is fierce!

Fees and Charges: The Biggest New Money Makers

Fees and charges have been growing like weeds. These ugly little demons keep taking more and more out of your wallet. How do banks get away with it? Simple. Customers focus mostly on interest rates, not on fees. The bank slips in a higher fee here, a new little charge there, and you hardly notice it.

Thirty bucks to bounce a check in some cities? A $35 penalty if you're one day late with your credit card payment? Another $30 if you exceed your credit limit? Yes. Fees have become so important to banks that they're now considered "profit centers" all by themselves. In recent years, the percentage of banks' income that comes from fees has almost doubled! In fact, one banker stood up at a big convention a few years ago and bragged that his institution had suddenly discovered they were making money hand-over-fist by charging people whose accounts were overdrawn.

The big secret is this: Today banks use sophisticated new computer techniques to identify which customers are profitable and which ones aren't. Joe Doaks who maintains a low balance, but keeps pestering live tellers for service, is slapped silly with an extra fee every time he makes a transaction. But Mrs. Gottrocks, who has accounts in the six figures, doesn't pay a dime to do her banking. The name of the game is soak the little guy, and give the freebies to the well-heeled customer on whom the bank makes money.

Fiscal Facts

A bank's **Fee Disclosure Statement** is a document that lists all fees and the reasons why they're imposed. It's required by law, and your bank must make a copy available to you on request.

> **Bank-beater secret:** Ask your bank for a copy of its *Fee Disclosure Statement.* Read every part of it, word for word. Then match it against your personal banking behavior and switch to a lower-fee outfit if necessary.

Big Bank Mergers: Everybody Wins but You

Bank mergers are common, and it's more than likely your bank has been absorbed one or two times in a merger. In years past, giant newspaper ads touting customer benefits of the new merger were rampant. More ATMs, more resources, more branches, two great institutions uniting, blah, blah, blah.

Here's what usually happens, aside from the CEOs of the two banks personally making a few million bucks from the merger:

1. Mighty Megabuck, to prevent Friendly Federal's nervous customers from fleeing out the door, dangles a few incentives and freebies to keep them happy temporarily, like a special CD rate or a discount on a loan rate.

2. All the other banks in the area, smelling blood, swoop down on Friendly Federal's customers and offer their own special incentives to steal away that business. Because of this competition, more savings rates in the market go up.

3. A couple of months after the merger, Megabuck announces it's closing 80 branches that overlap with Friendly Federal's locations and laying off 1,500 employees.

4. Six months after the merger, after the temporary rate competition dies down, Megabuck begins cutting all its CD and Money Market Account rates. It also raises some of its personal loan rates a tad. Because Mighty Megabuck is the market leader, other outfits in town do the same thing.

> ### The Road to Riches
>
> Get cash back when you use your debit card at the supermarket check-out line. That way, there's usually no cost.

> ### The Money Line
>
> While banks grumble that they need to raise fees to cover their costs of handling customer transactions, a recent study turned up this fact: It costs the average big bank only $1.07 to have a live teller care for a deposit, compared with 27¢ at an ATM.

Result: The little guy gets stiffed from the big bank marriage, and is worse off now than he was before. The example we gave you may vary by situation, but we've seen it happen enough times to know that there's more truth to it than make-believe.

Bank-beater secret: When you hear your bank is merging, start shopping around for a smaller community bank or credit union, because they charge less. Don't believe all the promises that Megabank will feed you.

ATMs: An Inexpensive Way to Do Your Banking

When ATMs first came out, it cost nothing to use them. Then it cost 25¢, then 50¢, then a buck, then $1.50. That's if you used a rival bank's machine; many banks still offered the service free to their own customers. In the mid-1990s, the "double-whammy" ATM charge came along. The rival bank also hit you with a $1.50 fee for using the ATM, so it cost you *a total of $3* to make a machine transaction. In other words, the banks want their cake and want to eat it, too. First you're told not to bother a live teller or you'll get hit by a fee of $1 to $3 at some banks. So you run outside to their machines. But once you get into the ATM habit—wham!—you get nailed there, too. Not once, but twice on the same transaction!

Multiply that by millions of customers using their ATMs three or four times per month, and you get an idea of how much money is involved. The latest estimate is that all those new ATM fees have netted the banks an additional $2 billion a year! And there are a number of new fees, besides. For example, many banks now charge customers $25 an hour for helping to balance their statements or just for digging up one of their old account records. Others charge you $10 or $15 to close your account or shift funds from one account to another.

Watch Your Wallet _____

Pay attention to your ATM usage. You might think that restricting yourself to withdrawals of $20 at a clip is a way to exercise self-control; but every time you take out $20, the bank socks you with a fee. If you must use the ATM, take out a reasonable sum in a single transaction. Better you get charged once for withdrawing $100, than make five separate withdrawals of $20 each and get charged for each one.

Gone are the days when your friendly teller handled all your transactions. It's not a conspiracy, exactly, because the whole world—including banks—is becoming more electronic. It helps efficiency and productivity. If some mechanical marvel can replace a human being, the bank saves money—and banks love that. Their tellers have to put up with fewer people acting like pests in front of a long teller line. Some outfits go so far as to charge customers $3 for a live teller transaction, $1 for a deposit slip, or $8 to cash your paycheck at your employer's bank if you don't have an account there.

On special checking accounts for low-balance customers, banks will charge you more for your transactions if they are not through an ATM. You could be clipped with a higher charge if you make a simple balance inquiry through a person instead of a machine. When banks close their doors at 3:00 P.M., they know you'll have to conduct your late business electronically.

How Banks Work the Rates

This section explains some tricks that banks use to make the interest rates work to their advantage.

First, banks often push long-term CDs when interest rates are low, and short-term CDs when interest rates are high. Remember that little front-door– back-door example of how banks make sure they mark up your money to earn their profit spread? Well, here's another sly maneuver. Banks want to rent your savings money at the lowest possible cost (see Chapter 10 for more information).

Let's say CD rates have been rising for several months. You're all excited to see a five-year account that used to earn 5 percent interest now paying 6 percent. That's a whole extra 1 percent, right? So you're tempted to grab the deal.

Bank interest rates dropped steadily between 2001 and 2004. But suppose you once again saw rates up where they were in the late 1990s. Say the five-year CD goes back up to 7 percent. If you lock in at 6 percent between now and then, you've bilked yourself out of that extra 1 percent. On a $10,000 five-year CD, you would lose $500 by not waiting. Here's why: By opening the account now, you earn $600 a year for all five years for a total of $3,000 in interest. But if you buy the CD next year instead, when the rate is up to 7 percent, you'll earn $3,500 on the same $10,000 investment. In other words, you'll earn $500 more.

> **Fiscal Facts**
>
> The **prime rate** is the bank's benchmark rate. Supposedly it's what banks charge their most favored business customers when they borrow. The little mom-and-pop store that doesn't have shiny credit will be charged a higher rate—such as 2 or 3 percent above the prime rate. The prime rate also influences what the bank pays you on savings accounts.

Keep in mind that the reverse is true when rates are falling. Banks then promote short-term CDs more heavily. If you lock up a long-term account, you'll protect yourself with a high yield for a longer stretch of time.

> **Bank-beater secret:** Buy short-term CDs when rates are rising; go long only when rates are declining.

Second, banks drag their heels in raising savings rates after they increase their prime rate. The banks' *prime rate* goes up or down depending on how well the economy is doing. That rate influences most of the bank's other interest rates, including savings and personal loans. In a perfect world, you'd expect that if the prime rate increases or decreases by, say, one half of a percent, then your savings and loans would change by the same amount, right?

But what typically happens is this: When the prime jumps by a half-percent, banks boost your CD rates more slowly. It may take months for your CDs to increase by as much as the prime rate. That way banks can increase their profit by lending at the higher rate for a while before increasing the amount they have to pay you in savings and CD interest. Score one for the banks.

> **Bank-beater secret:** When the prime rate goes up, take out the loans you need immediately. Go short with CDs until the prime goes down.

Third, banks pay you zip on interest checking, money market accounts, and passbook savings. For some strange reason, millions of Americans keep stashing more than *$1 trillion* in low-paying savings accounts and even lower-interest checking accounts.

These naive folks could make a bundle more by shifting to CDs. Chalk that up to old-fashioned American savings habits.

Banks are euphoric over that idiotic consumer behavior. They're getting the cheapest money of all through the front door by peddling 2 and 3 percent savings accounts that cost them way less than CDs. Then—they mark up the money and lend it out—often at a rate that's more then 10 times what the money cost them!

> **Bank-beater secret:** Don't keep a dime more than you need in low-rate money market accounts (MMAs) and passbooks. Figure how much you won't have to touch for a particular length of time; put that money into higher-paying CDs for that period of time.

The Truth About High Credit Card Rates

How come over the past decade, while your savings rates were jumping up and down like a Mexican jumping bean, banks kept their credit card rates sky-high? On fixed-rate cards, for instance, the rate never went lower than about 15.5 percent and was as high as 19 percent. At the same time, savings rates have plunged to between 1.7 and 5 percent, depending on the type of account.

Eventually, banks discovered they could make atrociously high profits on credit card fees, such as for late payments, and began bringing their credit card rates down. But in the meantime, the average card rate has still been nibbling at 14 percent. So wouldn't you like to be in the banks' position—paying the average Joe 0.29 percent on his checking, 2 or 3 percent on CDs, and still making 14 percent on credit cards?

The banks' "official" explanation is that they need those high card rates to cover their operating costs, and nasty things like card fraud, counterfeiting, bad debt, and so forth.

A more likely reason is that the banking lobbies fought hard for years to raise state usury laws (the maximum amount banks and other lenders in a state can charge on loans). They wound up getting three out of every four states to pass laws setting the usury ceiling at 18 percent.

Watch Your Wallet

> Don't jump too much. Some cardholders keep switching their credit cards to get a lower rate. That's okay, except that if you do it too many times it will show up on your credit report and may scare off future lenders.

Card issuers are now afraid that if they bring their rates down too low, the states might change their laws to something below 18 percent. And, if they did, well heck, the banks might not get those high usury ceilings back again. Do you suppose that's why so many of the giant banks have transferred their credit card operations to states such as Delaware and South Dakota, which have *no* usury ceilings? That's why they mail billions of high-rate credit card offers out of those states to your homes. They get away with it because it's legal to do that from those no-usury-limit locations. Don't ever expect the banks to admit any of this to you. They won't. They'll just continue to pull the wool over your eyes and cry about their costs that are caused by Americans' high debt and personal bankruptcy rates.

> **Bank-beater secret:** Get rid of all your credit cards or carry only one or two at the most—the lowest plastic you can find. Pay the cards off every month. *Never* pay only the minimum amount due. If, for example, you pay only the minimum 2 percent every month on a balance of $5,000, it will take 32 years to pay off the card—and the interest will cost you $7,700!

Banks have many tricks when it comes to lending money. One is to promote low introductory rates on loans. The reason that this trick works is that a lot of Americans are just plain suckers for what looks like a cheap deal, and they don't bother to notice the fine print before they sign up at their bank.

Fiscal Facts

Here are two good reasons for staying away from big banks: (1) They charge 16 percent more in fees than do small institutions; and (2) the average regular checking account at a big outfit costs $217.32 a year, versus only $111.59 at a credit union.

Suppose that other outfits peddle a variable-rate credit card at 15 percent, but Megabuck Bank pushes a 6 percent rate. Sounds good until you read the flyspeck footnote at the bottom of the ad. The rate is only good for six months, after which it rises to the banks' prime rate, plus, maybe 9 percentage points. If the prime is at 8.5 percent, the card rate eventually goes to 17.5 percent. On a $3,000 balance, that's a difference of $345 a year in interest.

In another example, Friendly Federal lures you into a home equity loan at 4 percent, which appears to be a lower interest rate than what other outfits offer. They're out to grab you before you decide to do business across the street. The same thing happens as in the Megabuck card offer. The rate applies only for a few months, and then—bingo—it jumps up like an antelope. In both situations, you definitely could have found a better deal at a different bank and saved hundreds of dollars. Don't get snookered. Remember that nothing is for nothing in this world.

> **Bank-beater secret:** If the deal looks too good to be true, it probably is. Study the fine print before you sign on the dotted line.

One strategy banks use to protect themselves on the money they lend out is *not* to lend you any money unless they think you *don't* need any. It used to happen this way, over and over again: Assume that two guys named Dick and Harry apply to the same institution for a loan. Dick's family is strapped. They got behind in their debts after Dick lost his job, and they've been living off their credit cards and savings accounts, which are almost dry. The family rents a small house, and has no expensive jewels or other collateral to pledge against a loan. Dick and the family go to church every week, have never told a lie, and have a child ready for college. They need $5,000 to tide them over and maybe start a small lawn-maintenance service until Dick gets another regular job. The problem is that Dick and his wife have spotty credit reports, which make them a Grade C risk to the bank.

Harry's situation is different. He's a sterling, Grade A credit risk. The family has $120,000 equity in their home, owns another piece of property, has $85,000 in CDs, $110,000 in stocks, four credit cards, and a car that's paid off. They want to borrow $50,000.

Question: Which loan application do you think would normally whistle through the bank, and which one would probably be rejected? That's right. Harry gets his money on the spot, but Dick might be turned down, or, in a worst-case scenario, pay a "subprime" lending rate that's 2 or 5 percentage points higher than Harry's rate. Moral: The worse off you are financially, the more the bank will charge you.

The Road to Riches

Here's a bank-beater secret: Contacting Consumer Credit Counseling Services (CCCS), 1-800-388-2227, to get your credit straightened out. CCCS will do it for little or no fee. The nonprofit organization will contact creditors and can help you and your family set up easy payment plans. And, in a case like the one Dick and his wife have, they should write out a detailed business plan for their new business and present it to the bank. The plan should include a financial projection of revenues, costs, and profits.

Banks argue that they need to raise fees to cover their costs of "expanding" their services, such as later hours, online banking, more ATMs, and branches in supermarkets. But, that's a lot of hooey and you know it. The fact is, banks have added billions of dollars in new profits by hiking the bank's fees. If you bounce a check, for example, you're charged between 11 and 32 times their cost of processing it. And, usually the bigger the institution, the higher the fees.

 Watch Your Wallet

Remember: Banks want your money, not you—your visits cost them time and money, so many of them will try to get it back in fees when you take up time at the teller's window. If your bank does this, keep your visits to a minimum—or better still, change banks!

How to Avoid Being Ripped Off

Why are people so complacent and gullible? Several reasons: The amounts are small; a buck here, a buck there. Hardly noticeable. When they need cash, no one gripes about paying $1.50 or $3 to get emergency money out of an ATM in the middle of the night. The father who wires $100 to his daughter at college pays $20 to send the wire, and the daughter pays $10 to receive it. In other words, a 30 percent interest rate. The person with a bad credit record who gets a secured credit card for him or herself doesn't complain about paying a sky-high annual fee. If someone withdraws any money from their CD before the maturity date, they get hit with a penalty of three to six months' worth of interest. The biggest mistake? Few people ever sit down and study their outfit's "fee disclosure" document, which, by law, must explain each and every fee or penalty on accounts. And few notice the sneaky way that banks sprinkle their little debit items on your monthly statement. The list goes on, yet all these charges add up ... *way* up! You, my friend, are being quietly and consistently ripped off.

Step 1: Beware of the Danger Zones

No one is going to tie a string around your finger with a sign on it saying, "Here's exactly how to avoid paying that next fee." You simply need to remember several things. First, be aware of the trouble areas where you're likely to encounter bank fees. They usually pop up if ...

- There are a lot of human transactions involved, such as making any (or too many) trips to a live teller during one month.

- You're a very-low-balance customer and make a lot of time-consuming transactions, or you don't keep several accounts at the same bank.

- You have a bad habit of always using another bank's ATMs.

- You're so much as one day late with your payment, or exceed your credit limit.

- You grab a checking account that pays interest, instead on one that doesn't. Truth is, the interest-bearing account requires a lot more money to open, and you must maintain a much larger average balance to escape big monthly fees. Plus the interest will be puny—at best. Bottom line: You're better off getting a checking account that doesn't pay interest.

Watch Your Wallet

Some banks charge as much as $24 for a box of 200 checks. You can get that same box for $7 or less by ordering direct from the printer. Visit the website of Checks-in-the-mail (www.checksinthemail.com; 1-800-733-4443) or Current Checks (www.currentchecks.com; 1-800-426-0822) for more information.

◆ You close out your MMA or passbook account only a few months after opening it or withdraw any of your CD money before the account's maturity date.

The newest and ugliest fees of all? A special charge if you don't use your credit card or home equity line of credit at all for six months or always pay your card balance off on time. You mean you pay a fee for being a Goody-Two-Shoes customer? That's right. You're penalized for *behaving yourself* or doing *nothing*, instead of doing *something*. Banks can't make a dime off you under those circumstances—unless they impose a fee.

The ugliest rates? Your credit card rate can zoom to 25 percent or 29 percent if your payment arrives late two times within a six-month period. Or you can get whacked $29 if you exceed your credit limit.

Step 2: Absolutely, Positively Shop Other Outfits

Here's a big mistake consumers make: For whatever reason—apathy, laziness, or because they say they don't have the time—they simply roll over and play dead instead of shopping other banks beyond their present one. It makes no difference how convenient your bank is, how much you like the folks who work there, or how stubbornly loyal you've been to the bank all these years. Odds are there's an institution out there whose fees are lower than what you've been paying. Ask yourself: Why would you *not* shop if you knew you could save money? It's *your* cash we're talking about, not the bank's!

Instead of being hung up only on interest rates, as most people are, tell yourself now that you're going to start looking at the rest of your banking picture— those outrageous fees and charges that are costing you more money every year. Ask your bank (and about four or five other institutions) for a copy of their Fee Disclosure document. They must offer it to you, by law. The document will be fairly short and look like a bunch of gobbledygook, but it breaks down all the fees, one by one, for each type of account such as checking, savings, and credit cards.

Step 3: Match Your Behavior Against the Fees

Next—this is critical—outline on paper *how you personally bank*. For instance, how many checks a month do you write? What's your average monthly balance? How often do you slip below that figure? How often do you reorder checks? What about late payments? How often do you visit a live teller? Make ATM transactions at another bank or your bank? How many times do you go over your credit limit or get a cash advance on your credit card? The list goes on and on. (Whatever you do, don't feel embarrassed. You're just going to bite the bullet this one time so you can slash your banking costs. And, it won't change the rest of your life one iota.)

Next, match your personal banking behavior against each bank's Fee Disclosure document. Add up the costs, bank by bank, based on that behavior. You'll be amazed by two things: The differences in all the banks' fees, and how much money you can save per year. It's a sure-fire method to cut your banking costs. But to really save the most, you must also discipline yourself a little bit by, for example, never using any ATMs except those owned by your bank. The bottom line here is, we're potentially talking savings of hundreds of dollars annually, not just nickels and dimes!

Worse Than Banks: Check-Cashing Stores

Neighborhood check-cashing stores claim they will cash any check for you, no matter what. They say they're providing a necessary service, especially in poor neighborhoods, and that there are 12 million Americans without a checking account. So what do those people do? They're forced to pay their bills by buying expensive money orders at the check-cashing company.

Let's say a gentleman needs cash to tide him over until he gets paid by his company 14 days from now. He runs to the check-cashing outfit and writes a post-dated check for $220. The check-casher gives him $200 for 14 days. At that time, if he can't make the check good or pay the $220 in cash, he rolls-over the amount for another two weeks, with another fee. Many folks get trapped that way for a year or more, and wind up paying more than $1,000 in interest on a $200 loan. On an annualized basis, the interest rate on these rip-off transactions can range from 300 percent to an astronomical 1,800 percent!

In some parts of the country, those same check-cashers are taking advantage of seniors who cash their Social Security checks. One expert estimated that it cost a retiree trying to live on $8,000 a year almost $200 a year to get his cash that way.

The Bigger They Are, the Worse It Gets

Free checking billboards grace interstate highways nationwide, but they are more the exception rather than the rule. One PIRG survey showed that only 15 out of every 100 banks offered it, while 41 out of 100 gave free checking with direct deposit of payroll, pension, or government checks. Then between the years 2001 and 2003 things changed: 17 percent more banks began offering free checking, thanks in part to the explosion in costly fees and penalties. Whatever happened to the big banks' promises that, by merging with another large outfit, they'd become more efficient and pass along the savings to you? Those were pipe dreams, friend. You're talking out-and-out greed and bankers' efforts to satisfy their shareholders.

Bouncing a Check Costs a Bundle

One poor soul had this happen to him: He inadvertently overdrew his checking account by $4.50 without knowing it, but needed cash. Over a two-day period he used his own bank's ATM three times (to avoid paying a surcharge). He withdrew $20, $20, and $40, for a total of $80. Nothing on the ATM screen warned him that he was overdrawing his account each time.

The bank nailed him with a $28.50 charge for each overdraw, or $85.50 altogether—the equivalent of paying an 85.5 percent interest rate on his money.

In another situation, a father asked a bank why it charged his nine-year-old daughter a $5 per month maintenance fee on her $75 savings account. Answer: She had to make a deposit every month to avoid the fee.

> **CAUTION**
>
> **Watch Your Wallet**
>
> Beware: Banks choose the order in which they process the day's deposits and checks on your account. Even when you know that you've gotten a deposit in on the right day to cover your outstanding checks— if it's processed after the checks are, you *still* get hit with a bounced-check fee.

If you want to avoid this kind of banditry, run—don't walk—to the closest credit union that will permit you to sign up as a member. Because if you don't, sooner or later your bank is going to get you, too!

The cost of bouncing a check depends on where you live. The average is about $28 nationwide, but in Philadelphia it's about $30, while California is lowest at around $11. One way banks really slap it to customers is by paying the largest check first when several of your checks come in for payment at the same time. This increases the odds that one or more of your other checks will bounce. And each time one bounces, you get nicked with a fee. By the way, guess how much profit banks make off bounced checks? Would you believe $5.2 billion a year from people who wrote the rubber checks and another $900 million off the people who tried to cash them?

How You Can Negotiate

Once upon a time, banks were as rigid as granite when you wanted them to change a rate or waive a fee. Not any more. Most folks aren't aware of it, but because banks today are being hit from all sides by competition, they'll probably cut your credit card rate right on the spot if you complain loudly enough.

You don't like the fee you've just been hit with after giving the bank your business for the past 10 years? You don't like the interest rate they advertise, especially considering the size of the deposit you're contemplating for a CD account? Think you're being overcharged on the home equity loan that you want to take out?

Stand up and bark and tell the bank you're not satisfied, that you feel you need to consider taking your business elsewhere, by shopping other institutions in the area. This nice little aggressive strategy may not work 100 percent of the time, but the odds are more in your favor today than ever before. We've heard of banks cutting a customer's credit card rate from 18 percent to 9.9 percent on the spot.

Don't be bashful. Give it a try. After all, it's your money—not theirs—and you have every right to complain about any part of a deal you don't like. You just might be surprised by the positive reaction you get.

> **A bank-beater secret that can't be beat**: Don't try the negotiation strategy with a bank teller, account representative or platform personnel. Go straight to the branch manager or another officer—and nobody else.

The bottom line is that too many consumers hurt themselves by not taking the time to negotiate with banks and complain about rates, fees, and other charges. You have nothing to lose by trying and odds are that the bank will give you a break and change its terms, just because you asked.

The Least You Need to Know

- All bank fees are going up, and banks keep inventing new ones.

- Some banks charge new fees for doing nothing; that is, having an inactive account, as opposed to doing something bad.

- You need to be aware of which banking areas are liable to hit you with a fee. For example, the less you bother the bank's employees and the more you conduct all your banking electronically, the lower your fees will be.

- You can switch institutions and easily save a couple hundred dollars a year by shopping five or six banks and matching their fees against your personal banking behavior.

- Big banks charge higher fees than small institutions and credit unions.

Chapter 7

Interest Rates 101

In This Chapter

- How banks calculate the interest on your money
- What "APY" and "APR" mean in rates—in simple English
- The key difference between rate and yield
- Bank compounding explained the *easy* way
- How banks play with the numbers
- The most important rates you should watch

Let's face it. The average Joe and Jane know zip about how interest rates work. They read tons of page-one stories about rates going up or down. They hear about Wall Street analysts having heart attacks if rates suddenly jump, and they hang on every word that comes out of the mouth of the chairman of the Federal Reserve Board. Meanwhile, across America, guys are hanging over their back fences, asking their neighbor, "What do you think is gonna happen to mortgage rates?"

Today, interest rates run our lives just as much if not more than the economy. But, people don't have the foggiest about what makes rates behave the way they do, or how they can affect their wallets. Yet by knowing just the few basics outlined in this chapter, you'll be able to take much of the mystery out of the rate subject. It breaks this complicated subject down into Main Street language that you can easily understand so you can apply it to savings, mortgages, credit cards, you name it.

Understanding How Banks Are Cashing In on Your Ignorance

How many people do you know who can walk into a bank, discuss opening a new savings account, and figure exactly how their interest rate will be computed? Not many. Banks have been around for hundreds of years, and lately they've been inventing a slew of different, complex formulas for every kind of account they offer.

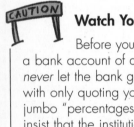

Watch Your Wallet

Before you sign up for a bank account of any type, *never* let the bank get away with only quoting you mumbo-jumbo "percentages." Instead, insist that the institution explain the deal in dollars and cents, nothing else. This rule should apply to both your investing *and* your borrowing.

Few customers ever ask how the numbers work. That gives banks a big advantage. They can sell you an account based on a complicated mathematical computation that really earns you less money than you can earn somewhere else. You may never realize you've been had. As one bank customer complained, "I'm getting smoked by all those numbers."

Even if you have a degree from Harvard or the Wharton School, you might not understand all the account rates. Worse still, the rising tide of fees and charges hit the little guy more than people who maintain big balances. But if you take some time to learn the inside tricks of what the banks are up to, we guarantee you'll come out ahead, dollar-wise.

Learning the Rate Basics and the Lingo

A rate is nothing more than a percentage number. Your bank pays you one rate when it borrows some of your money in the form of a savings account or CD, and it charges another customer a higher rate when that person borrows from the bank. The difference is the bank's profit. Your game plan is to earn as high an interest rate as you can when you save, and pay the lowest possible rate when you take out a mortgage, auto or home equity loan, or get a credit card.

But as you learn more about what makes rates tick, remember that another big secret to making money at the bank is to pay attention to other critical factors as well. One key is to slash those disgusting fees and charges. Another is to beware of introductory come-on rates that look great, but disappear after a few months. A "fantastic" rate means zilch if it goes "poof" in the night and you get pounded by ridiculous extra costs!

Everybody uses the word "rate" when they talk about banking, but that's not 100 percent accurate. By law, your banker must use a few other words to describe what you earn on savings or pay on loans. These are the key terms:

"Rate" vs. "Yield," and That Thing Called "APR": Knowing the Difference

It's important to know the difference between an annual percentage rate and an annual percentage yield. One easy way of distinguishing them is as follows:

◆ **Annual percentage yield**, or APY, applies to savings and CD accounts.

◆ **Annual percent rate,** APR, on the other hand, applies to loan accounts.

The Money Line _____

Which would you rather have? An outright gift of $1 million, or a penny in a savings account that doubles every day for 30 days? Better think this one through before you answer. At the end of the 30 days, the $1 million will still be worth a million bucks, but the penny will have grown to an astounding $5.37 million! That's not a misprint: Get out your calculator and check it for yourself.

First, APY:

◆ A rate is what the account earns before any interest is added. In other words, it's just a naked number.

◆ More important, the APY is what the account actually pays you in *one year*, after all the interest is added to your original deposit. The key words are "one year." That's the APY—expressed as a one-year number—regardless of the CD term of six months, one year, five years or whatever. It's the only way to accurately compare different deals at different banks because it includes the *interest* you earn. You're able to compare apples versus apples, on a one-year basis, without going berserk over a zillion different numbers.

◆ Compounding is the mathematical formula the bank uses to figure your yield based on the rate. It simply means interest added to interest. *The more frequently the bank compounds your money, the more interest you earn and the higher the yield.* For instance, daily compounding is better than monthly or quarterly compounding (see the table, "How Compounding Works," in this chapter).

And here's how APR works:

◆ The percentage rate, the amount you borrow, and the number of years you pay back the loan influence your monthly payment. The more you borrow and/or the higher your rate, the higher your payment will be. The longer you take to repay the loan, the lower your monthly payment, but the more you'll pay in total interest. Remember: The APR is *not* the rate of interest you pay on a loan, because it includes other costs as well.

◆ By law, on many loans such as those for new and used cars and credit cards, lenders must also show an APR in addition to the basic borrowing rate. The APR is always higher than the basic rate because it also includes certain fees and charges on the loan. Hence, it does a better job of revealing the total cost of your loan.

Fixed vs. Variable Rates

On all bank accounts, you need to know whether your rate is fixed or variable. It can make a whale of a difference in what you pay the bank, or what the bank pays you. A fixed rate is fixed, period. It can't ever change over the life of an account, or so you think. Strangely, banks have been known to change the so-called "fixed rate" on a credit card. If, say, you lock in a fixed mortgage rate while rates are low, that's all you'll be charged, regardless of how high market rates go in the future. But with an adjustable-rate mortgage (ARM), the bank ties your rate to an index, such as its prime rate, a Treasury bill, or another index. If that index rate changes, so does the rate you pay. In a period of rising interest rates, ARMs work against the homeowner because as time goes by, the monthly payments will increase. But if mortgage rates plunge, as they did in the early 2000s, it's best to lock up a low fixed rate and know that's all you'll pay over the life of the loan.

Variable rates aren't as frequent on savings accounts as on loan accounts. You might occasionally run across an MMA whose rate is tied to what the average money fund pays, or the latest yield on a Treasury bill—plus an extra fraction of a percentage point to make you think you're earning more than you could with other investments. But with some loans, such as adjustable-rate mortgages, the rate is always variable and is tied to whatever index the lender uses.

Once again, it's the bottom line in dollars-and-cents that counts, not the particular rate.

Compounding = Interest on Top of Interest

Relax. There aren't 10 guys in your neighborhood that know how bank compounding works. Here's the easy way to understand it: Say you open a new $10,000 savings account that earns 6 percent, with daily compounding. On the second day, the bank adds interest of $1.64 (6 percent times 10,000 divided by 365 days in a year). That increases your balance to $10,001.64. The next day, it figures interest the same way on top of the $10,001.64, and continues the same process each day thereafter. Your balance gets bigger and bigger.

With daily compounding, you'd have $10,618 in the account at the end of one year. That's a few more dollars than you would have received if the bank had compounded your money less frequently, such as quarterly or annually (see the following table, "How Compounding Works.")

Note that there is no difference in the amounts ($10,600) for "simple interest" and "annual compounding," both of which pay interest at the end of the year. But, there *would* be a difference if you left the money in the account for a second year. Here's why: With annual compounding, the interest in the second year would be added to the interest in the first year. But under the simple interest method, in the second year you'd only earn interest on your original $10,000 investment. In other words, on a multi-year CD—everything else being equal—annual compounding pays more than simple interest.

Here are the quarter-by-quarter comparisons:

How Compounding Works

Compound	First Quarter	Second Quarter	Third Quarter	Fourth Quarter
Continuous	$10,152	$10,305	$10,460	$10,618
Daily	$10,151	$10,305	$10,460	$10,618
Weekly	$10,151	$10,304	$10,460	$10,618
Monthly	$10,151	$10,304	$10,459	$10,617
Quarterly	$10,150	$10,302	$10,457	$10,614
Annual	$10,000	$10,000	$10,000	$10,600
Simple interest	$10,000	$10,000	$10,000	$10,600

Knowing How Banks Create (and Play With) Their Numbers

Many folks foolishly park their money at a bank without ever knowing how and why one bank's yields are higher than another's, even when everything else about the accounts may look the same. By learning how banks design their rate offers, you can easily earn a lot more in interest on a good-size investment.

Time Is Money

On a savings account, the longer you agree to lock up your money, the higher the interest rate. One-year CDs usually pay more than six-month accounts. Five-year CD yields are higher than those on two-year accounts, and so on. Why do banks do this? It's an enticement to keep your cash in their vaults for a longer period. The bank can count on the money staying there, instead of having to replace those deposits every few months or every year.

Banks Use a Crystal Ball

Other factors also influence what banks pay on CDs—such as where they think interest rates might be months or years from now. And, here's where you can become your own rate expert. Usually, when banks believe interest rates will rise over the next several months or years, they raise their long-term CD yields (such as on five-year accounts) faster than those on short-term accounts (such as six months and one year). Why? Because they would rather start paying you a little more today to lock up a five-year account, than pay you an even higher yield later on.

Supply and Demand Affect Your Rates, Too

Banks try to balance their savings-account maturities against their loan maturities. In other words, they might want to match the money in their four-year or five-year CD accounts against their volume of four-year and five-year auto loans. If, for instance, they're super-heavy in auto loans, they'll probably offer a slightly higher rate on five-year CDs to bring their deposit portfolio in line with their loan portfolio.

Understanding How Banks Brew Up Their Rates

With all that as a backdrop, let's pretend we're looking in on Megabuck Bank over a typical week to see how it sets its interest rates. In effect, we'll be peeking into their kitchen to see how they make their soup.

The first thing you should know is that banks typically change CD rates every week, generally on Tuesday or Wednesday. Let's say it's Thursday. When you waltzed into the lobby, you noticed Megabuck's rate numbers on their plastic sign are higher than they were last week. The one-year CD that paid 5 percent last week has edged up to 5.50 percent. How come? Nobody in the bank is going to tell you. Chances are, the bank didn't even explain why to its employees.

What might have happened is that two days ago, on Tuesday, when Megabuck's rate-setting committee met, they noticed that a whole bunch of things occurred since last week. For example, let's say ...

♦ Treasury rates moved up at the federal government's Monday auction.

♦ Many of the country's biggest banks have been raising rates.

♦ Just before the Tuesday meeting, a Megabuck secretary made cold calls to eight other local banks and found their rates, too, had climbed.

♦ The morning paper said unemployment is down, and consumer prices and housing starts were higher last month than the month before—signaling that the economy is getting stronger.

♦ Megabuck's loan officer reports more of the bank's consumer and business customers have been borrowing, which means the bank has to pull in some new money to replace what has been loaned out.

That's why Megabuck's committee raised rates. But had the bank gotten different information, if, for example, consumer prices and housing were down instead of up, and if other banks were dropping their rates, Megabuck also might have lowered its numbers.

What Banks Watch to Set Their Rates

Banks don't set rates in a vacuum. There are key things they watch (which you can easily watch, too) to see which way the numbers will probably go. The average person may not realize it, but certain economic indicators will dictate whether a bank will raise or lower its rates, or leave them alone. It's based on how the Federal Reserve reacts to changes in the economic numbers.

The problem is, unless the average person knows what to look for, he or she will go nuts trying to sift through all the latest rumors by analysts, advisers, brokers, and banks by themselves. One day some pundit says the Fed might raise rates, the next day another wag swears the Fed is going to lower them. That shows you how confused the "experts" really are. They have a lousy batting average trying to predict rate direction, so you mustn't trust everything they say when you're wondering if CD and mortgage rates will go up, down, or sideways.

Here's what you should watch:

The Federal Reserve's two key rates. They are the Fed discount rate (what it charges banks to borrow from the Fed) and the Fed overnight funds rate (what banks charge to borrow money from each other). At its meetings, which happen about once a month or so, the Fed may raise or lower one or both of those rates. If it raises a rate, it means the Fed thinks the economy is getting too hot, and it must, therefore, cool things down to head off inflation. If it lowers a rate, the Fed is trying to stimulate a lagging economy by making it cheaper for businesses to borrow money, thus stimulating business activity. Fed rates don't affect you directly, but they do influence the rates that banks set for your deposits and loans.

Watch Your Wallet

Just because the Fed lowers its key rates doesn't mean that mortgage lenders will automatically drop their rates by the same margin. That's where home buyers make a huge mistake. The same thing once happened when the Fed cut rates many times, but variable-rate credit cards stopped dropping all of a sudden.

The Money Line

If your credit history is less than stellar, don't expect banks to lower your rate just because it's dropped its prime rate. You'll still get socked with a "subprime" rate much higher than what credit-worthy applicants pay.

Key economic indicators. These are the numbers the Fed watches to decide what to do with its key rates. Its economists study every piece of economic information they can get their hands on, especially unemployment figures, wages, producer prices, consumer prices, retail sales, new plant equipment, housing starts, you name it. Even the federal deficit and the soundness of the dollar have an influence on the Fed's decisions. When the data show very strong gains, the economy may be tilting toward inflation. Data suggesting a weaker economy, such as higher unemployment figures and lower housing starts, could lead to a Fed rate cut.

The prime rate. When the Fed raises or lowers its key rates, the banks fall in line by increasing or decreasing their prime rate by the same margin. For example, a one-quarter percentage point decrease by the Fed would prompt the banks to change the prime from 8.50 percent to 8.25 percent. The prime rate is supposedly what banks charge their most creditworthy business customers to borrow money. When that rate changes, your savings and loan rates do, too. For example, a quarter-point drop in variable-rate credit cards and home equity loans, whose rates are tied to the prime rate, would result in these consumer loan rates also falling. Conversely, when the prime rate rises, so do these loan rates.

Local savings rate direction. In local rate tables that run weekly in your newspaper, pick out 5 to 10 of the largest area banks to follow. Track their 6-month, 1-year and 5-year CD yields week after week. Note which rates seem to be falling, and which ones appear to be rising, especially on longer-term accounts. That trend is usually a hint of where banks expect rates to be down the road. One thing that influences savings rates in a particular market is the strength of the local economy. If the economy is brisk, banks are lending more money to businesses for growth and expansion. This creates a need to attract new funds to replace those that the banks lent out, meaning they must offer higher rates on MMAs and CDs.

Long-term bond yields. They'll tell you whether mortgage rates are on the way up or down. Specifically, follow 10-year Treasury bond yields because that's what the mortgage market uses to set fixed-rate home loans. Why? Because long bond yields are based on what's likely to happen years from now, and that scenario can change by the hour or by the minute. In other words, as dumb as it sounds, the experts are continually making their best guess on the *future*, as opposed to the present or what happened five minutes ago. Anticipation plays a big part in the picture. If some new economic indicator suggests inflation is in the wind-bingo-long bond yields will jump, and so will mortgage rates. But if economic data suggest the economy is slowing down, bond and mortgage numbers will drop.

The Money Line

What some people don't know: It's the 10-year bond yield, not changes in the prime rate, that directly influences mortgage rates. However, the prime rate is a general indicator of overall rate movement, which can include mortgages.

The Money Line

Interest rates can vary greatly across America, and by type of institution. For example, on the same given day mortgage rates might be three fourths of a percentage point higher in Wisconsin than in Connecticut. And also the same day, the average yield on a five-year CD at a credit union may be 1 percent higher than at a bank or thrift.

Don't Kid Yourself–What Happens in Tokyo Now Affects You in Peoria

There's an enormous new influence on interest rates in the United States. It's how well other countries are doing in the global economy. When the economy of one distant country slips, such as Malaysia in the late 1990s, the currencies of other nations in the region start falling like dominos.

Once upon a time, that would have had no effect on America. Not so today. Countries are so economically linked that news 10,000 miles away can have a direct effect on your mortgage rates, as well as your job.

For example, let's say Asian economic markets crumble because of a Japanese bank crisis or Malaysian revolt. Currencies are devalued. The dollar is worth more than it was a few weeks ago. U.S. manufacturers can't sell their goods in Asia because our prices go up, and those nations cut back on their buying. But Asian countries, to survive, begin exporting more to the United States. The competition forces U.S. manufacturers to cut prices and it drives up their inventories. Plants lay off employees. America's economy gets weaker, and economists foresee a downturn.

The Federal Reserve cuts interest rates to stimulate business. Savings and loan rates drop. Long-term bond yields also fall on the recessionary news, taking mortgage rates with them. Maybe that won't happen, but America no longer lives in a vacuum. Financially, it's tied to the rest of the world.

Chiseling Gets Down to Pennies

Wait until you hear this one. We all know there are 365 days in a year. Well, not all banks use that many days when they compute your interest. Some work with a 360-day year. That shaves your earnings by only pennies, but it saves the banks millions of dollars a year.

Say you deposit $10,000 in an account that pays 3 percent interest, compounded daily. If the bank uses a 365-day calculation method, you earn $304.53 in annual interest; with a 360-day method, the interest comes to $300.30 on the same account.

"Indexed" Accounts Protect the Bank More Than They Protect You

Indexed accounts have become the rage in the past decade because they allow the bank to set the rates they pay you on savings or charge you on loans, based on a known benchmark. It can be the bank's prime rate, a U.S. Treasury bill, or some other known index that moves up or down with the economy.

An index gives the banks a predictable, controlled device that protects the bank from swings in interest rates. If their costs rise (such as having to pay you higher interest on CDs when the economy gets stronger), their indexes on rates for credit cards, home equity credit lines, mortgages and other loans will also rise. If banks didn't protect themselves that way, it would cut into their profits.

Key Math Questions You Should Ask

Consumers tend to forget to ask the most important, basic questions before depositing funds or borrowing money from a bank. Yet the answers to the following questions are critical when you shop around for the best deals. The moral is, if you don't compare institutions and ask the following questions, you could easily wind up with less money in your pocket:

- On savings accounts and CDs, what are the interest rate and the annual percentage yield (APY)?

- Based on the compounding method, how much money will I have in the account, in dollars and cents, at the end of the first year (or when my CD matures, if the account is less than one year)?

- Is the interest rate tied to an index? If so, how often can the index change?

- How often is the account compounded? Daily? Quarterly? Annually?

- On loans, what is the rate and what is the APR? What does the APR include?

There are a lot of different kinds of interest rates out there, but if you learn the basics we discussed in this chapter, you can find the best deal for your money.

The Least You Need to Know

- Use the Annual Percentage Yield (APY) to compare CDs of different terms and figure out which really offers you the best deal.

- The Annual Percentage Rate (APR) includes the rate and certain fees and charges on loans.

- Rates on many loan accounts and a few deposit accounts are variable and are tied to an index.

- Keep your eye on Fed rates, the banks' prime rate, and long-term bond yields, as they dictate the rates banks set on your personal accounts.

◆ The more frequently the bank compounds your money, the more interest you earn. Accounts that compound daily are best.

◆ Always get the bank to explain every deal to you in dollars and cents, instead of percentages.

Chapter 8

How to Get the Best Deal on a Checking Account

In This Chapter

- ◆ How the right checking deal can save you hundreds of dollars
- ◆ Why a noninterest account can be better than one paying interest
- ◆ How to avoid getting nickel-and-dimed to death by checking fees
- ◆ How outrageous ATM charges are robbing you blind
- ◆ The secrets to shrewd checking shopping—including getting the cheapest account

You may not realize it, but aside from credit cards nowhere are you getting clobbered as badly on bank fees as on your checking account. While you've been using your checkbook to pay bills and buy things, banks have been slowly, but steadily, jacking up just about every checking fee you can think of. For example, today it costs as much as $30 if you bounce a check.

A checkbook is a basic part of American life; no one wants to be without one, yet few people complain about the rising costs because they're used to checking "convenience." In fact, not shopping around for a better checking deal could be costing you $200 to $300 extra per year! You could easily keep that money in your wallet simply by changing banks.

Do too many consumers take checking for granted? You bet. This makes it easier for banks to slip in fees and charges that you don't notice. This chapter shows you how to get the most out of your checking by explaining how banks exploit these accounts, how to figure out exactly what kind of account you need, how to locate the best deal in town, and how to avoid those ugly fees.

Checking Account Basics

Ever wonder why banks run so many ads promoting checking deals? They want to get their hands on your checking account because it's their "core" business. They figure that if they can grab your checking, they've also got the best shot at landing your CD, personal loan, and mortgage business. And if you're a high-balance checking customer (instead of somebody whose balance consistently runs below $1,000), then all the better for them. They have more money to lend out at a profit while they're paying you zip in interest. No wonder there's been an explosion of so-called "free" checking accounts in recent years. Currently more than 60 percent of banks offer them, but you must dig deeply to find out about the hidden fees.

Watch Your Wallet _____

The cop on the block is watching you. A company called ChexSystems keeps tabs on U.S. consumers who collectively write more than 60 billion checks a year. Specifically, it maintains lists of those who write bad checks, don't pay the bank if they do, or otherwise cheat the institution. This way, banks can weed out the naughty people who apply for a checking account. The real bad news is that if you land in ChexSystem's data base, you stay there for *five years!* Eighty percent of all U.S. banks and credit unions belong to ChexSystem's network, so, if you're rejected when you apply for a new checking account, now you know the reason why.

The average interest-paying checking account earns only 1.05 percent, whereas the typical noninterest account pays only 0.27 percent. The average monthly fee on an interest-bearing account is $5.86 versus $10.86 on a no-interest deal. But the average balance you need to avoid fees is way high: $1,088 on an interest-bearing account as opposed to a big $2,258 on non-interest. You'll find better deals by searching Bankrate.com on the Internet, such as 2.75 percent on an interest account at Presidential Bank, with $1,500 to open and maintaining at least a $1,000 balance. On the other hand, you can get a free checking account at Wachovia Bank, for example, with only $50 to open. An example on the high end is Crown Banking, where you must keep a $5,000 balance to avoid a $20 per month fee, and the account pays only 0.10 percent interest. To figure out how much your current checking account is costing you—and how you can get a better deal—you need to do a little homework that will pay off! This section explains the different types of checking accounts, how to figure out fees, and how banks calculate your checking account balance.

Why Banking Costs So Much

You hardly notice it, but as you keep writing checks month after month, the fat fees add up. Monthly service fees ranging from $5 to $25. Another $10 to $25 any time your balance falls below the minimum requirement. Probably $20 to $30 if you bounce a check. Plus banks have even started charging $5 to $8 for cashing your paycheck at the institution where your employer has its account.

Your banker is getting away with financial murder, because the average Joe doesn't realize the charges unless he studies his monthly statement very carefully. A recent Bankrate.com survey of the worst checking deals in America showed that, based on a $1,500 monthly balance, 12 written checks per month, and one bounced check a year, it cost $315 a year to have an account at one outfit.

Also, even if a bank pays you interest on checking, you could wind up losing money because of fees.

Mistakes You Should Avoid from Day One

The biggest error is walking into a bank to open a checking account without asking the right questions and demanding to see a copy of the bank's "Terms and Conditions," sometimes called "Fees and Disclosures." It's a little, tiny brochure whose wording is so small that an ant would have a tough time reading it. But every nitty-gritty penalty and fee is right there for you to see. It's best that you take it home and study it—*before* you sign up—instead of getting clobbered later on.

By law, banks have to give you that document, but more than likely they hope you won't read it. They just want you to sit down with their account representative and fill out an application.

The Money Line

You're apt to see free checking accounts pop up when one big bank acquires another major institution in a different state. To make quick points with consumers and steal away business, the new bank in town might offer special deals, such as accounts with no minimum balance.

The second mistake is to open a checking account that doesn't fit your habits, your financial lifestyle, and your wallet. Review with the account rep your month-by-month checking behavior so that you can match it against the different types of fees on the types of accounts the bank has available.

Unless you ask, dollars-to-donuts you won't be told the pluses and minuses of interest-checking versus noninterest checking.

Different Types of Checking Accounts

It's enough to blow your mind. Some banks offer as many as seven different checking accounts, all with weird names like "Master Checking," "Super Value Checking," "Special Checking," and "Regular Checking". And you're supposed to decide on one, with no road map to guide you. Even worse, some banks try to palm off slightly higher-interest Money Market Accounts (MMAs) as checking accounts by giving them a weasel-worded name like "Money Market Checking" or "Money Fund Checking." MMAs are basically savings accounts, not checking, which only allow you to write up to three checks a month. (See Chapter 10, "Savings and CD Accounts: Beating the Averages," for more information on MMAs and other savings accounts.)

Here's the easy way to cut through the confusion. Just remember that most checking accounts generally fall into one of three broad categories:

♦ **Basic checking**. This is a Plain Jane account for people who only use checking to pay bills and cover their basic expenses. A high balance isn't required, but the account may require direct deposit of your paycheck and a bare minimum balance to escape fees.

♦ **Interest-bearing checking**. Typically you'll need a minimum balance to open, and an even higher balance to maintain in order to avoid fees. Don't be surprised if the bank requires an opening deposit of only $100, but charges $25 each month if your balance sinks below $10,000 only one day during the month. The interest rate will be terrible—an average 1.05 percent—but at some outfits (notably Internet banks) you can earn 2 percent or more.

♦ **"Lifeline" accounts**. These are for low-income folks such a senior citizens, with monthly fees anywhere from $0 to $6. There's no minimum deposit or maybe a very low one, and you're allowed a certain number of checks per month. They're offered by many banks, thrifts, and credit unions, and some states have laws requiring them.

What does that translate into, dollar-wise, on the different accounts? According to Bankrate.com, on the average noninterest checking, you'll need $105 to open the account, versus $591 for an interest-bearing version.

Debit Cards

More Americans are using debit cards instead of credit cards to control their spending. A debit card looks just like a regular credit card, but when you use it to buy groceries, gas, or merchandise, the money comes out of your account electronically and immediately. You don't "pay later," as with a credit card. Hence, you must pay close attention to your balance and record your purchases to avoid bouncing checks. Some debit cards require a four-digit personal identification number (PIN); others require your signature when you make a purchase. You enter your PIN when you make a purchase at a store. The cards carry a MasterCard or Visa logo and are accepted anywhere that those two credit cards are accepted. Some banks charge debit customers a monthly fee; others charge a fee for each debit transaction. The big pluses with debit cards are that you aren't paying big credit card interest rates, and you don't spend money that you don't have. Also you can use your debit card to get cash back from a grocery store or drug store, often without paying an ATM fee. The minuses are that unless you keep good records you could overdraw your checking account, and if a thief steals your debit card and somehow also gets your PIN, he could easily drain your account dry overnight.

Dropping Interest Rates: How Low Can They Go?

Once upon a time, many banks paid yields as high as 6 percent on interest checking. But, when all interest rates plunged in the late 1990s and early 2000s, checking rates hit the basement and never came back up; CD rates did rise slightly, but then fell back down.

Since then, checking rates bottomed out and have stayed under 1 percent for years. So now, using the 1.05 percent average with a balance of $1,000, the typical customer has been earning only $10.05 in interest per year. If that customer pays a monthly maintenance fee of $12 just to have the account, he's already $133.50 in the hole. And, that's not counting other checking fees, either!

The following table lists some banks that do offer good interest-bearing checking accounts.

Some of the Best Interest-Bearing Deals (Average Yield)

Institution	Yield	Minimum to Open	Minimum to avoid fees	Monthly Service Fees	NSF
Newton Federal of Atlanta, GA	2.28%	$100	$500	$12	$22
Arundern Federal of Baltimore, MD	2.78%	$250	$250	$5	$20
Middlesex Savings of Boston, MA	.075%	$1	$1,000	$5	$15
Alden State Bank of Buffalo, N.Y.	2.02%	$1,000	$1,000	$5	$15
Gasten State Bank of Charlotte, NC	1.50%	$50	$100	$9	$22

Source: Bankrate.com

Odds are that you'll earn the highest rate on your interest-bearing checking account from Internet banks. They dominate the list of top payers in the country. Reason: They don't have the high brick-and-mortar overhead of bank branches. Not only are their rates higher, they require less money to open an account and their fees are generally lower—although they've begun raising some of their fees in recent years. For example, the average threshold to avoid monthly fees at an online, interest-bearing account will probably be slightly more than $1,000. But at a brick-and-mortar bank you'll need to keep more than $2,200 in checking. Will Internet banks do business with out-of-state customers? Yes. And, even though those Internet banks don't have any ATMS, many of them will reimburse you for up to four ATM surcharges a month at $1.50 each when you use some other outfit's machine.

Instead of keeping all your money in a checking account that might earn only 1 percent interest, put most of your loose funds in a higher-paying Money Market Account (MMA). Some out-of-state, federally-insured MMAs pay 5.5 percent and higher. Locally, you're apt to earn only 3 to 4 percent, or slightly higher with deposits of $20,000 or more. Because an MMA permits you to write up to three checks a month to parties other than yourself, here's the best strategy: Once a month, move enough money from your MMA to your local checking account to pay bills. You won't pay a penalty to transfer the funds, but be sure to allow at least five days for your check to clear.

Finally, get your checking account through a small community bank or credit union (CU) instead of at a giant bank or thrift. CUs typically pay more than banks do, plus, their fees are lower. At a small bank, you're apt to get better service and will probably be able to negotiate the rate and certain fees.

Those Frightening Fees

According to a study of big banks by the Federal Reserve, in recent years the banks' internal cost of maintaining a checking account has fallen from $7.38 to $6.82 a month. By earning money on your money through lending, they're able to reduce their cost to only about $4 a month. Your costs, meanwhile, have been steadily inching up to where some of your one-time fees can range as high as $30. In other words, you're riding a down escalator, while the bank's is going up. This is why you need a defensive plan to keep more of your cash.

The following list contains some interesting bank fee facts:

◆ Banks are making a fortune from fees of all types. Once upon a time, fees accounted for only 14 percent of their profits. Now the figure is more than 25 percent, and the end to their fee-raising is nowhere in sight.

◆ Banks have been raising fees at a much faster rate than inflation. For example, over the past several years their income from fees has nearly doubled, while the rate of inflation has been hovering somewhere between 2 and 3 percent per year.

◆ According to the newsletter *Fee Income Report*, in one recent year, banks charged 225 fees of all types, up from 15 years ago. Among the Fee Disclosure documents that banks hand out to new customers, we've seen one that listed *64 separate fees!* That's enough to throw an accounting major for a loop, much less the average Joe or Jane from Dubuque. To help you focus on fees, see Chapter 6.

How much money do you usually keep in your account? The less you keep, the more you're charged. Banks will often waive fees for higher-balance customers. It's when you drop below the "threshold" (a certain balance level) that you get whacked. Banks also may waive fees if you maintain several different accounts in one "relationship package," (in other words, savings, checking, and a loan) or if they're trying to keep old customers or lure new ones. That happens, for example, right after a bank merger, when the surviving institution is afraid that customers of the acquired bank may flee out the back door.

The key to what banks charge for banking is this: They classify you as to whether you are a "low-balance," "medium-balance," or "high-balance" customer, and their fees favor—you guessed it—the high-balance crowd. For example:

◆ Mrs. Gottrocks is a wealthy, high-balance customer. Because she keeps $5,000 or $10,000 in her account, she's given a better break, such as having many of her fees waived, including her monthly balance charge.

◆ Susie Smith, with $1,000, is considered a medium-balance customer. She doesn't go below her required balance during the month, so she's charged normal fees, such as "monthly maintenance."

◆ Joe Doaks, with a $400 balance, is a low-balance guy, so the bank discourages him from making too many transactions that cost the bank money. How? They hit him with charges on a slew of services. His monthly maintenance charge may be a few bucks higher than what Susie Smith pays.

It doesn't seem fair, the rich are getting richer and the poor getting poorer, but that's the way banks play the game. Your job is to beat the system by making decisions that will tilt things your way.

The Clearing Game

Just because you deposited the $100 check from Uncle Louie in your bank one hour ago, doesn't mean you can draw on any of the funds today. The process can take up to five days until the check clears through the national banking system. Meanwhile, one of your checks could bounce. The reason it takes so long is that Uncle Louie's bank needs time to get the check back and reduce his account balance by the amount of the check. The same thing applies to the $500 check from Aunt Nellie, but in this case, many banks let you draw against the first $100 on the next business day, and hold the other $400 until the check clears her bank. (Regulations may *require* local checks to clear in one day. It all depends on location.) The big "but" is that, despite federal laws on check-holds, your bank has plenty of elbow-room to do what it wants.

The following list shows how much you can withdraw against the deposit of a $1,000 check into your account (depending upon what kind of check it is):

◆ One day later, you can usually withdraw all $1,000 if it's a federal, state, or local government check; a bank check, certified check, or traveler's check; a check written on your bank by someone else; or an electronic funds transfer.

◆ If the check was written on a local bank, you should be able to withdraw $100 of the $1,000 one day later, $400 on the second day, and the remaining $500 on the third day.

◆ On an out-of-town check, you can withdraw $100 one day later and the other $900 five days later.

Remember that if you write checks against somebody else's check that you deposited to your account, that person's check may not clear in time for your check to be honored. If this happens, it may overdraw your account and you'll wind up paying a bounced-check fee.

There are exceptions. If you keep beaucoup bucks in your accounts and know the branch manager by name, the bank may stroke you by letting you draw immediately on any type of check you deposit.

Whatever you do, read the fine print in the bank's check-hold policy. Ask the branch manager for a shorter hold, or no hold at all, if you've been a good customer. Use direct deposit for payroll and government checks such as Social Security.

The Balancing Act

Finding out how banks calculate your balance sounds like an exercise for Einstein, but it's not. You simply need to know which method a bank uses, because it will tell you when a fee will kick in on your account. The institution calculates one of two ways:

- Using your low-minimum balance, which activates a fee if the balance falls below a certain level at any time during the month.

- Using your average-daily balance, where the fee kicks in if the monthly average of each day's balance drops below a certain amount.

The average-daily balance method is better because it protects you if your balance takes a sudden, temporary dive during the month. By contrast, if you choose an account using the low-minimum method, and your balance sinks to $10 one day, but is $1,000 on all the other days of the month, you will still get hit with a penalty. The dollar difference between the two kinds of accounts can be substantial, as shown in the following example.

Mary and Thelma, who have checking accounts at two different banks, normally keep about $600 each in their accounts, give or take a few hundred dollars either way. Mary's bank uses the low-minimum balance method, and charges her a $10 fee if her balance falls below $300 any day of the month. Mary deposited her paycheck the first week of the month and her account balance went up to $950. Ten days later, after she paid her rent and other bills, Mary's balance sank to $285 for one day. But, the next day she deposited another paycheck that pushed the balance up to $700. Mary's average balance for the whole month was $600, but the bank still whacked her with the $10 charge because it uses the low-minimum-balance method. Multiply that situation times 12 months a year, and you'll begin to understand why it pays to shop banks and ask the right questions.

Let's pretend Thelma's numbers were the same as Mary's—same pay, same rent, same bills, same everything. Thelma's balance dropped to $285 for just one day, just like Mary's. Even her average monthly balance was the same, $600. But she wasn't charged any fee because her bank uses the average-daily balance method. The $600 figure was all that mattered.

Identifying What Kind of Checking Creature You Are

No one wants to go through the nuisance of analyzing his or her personal behavior, especially on something as small and common as a checking account. When people need to write a check, they write one, period, and once a month they balance their statement and pray they have enough in the account to get through next week.

When you dashed over to the ATM last Sunday to get some emergency cash, you may not have thought about how many similar trips you made in the past month, or about whose automatic teller you were using—your bank's, or a different outfit's machine across the street. But those kinds of individual actions form a pattern of your personal checking behavior. The account that's just right for you probably won't be the one that's right for your child in college or for your neighbor. They're going to need one that fits their financial lifestyles.

Take stock of how you do things. Ask yourself:

The Money Line

Eighty-three percent of consumers believe checking is the most convenient way to pay bills, according to the Gallup organization. Cash comes in second at 8 percent, followed by electronic banking at 4 percent.

Fiscal Facts

According to the Federal Reserve, 88 percent of U.S. families use checks today. The 12 percent of those who didn't use checks said service charges were too high, compared with 7.4 percent who said that in 1989.

- How do I usually buy merchandise and pay my bills? By check, credit card, debit card, online banking, or a combination of those methods?

- What's the average amount of money I keep in checking every month?

- How likely am I to let my balance slip below that level?

- How many checks a month do I write?

- How often do I use an ATM?

- Which bank's ATM do I use? My own bank's? Another bank's machine in the same town? An out-of-town ATM? How much do I usually withdraw each time?

♦ Where do I buy my check reorders?

♦ Do I bounce checks or issue stop-payment orders?

♦ Do I ever ask the bank for back copies of my statement or copies of old checks?

♦ Have I ever investigated Internet banks or a credit union for my checking?

Next, haul out your last three or four monthly checking statements and add up all the various fees, including ATM deposits and withdrawals, check reorders—the works. Then estimate what your checking is costing you per month and per year, because those are the bottom-line costs you want to cut to ribbons. Tape that information on your refrigerator door (or put it on your desk) and get ready to play hardball with the banks. Believe it or not, you're on your way to putting extra money in your pocketbook.

Finally, don't make the same mistake that many other consumers make by being too lazy to balance your checkbook or close out a costly account. Get ready to switch banks by keeping a record of how many checks are outstanding and how much money you'll need to cover them. Then you won't sweat the transition.

If you don't prepare, you can wind up costing yourself some money. For example, a fellow we know wrote his ex-wife a check that she didn't cash for two months. After he closed out his account (forgetting about the check), the ex deposited the check and it came back marked NSF (nonsufficient funds), whereupon she nailed him for issuing a bounced check.

Banks were making $2.2 billion a year in profits before they started adding surcharges" to ATM transactions. Now, ATMs where you don't bank charge as much as $1.75 per transaction, plus, there's probably a $1.50 fee at your own institution, making a total of more than $3. It gets worse in places such as Las Vegas casinos, gas stations, and sports arenas, where the ATM fee can be as high as $10. Ridiculous!

When surcharging came along, that increased the banks' profits by $2.7 billion, according to the Center for the Study of Responsive Law.

Understanding Fees: You'd Better Shop Around

Outside of mortgages, a checking account, yes, little old checking, is one of the trickiest accounts to shop for. "How can that be?" you ask. "What else are there besides a few fees, and maybe an interest rate?"

Plenty. Instead of just "a few" fees, you're going to come across dozens and dozens of different ones. Rarely will you see even two banks whose fees are exactly alike, or whose account requirements are absolutely identical. The trick is to ignore all the gimmicks and focus on these two key points:

◆ The account you're looking for is the one whose low-cost features match your personal checking behavior. Nothing else.

◆ Pretend you're shopping for a computer or a television set, not a checking account. You wouldn't buy a TV if it cost you a buck every time you turned it on, would you? Use the same demanding buying principles when you open a checking account.

You'll never be a checking idiot if you follow these two simple rules.

Basic Shopping Tips

When you shop, don't try to compare every single, cotton-picking fee charged by every institution. Otherwise, you'll go berserk and wind up in a straitjacket. There are simply too many different fees to cope with. So what do you do? You limit your comparisons to only the most common fees and charges that are apt to affect you, such as monthly maintenance, and so on.

Do this: Instead of scribbling notes on the backs of fee schedules the banks give you, organize the information on a piece of paper with headings for each fee type, *bank by bank*. Jot down each outfit's information under the appropriate heading, but remember to base each fee on the average monthly balance you carry in your account.

Match the fees on your shopping chart with your checking behavior that you determined earlier. Based on what you usually do with your account, what would Bank "A" cost you per month? What about Banks "B," "C," and the others? Also ask yourself if your financial condition will likely change in any way that might affect your decision on where to take your business. Can you change any of your old checking habits, such as reducing the number of ATM transactions or checks you write, to cut costs even further?

The more banks you shop, the better your chances of cutting your checking costs. Keep your pencil sharpened and your eye on the bottom line. One of those outfits is going to wind up being the cheapest place to do your checking, and it probably won't be your old bank!

Before Signing on the Dotted Line

Banks have been adding so many new fees—and increasing their old ones—that almost everything you do with checks today is going to cost you. It's critical to ask the right questions up front, before you sign on the dotted line. These are the most important ones:

- What is the minimum deposit to open the account?

- Does the account pay interest? If not, what are the differences in fees between this account and an account that does pay interest?

- Is the account tiered? If so, what interest rate does each tier pay?

- What minimum balance must I maintain to avoid paying a fee?

- Under what conditions would you waive my fee?

- What is the cost per check?

- How much do check reorders cost?

- What are the ATM costs if I use this bank's machine or another bank's machine?

- How much is the bounced-check fee?

- Do you return my cancelled checks with each monthly statement? If not, how much extra would it cost?

The Road to Riches

In a bid to get your business, many institutions offer "free" checking with "package accounts" that combine several of your accounts, such as savings and CDs, on one monthly statement. Even though the free checking part of the package many seem to be a good deal, the rest of the package may not be. You'd probably be better off splitting your accounts among several outfits.

When Free Checking Really Costs Money

Banking associations claim that today you can find a so-called free, "no-frills" checking account at 8 out of 10 outfits. Oh, yeah? Let's say you just saw an ad for "free checking." Better read the fine print. Even though a Truth in Savings law (which was supposed to reduce the number of tricks that banks can pull when they advertise the word "free") went into effect in 1993, it's still fairly easy for banks to mislead you. For one thing, although they can't say an account is free if they sock you with a fee for allowing your account balance to fall below a certain minimum (or if they require you to open another account to get free checking), they can peddle the account as being "free" if there are ATM or debit card charges associated with checking. Also if you bounce a check with a no-frills account, your fee penalty could be double that of a regular checking account.

Here are some examples of when a free checking account isn't so free:

♦ You get an ATM card with your checking, but when you sign up, the small print in the agreement says that you'll pay a fee for using another bank's automatic teller. If your balance slides below the minimum, you'll also pay a fee when you use your bank's machine.

♦ The bank promotes free checking even though you pay an annual fee on a debit card (which electronically withdraws funds from your checking when you buy something).

♦ The bank can still claim the checking account is free if you do your banking electronically from your computer and are charged a fee for the service.

> ### The Road to Riches
>
> Here's why having your checks, especially Social Security and payroll checks, deposited directly into your bank accounts is important. As long as ten years ago, when Hurricane Andrew hit Homestead, Florida, although everything was being destroyed by the storm, receipt of direct-deposit payments was not interrupted.

How come banks can circumvent the rules? Because the Truth in Savings law says that if the transaction is electronic, it's not really part of the checking account. Rather crafty, don't you think?

Using Your Checking Account Wisely

The biggest mistake consumers make, over and over again, is that they don't understand that there's a cost almost every time they engage in checking activity. For example, Joe Doaks thinks he's exercising discipline by taking out only $10 whenever he withdraws checking funds from an ATM. Say he takes out 10 bucks a day for five days in a row. He forgets that each time he does this, the bank is charging him $1.50, for a total of $7.50 in transaction fees. Had he withdrawn the $50 all at once, he would have been nicked only $1.50.

> ### Fiscal Facts
>
> When ATMs first appeared nearly 25 years ago, banks enticed consumers to try the newfangled machines by offering free hamburger coupons, cotton candy, and balloons for the kids. It was sort of a try-it-you'll-like-it campaign to get us addicted—and all the ATM transactions were free. Then, they began their big spree with fees.

It could even get worse. If Joe uses an ATM other than his own bank's, the foreign bank will also hit him with a $1.50 "surcharge," raising his total cost per transaction to $3. Now the five withdrawals cost him a total of $15, or the equivalent of 30 percent interest on the 50 bucks he withdrew. This next section tells you how to avoid such costly mistakes and provides additional money-saving tips.

Using ATMs

A machine's a machine, but whose ATM you use will make a difference in the fees you're charged. Here's the lingo banks use in their literature:

◆ **Proprietary ATM.** It means your bank owns the machine. Nine out of 10 banks don't charge customers for using their ATMs, but of those that do, most charge nearly $1.

◆ **Non-Proprietary ATM.** The machine belongs to another outfit. Expect to pay $1 to $1.50 per transaction charged by your own bank. Plus, the new costly wrinkle is a $1 to $1.50 "surcharge" by the bank whose machine you're using—that's *on top of* what your bank charges for you using a foreign or non-proprietary ATM. Eight of every 10 outfits now surcharge.

◆ **National ATM.** The bank's machine is hooked up to a national or regional network such as Cirrus, Plus, or MasterCard. You'll see their emblems on the machine. When you make an out-of-town transaction on these ATMs, the fee rises to $1.50 or $2.50.

◆ **"Foreign" ATMs.** Another way of saying "non-proprietary."

Even retailers are cashing in on ATM profits. Grocery stores, convenience outlets, gas stations and even hotels want a piece of the high-profit ATM action. They're acting like banks by putting thousands of machines everywhere, just so you can get some fast cash when you need it. If you fall for this convenience, expect to get nailed a total of $2.50 to $3 every time you withdraw money. At gambling casinos, the robbery will be higher, like $5 or more. Who benefits? They do. Who loses money? You do.

Reducing Your ATM Charges

You can reduce your ATM charges if you keep the following in mind:

◆ Keep your checking account at a bank that doesn't charge you for using its machines.

◆ Don't use an ATM belonging to an institution where you don't bank.

◆ Withdraw all the cash you'll need for the next few weeks, instead of making several small transactions that run up your total ATM fees.

Using ATMs can be dangerous as well as expensive. To protect your money—and your personal privacy—follow these rules:

◆ Memorize your Personal Identification Number (PIN) and keep it to yourself. Don't keep it in your wallet.

◆ Keep your ATM card in a safe place. It's as valuable to you as your credit card. If the ATM card is lost or stolen, report it to your bank immediately.

◆ Keep extra deposit envelopes in your car so you can fill them out before approaching the ATM.

◆ Have your paperwork and your ATM card ready when you reach the ATM so you won't have to reach into your purse or wallet.

◆ Stand between the ATM and people waiting in line so no one can see your PIN number or your transaction.

◆ Don't accept help from strangers while you're using the ATM. If you have a problem, contact the bank.

◆ Take your ATM receipt. Put away your cash, ATM card, and receipt *before* you leave the ATM.

◆ Report all crimes to the ATM owner and local law enforcement officers immediately.

Identifying Cost-Cutting Tips

As big as the world of check fees is getting, there are still a few ways to get around those little buggers. This is especially true now, as the merger pace quickens and banks try to romance you to do business at their place instead of someone else's.

For example, many banks will waive certain checking fees if you …

◆ Keep a big balance in your account.

◆ Agree to forego getting your cancelled checks back with your monthly statement.

◆ Are older than 50 or 55 years, depending on the bank's senior checking requirements.

◆ Open a package account that combines several of your accounts, such as CDs and passbooks, under one statement.

◆ Limit the number of checks you write per month to the maximum allowed without a fee.

◆ Don't exceed a certain number of ATM transactions per month.

Understanding the Ugliest Fee of Them All

The one fee you should absolutely try to avoid is the bounced-check charge. The banks call these checks "NSFs" (nonsufficient funds). The latest figures show that banks are raking in an astounding $6.2 billion in profits from rubber checks that people write, and fees collected from people who deposit them. In fact, consumer watchdogs say that banks have set "traps" so that checks are more apt to bounce, such as paying the biggest items first so there won't be enough money left to pay off the smaller items.

Though industry studies show it costs a bank less than $2 to handle a bounced check, the average NSF costs about $25.

In some cities such as Philadelphia, banks charge as high as $32. Across America, the bigger the bank, the higher the NSF charge.

Watch Your Wallet _____

You can prevent getting hit by bounced-check fees if you have "overdraft protection" from your bank. This means that if you don't have enough money in your account to cover a check, the bank will pay it. It might offer you, say, up to $5,000 worth of protection in the form of a line of credit from a separate account. When the overdraft occurs, the bank transfers enough money to your checking to cover it. But, the interest rate on the transferred amount might be 18 percent, plus there could be an annual fee of maybe $20 for the service. Another way to get overdraft protection is to link your checking to your credit card.

If a bank decides to honor a check instead of letting it bounce, it will cost you about $20 in addition to the amount of the check. If it pays the check against your funds that haven't yet cleared, the charge is around $13.

An outrage? You ain't heard nothin' yet. More outfits have begun to hit consumers with an NSF charge if they deposit someone else's rubber check to their account, regardless of their own balance. That cost averages about $5.50. One Chicago outfit charges a $20 fee.

Remember that if you don't have enough funds in your account, every check you write beyond your balance will bounce. If, say, your balance is $15 and you write three checks for $25 each, the bank will charge you a fee for each one. The fee will be between $10 and $30, so you could wind up with the bad checks costing a total of as much as $90!

Bounced-check charges are so out of control that it's possible for this to happen: A person writes a bad check for $10. The check is presented to his or her bank not once, but twice, and the customer gets nicked $20 each time. Plus the person whose name is on the check gets charged $5. The fees add up to $45 in all—just for a $10 check. Consider yourself warned!

Banks argue that they need those charges to dissuade people from writing bad checks, but that's a lot of hooey. An independent study showed that only 5 percent of institutions reported a decline in NSFs after they raised their fees. Meanwhile, other studies show that the average bounced-check charge is 84 percent more than the bank's cost of handling the check!

Knowing When to Use Stop Payments

You just issued a check to Big Bubba's garage for a new transmission in old Betsy. On your way home, the transmission sounds likes a blender full of rocks, and you don't want Bubba to pocket the money until he makes good on the deal. What do you do? Immediately inform the bank to stop payment on the check. Tell them your account number, the check number, the exact amount (in dollars and cents), date of the check, and the name of the person or company you wrote it to.

The problem with stop payments is that they don't come cheap. They'll cost you as much as $35, and the fees have been going up. You will have to decide whether the action is worth it, by considering whom you're doing business with on the other end, and how important it is that the other party not cash the check.

 Fiscal Facts

Attempted check fraud at the biggest U.S. banks has doubled in the last two years, to a staggering $2.2 billion. But actual dollar losses were $679 million, says the American Bankers Association. Over the same two-year period, the number of check fraud *cases* rose to 447,342, with the average loss being $1,518. The largest institutions are hit hardest by check fraud.

A Savings Tip That Might Not Save You Anything

Earlier we told you that you could reduce your account fees by not getting your cancelled checks back every month. The banks call this "truncation" or "check storage." It works like this: You receive only your statement, and they keep your checks in their warehouse. That will shave a few bucks off your checking fees, but if you suddenly need a copy of one of the checks—zing!—you may be charged about $3 to $5 per copy. And the process will take a few days.

Then there's something called check imaging where you get back miniature photos of the fronts of the checks you issued last month, printed out on a large sheet. The banks charge a couple of dollars for the service, and still keep the real checks.

Before you grab the bank's bait, ask yourself: Wouldn't the cancelled checks come in handy when you prepare your taxes or if you ever get entangled in a lawsuit?

Protecting Yourself Against Forgery

The number one rule is *never imprint your Social Security or driver's license number on your checks!* Some people do, and they're only inviting thieves to rip them off. There are 700,000 cases of identity theft per year in the United States, many of which are caused by sloppy handling of checks.

You also can prevent check forgery by keeping your checks in a locked drawer or safe deposit box. The institution should try to protect you by comparing the signature on the checks it receives with the signature card you filled out when you opened your account. You should have a copy of that card. It's also your proof of your legal signature.

Once a forgery is committed and it gets by the institution, there's no automatic protection. Almost all states have adopted a uniform code on forgeries, but the interpretation and execution varies by state.

As soon as possible, notify the bank if a check is forged. You'll likely discover it when reviewing your statement. Your obligation to notify the institution may be spelled out on the back of the statement. In some states, it's as short as 14 days. You can call the outfit, but your rights are protected only if you put the claim in writing.

The institution may investigate, or it may not respond. If it doesn't respond, make follow-up phone calls and write more letters. The bank may claim that you failed to notify it on time or that you were negligent by letting other people use your checkbook.

In that case, you may be forced to sue the bank. That will be a headache if a small sum is involved. You may be able to raise enough ruckus with your letters to get some action. But if you were careless in leaving your blank checks lying around, you may have to swallow the loss yourself. The lesson? Protect your checks as if they were cash.

The Least You Need to Know

- Get a copy of your bank's Fee Disclosure document on checking and read it with a fine-tooth comb.

- Interest checking often costs more money than noninterest checking because the fees are higher, and the minimum deposit and average monthly balance requirements are greater.

- Compare your personal check habits against the fees charged by different financial institutions to minimize your checking account costs and find the right account for you.

- Be wary of offers of "super-high interest rates" and "free checking."

- Get your checking account through a credit union, or put some of your money in an MMA: It can boost your interest rate.

- Remember that there's a cost almost every time you engage in checking activity.

Chapter

Investing Safely with Uncle Sam

In This Chapter

♦ Which investments are super-safe

♦ Why the highest-yielding investments are always riskier

♦ How to easily set up a safe Treasury securities account

♦ How the government sets U.S. Savings Bond rates

♦ How one family can insure up to $1.4 million at the same FDIC institution

It's a chancy thing, pumping money into the sometimes-high-flying stock market, or investing in bonds, gold, foreign currencies, or windmill farms. In the years 2000 and 2001 alone, American investors lost a total of $3 trillion when the stock market went *thunk!* There's lots of money to be made—*if* an investment performs and doesn't fall on its face. Because if it does, you'll be out the original cash you put up, along with any possible earnings on your money. That's the bottom line in the risk versus reward money game; you could make a mint if things go right, or lose your shirt if they don't.

The cautious, conservative crowd doesn't invest that way. They play it safe. They plunk down their money for investments that may not earn nearly as much as the stock market does, but they sleep better at night knowing their money is fully protected by the federal government. Getting only 1 or 2 percent on a bank account, U.S. Savings Bond, or money fund may appear to be a dinky return next to the 10 percent you can get from, say, Amalgamated World's stock shares, but when you wake up in the morning, you know the money's there! This chapter looks at four of the basic investments that are fully backed by Uncle Sam, and explains how to build a 100 percent safe portfolio.

Two Choices: Your Money's Safe or It Isn't

Learn this right off the bat, because it's critical: When it comes to how safe your money is, there are, broadly speaking, only two kinds of things to invest in:

◆ Investments that are guaranteed and protected by the federal government, such FDIC-insured accounts, and others, such as Treasuries, that are backed by the full faith and credit of Uncle Sam.

◆ Investments where you could lose your shirt if things don't pan out the way you hope. That includes stocks, bonds, mutual funds, and a host of other places where you can park your cash. Sure, millions of people have made tons of money from these investments, but there's no guarantee of how they will perform in the future. In other words, it's a risk versus reward situation; the riskier an investment is, the more you might make—and vice-versa.

This chapter deals with only the first type of investing (#1, above), where you'll *never* take a financial bath, because you kept your money in one of these four places:

◆ Treasuries

◆ U.S. Savings Bonds

◆ FDIC-insured bank savings and CD accounts

◆ Government-only money funds

He Who Laughs Last ...

When the economy is great and the stock market is roaring, your friendly broker laughs at anyone who puts his or her money in a low-paying instrument such as a

2 percent bank CD account. The broker pushes you into stocks, bonds, and funds instead. But, when the Dow Jones average plunges by 20 percent, the broker doesn't laugh any more. He panics. Suddenly, every business writer in the country begins reporting on how safe U.S. Treasury investments are, by comparison. Investors begin calling high-yielding banks around the country to ask about FDIC-insured CDs and U.S. Savings Bonds.

Ask yourself this question: What would happen if there was a real economic catastrophe around the world, and the market sank by 65 percent with the Dow plunging from, say, 10,000 to 5,000? Some gloom-and-doom prophets think that might happen one day. Millions of people's savings would be wiped out, but any money you had stashed away in a safe, federally-protected account would look like a lifeboat.

Enter the subject of safety. With a safe, U.S.-backed investment, you won't become a millionaire overnight, but you'll sure sleep better.

Many consumers tend to forget that advice, especially when times are good with the economy. Even though the American economies recovered from financial debacles such as the bank runs during the Great Depression and savings and loan crisis in the late 1980s, some people are still nervous about whether their institution is safer than the one across the street.

You Shouldn't Overdo the Safety Angle

Want to know how foolish some people are? They're creatures of habit, taught as kids to "save in a nice, safe place for a rainy day." So they keep more money in bank passbooks and Money Market Accounts that only pay a measly 1.75 percent on average, than they keep in CDs paying 2 to 3 percent! Why? Because the basic savings account with a little old passbook is what they had when they were young. It's their security blanket. Where they're missing out on is not shopping FDIC-insured, out-of-state banks that pay more than their local institutions do. You find out more about CD and high-interest savings accounts in Chapter 10.

A study by the Consumer Federation of America notes that millions of bank customers are missing out on up to $50 billion each year in additional interest that could have been earned on those deposits with equal safety.

The Money Line

According to the Federal Reserve, in 2003 consumers had deposited a total of $3.16 billion in low-paying savings vs. $809 trillion in higher-paying CDs. By contrast, Americans had $6.2 trillion invested in stocks, $2.2 trillion in bonds and $4 trillion in mutual funds.

While there is nothing wrong with leaving money in the bank, as it's money you can't afford to lose, it doesn't mean you should lose out on earning the best-insured interest rates. As you'll learn in Part 3, there are different types of bank accounts to stash your cash in during volatile market times:

◆ Bank passbook savings accounts

◆ Certificates of deposit (CDs)

◆ Money market accounts

In addition, you will learn where to find the highest interest rates on bank products nationwide.

Uncle Sam Is As Solid As the Rock of Gibraltar

If you're looking for a safe way to double your money, consider folding it over once and putting it in your pocket. Of course, you really don't earn a 100 percent return this way, but you can count on keeping all of your principal.

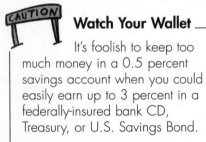

Watch Your Wallet

It's foolish to keep too much money in a 0.5 percent savings account when you could easily earn up to 3 percent in a federally-insured bank CD, Treasury, or U.S. Savings Bond.

The Road to Riches

Treasury bills, notes, and bonds are debt obligations of the U.S. government, issued through the Treasury Department. These securities are auctioned at different times when you can bid on them. You can now buy Treasuries for as little as $1,000, and your investment is super-safe because it is guaranteed by the full faith and credit of the United States of America.

There's another strategy to keeping your money safe: Invest in Uncle Sam. The ol' red, white, and blue puts its full faith and credit in the types of investments its financial arm, the Treasury Department, issues, known as Treasury securities.

The Treasury issues debt instruments (securities) in the form of Treasury bills, Treasury notes, and Treasury bonds to finance its deficit spending. Maturities on these securities range from three-month Treasury bills to five-year notes to 30-year Treasury bonds.

That's right—what Uncle Sam is doing is borrowing money from consumers. So, when you invest in any of these Treasury securities, you are loaning the government your money.

Currently, there are close to $4.2 trillion dollars worth of Treasury securities held by the public. That's what it takes to help fund America's debt.

One of the biggest reasons people invest in Treasury securities is because anyone who invests in them will receive their money back when promised.

Guaranteed. There really isn't any credit risk when you invest in Treasury securities. That's why the interest rates paid on Treasuries (remember, they're nothing but loans from consumers to the government) are lower than those on comparable bonds from different issuers, such as a corporation.

Of course, Treasuries do experience a lot of price volatility. When interest rates rise, bond prices fall. That means the value of your bonds fluctuates either higher or lower than the original purchase price, depending on the general direction of interest rates.

Getting a "Discount" or a "Coupon"

Treasury bills are considered a discount security because they don't pay any interest. You purchase the security at a "discount" from its face value, and at maturity (the day that the money you loaned the government has to be paid back) you receive the full face value. The difference between the discount price and the face value received at maturity is the "interest" earned on the investment.

Coupon securities, such as T-notes and T-bonds, pay interest semi-annually and the face value at maturity. The interest payments you receive are federally taxable, but exempt from state and local taxes.

The Money Line

Treasury bills don't "pay interest." Rather, they're sold at a discount off the face value that appears on the security, such as paying $500 for a $1,000-face-value T-bill that you redeem for that amount at maturity.

Opening a "Treasury Direct" Account

Buying Treasury securities directly from the Fed, by setting up what's called a Treasury Direct account, is the easiest and most cost-effective way to purchase them. You don't have to live near the Fed or one of its branches either, but you can go there if it's convenient. Contact the Bureau of Public Debt via email at is-mab@bpd.treas.gov to find out more about purchasing Treasury securities. Now people with Treasury Direct accounts can also buy Treasuries over the Internet at www.treas.gov, or by phone at 1-800-722-2678. You can arrange to have the Treasury deduct the cost of your investment electronically from your bank or brokerage account, or mail them a certified or cashier's check.

Going, Going ...

Buying a Treasury security is a lot different than buying a CD from a bank. Everything is explained to you in simple English at a good Internet website (www.publicdebt. treas.gov.) maintained by the U.S. Bureau of Public Debt.

Here are the basics:

◆ Treasury securities are auctioned off (sold) from the Federal Reserve Bank, or a Fed branch, at more than 150 auctions a year. They're not sold by the Treasury Department in Washington, D.C., but that department does issue a press release about one week before each auction announcing the auction date, amount to be sold, and other details. The previous Internet address gives you all the details about how to get information on the auctions in advance.

◆ To purchase a bill, note, or bond, you put in a noncompetitive bid at one of the Treasury auctions, which means you accept whatever average rate you get for the securities you want to buy. After you buy a Treasury security, whether it's a bill, note, or bond, your purchase will be noted as being in book-entry form, which means that you don't receive the certificate, but rather are "on the books" with the Treasury Department and your interest payments are sent directly to your home.

Following is the rundown on the different types of Treasury securities, how often they are auctioned, and minimum purchase amounts.

Purchasing T-Bills, T-Bonds, and T-Notes

Maturity	Minimum Amount
Three-month and six-month Treasury bills are auctioned every Monday; the one-year T-bill is auctioned every quarter.	$10,000
Two-year and five-year Treasury notes are auctioned toward the end of each month; three-year and seven-year Treasury notes are auctioned quarterly, in early February, May, August, and November.	$5,000
Treasury bonds with maturities of 10 years and 30 years are auctioned on the second month of each calendar quarter. Note: If you wanted to buy a 25-year T-bond, you would buy a 30-year T-bond that is five years old.	$1,000

But I Don't Have $10 Grand!

The government has made it easier for small savers to get in on the Treasuries action. Instead of needing $5,000 or $10,000, as in the past, now you only need as little as

$1,000 to buy a short-term or intermediate-term Treasury security. Before, longer-term securities of five years or more required only $1,000, but the downside was that some investors didn't want to tie up their money that long.

How much can you earn with Treasuries? Generally, a trifle more than what the average bank will pay you on a CD with a comparable maturity, but not as much as what the highest-paying banks will offer (see Chapter 11 for tips on finding the high-yielding CDs).

Treasury Money Funds Are an Option

There's another way to chase higher yields and keep your money safe. That's by investing in Treasury-only money funds. Most of them yield up to 5 percent, or about double what the typical bank Money Market Account (MMA) pays, and 2½ times what an interest checking account pays. Also when a Treasury-only money fund yield is quoted, it has already taken into account its fees and expenses—unlike a bank which quotes yields before any fees and charges are assessed. And you don't pay any commission with your fund.

Other advantages of Treasury-only money funds include exemption from state and local income taxes and check-writing features, although minimum amounts of usually $100 are required for each check. By contrast, your earnings on bank CDs are taxable.

If you're looking for Treasury-only money funds, consider the following:

> Other advantages of Treasury-only money funds include exemption from state and local income taxes and check-writing features, although minimum amounts of usually $100 are required for each check. By contrast, your earnings on bank CDs are taxable.

If you're looking for Treasury-only money funds, consider the following:

♦ One Group Treasury & Bond Agency I, 1-800-480-4111, which had a year-to-date return of 1.30 percent as of October 2004, invests in U.S. Treasury notes, bonds, and government agency obligations. Get online and pull up their web-site at www.onegroup.com.

The Road to Riches
It's easy and inexpensive to buy Treasury securities directly from the Federal Reserve by setting up your own "Treasury Direct" account. The cost of your investments can be deducted electronically from your bank or brokerage account, or you can mail a certified or cashier's check.

◆ American Century Target Maturity 2010, 1-800-345-2021, which had a return of 3.52 percent as of October 2004. The fund invests in zero-coupon Treasuries and other Treasury securities all timed toward maturity in 2010. You can learn more at www.americancentury.com.

◆ Federated Government Ultrashort, 1-800-341-7000, requires a minimum $25,000 initial investment and invests in U.S. government securities. The year-to-date return as of October 2004 is 1.19 percent.

For the latest, highest-yielding Treasury-only money funds, and the basics of how all types of money funds work, check out IBC Financial Data's Web site at www. ibcdata.com.

Any Savings Bonds Today?

Historically, U.S. Savings Bonds are the most patriotic of all investments. Uncle Sam has sold them through big promotions and publicity to finance previous war efforts, such as during World War II. Parents and grandparents purchase bonds to sock money away for children's college tuition, and in these cases, the interest may be tax-exempt. And the best part is that these conservative investments, though they only pay about what long-term bank CDs offer, are backed by the full faith and credit of Uncle Sam.

The most popular is the Series EE bond. But the newer version is an I-Bond, so-called because the rate is partly tied to the inflation rate, which we describe in this chapter. The HH/H bond was discontinued on August 31, 2004.

Besides safety, a big benefit is that your interest earnings are exempt from state and local taxes. And, you can defer paying federal income tax on the interest until you cash the bond, or until it stops earning interest in 30 years. As of 1997, early redemption penalties were added to Series EE bonds. Older bonds paid interest every six months. If you redeem your bond a day early, you could lose up to half your interest for the year. To find out more information, log onto www.savingsbonds.gov.

How the Rate Formula Works

How Series EE Savings Bond rates are calculated every six months can throw the unknowing investor for a loop, but it's not that difficult.

◆ The rate changes twice a year, on May 1 and November 1.

◆ The rate is based on the average of the five-year Treasury securities yields for the previous six months, multiplied by 90 percent.

So when you buy a Savings Bond that earns interest for 30 years, every six months, the rate you get on the bond will change. You may cash the bond anytime six months after the date you bought it. The amount printed on the bond is its "face value," or denomination. Your purchase price is 50 percent of the face value amount (for instance, a $50 bond will cost you $25) but if you hold the bond until maturity, you'll be paid its face value. As of September 2004, interest rates range from 2.84 percent for an EE bond to 3.39 percent for an I-Bond.

Where to Buy Bonds

Series EE is the only type of Savings Bond you can buy for cash. Purchases are usually done through a bank, or in denominations of at least $100 via a payroll savings plan where you work. Don't expect your bank to jump for joy when you tell them you want to buy a Savings Bond. Why? The bonds compete directly with the bank's own CDs. No wonder you never see banks advertising bonds, even though they're every bit as safe as CDs. Because there's no risk, the Treasury Department is puzzled that more consumers aren't aware of them.

The Money Line

Savings Bonds are exempt from state and local taxes, and you can defer paying federal income tax on them until the bonds are cashed. They can be bought through a bank or a payroll savings plan in denominations of at least $100.

How to Generate Tax Savings—*If* the Money Is for Junior's College

Here's a tip: The interest you earn on Savings Bonds is eligible for a special federal income tax exclusion when you use the bond redemption proceeds to finance higher education. The bonds must be registered in the name of the taxpayer (or taxpayer and spouse) for whom the child is a dependent. If the bonds are issued in the name of the child, or the child as a co-owner, they're not eligible for the tax exclusion. Also, the cost of the college tuition must be greater than the amount (principal and interest) of the bonds you're redeeming to pay for tuition.

Note: You can buy up to $30,000 (face amount) worth of bonds in a calendar year.

"I" Is for "Inflation"

Almost seven years ago, the government began giving the average Joe an opportunity to buy a U.S.-guaranteed investment that protected him or her against inflation. It started selling Savings Bonds indexed to the Consumer Price Index, or CPI, in denominations as low as $50.

I-Bonds, as they're called, have face values of $50, $75, $100, $200, $500, $1,000, $5,000, and $10,000. Instead of bearing the familiar faces of our Founding Fathers, such as George Washington, Thomas Jefferson, and John Adams, they carry the likeness of more modern heroes such as Albert Einstein and Martin Luther King.

The rate you earn on I-Bonds comes in a two-part combination: First, the rate the government pays on the most recent auction of five-year Treasury notes; and second, the rise in the Consumer Price Index adjusted every six months. Another difference is that while Series EE Savings Bonds, as described earlier, are sold at half their face value (for example, a $50 bond costs $25), I-Bonds are sold at their full face value and carry a fixed rate of return, as of May 2004 the fixed rate hovered around 1 percent. While bond investors have to pony up the full face value of an I-Bond compared to a Series EE savings bond, the Series I-Bond savings bond yield may continue to be higher than the Series EE, which is tied to Treasury bill yields.

Like the Series EE, the interest on I-Bonds is tax-deferred until the bonds are cashed, or if the money is used for college tuition provided the taxpayer meets certain income limits. If you cash in either type of bond within five years after purchasing it, you incur a three-month interest penalty.

The I-Bond's biggest downside? When the U.S. inflation rate isn't rising, neither is the rate on the I-Bond. When deflation occurs, which is when the economy is shrinking, economic indicators such as the CPI (consumer price index) negatively impact the I-Bond rate and its yield falls.

One expert source on these investments is Savings Bond Informer, 1-800-927-1901, a Detroit-based company run by an ex-Federal Reserve man, Dan Pederson, who offers bond holders a customized report that projects rates, values, dates of changes, and accrued interest over the next two years and five years. Cost ranges from $15 to $69 per report, depending on the number of bonds involved. Savings Bond Informer also has an over-the-phone consultation service, and its descriptive brochure is free.

FDIC Protects Your Bank Deposits up to $100 Grand

After the big debacle of savings and loans dropping like flies in the late 1980s and early '90s, you'd think that by now, everybody would understand federal insurance protection A through Z. Wrong. There are still a lot of misconceptions about how the Federal Deposit Insurance Corporation (FDIC) works. This will simplify it for you:

♦ **The "Rule of 1's":** Here's the easy way to remember it: FDIC insurance covers one person at one institution for up to $100,000, including principal and interest. That last part is important. If you deposit $100,000 in a CD earning 6 percent for one year, at the end of the year you'll have $106,000 in the account, right? But the $6,000 in interest *won't* be protected because FDIC's insurance limit is $100,000.

But if you deposit only $92,000 at 6 percent interest, the account will earn $5,520, so at the end of the year there will be a total of $97,520 in your account. Every single dollar, including the interest, will be insured because there will be less than $100,000 in one person's name at that bank. *Note*: Credit union deposits also are insured up to $100,000, by the National Credit Union Administration (NCUA).

♦ **Which bank products are (or aren't) insured:** At FDIC-insured banks and NCUA-insured credit unions, the deposits that are protected include passbook accounts, statement savings accounts, Money Market Accounts, checking accounts, and CD accounts. Mutual funds sold by banks are *not* FDIC-insured, even though some banks may try to deceive you by saying, in the same breath, that they will sell you a mutual fund and that, "We're a member of the FDIC." Repeat: Your mutual fund will not be protected by Uncle Sam.

♦ **IRAs are insured separately:** Let's say you have several savings and CD accounts at one bank, plus an Individual Retirement Account at the same institution. The IRA is insured separately for $100,000 by the FDIC. So for insurance purposes, the amount in your IRA won't count toward the money you have in savings and CDs. It will have its own $100,000 protection.

How to Beat the $100,000 Insurance Limit

Believe it or not, by creating different kinds of joint accounts and trust accounts, it's possible for a family of four to have a total of $1.4 million of FDIC-insured protection at the same institution. *Tip*: Lots of people think the FDIC $100,000 limit applies to a person's total bank investments, regardless of how many institutions they keep their money in. Not so. The key is the $100,000 *per-institution* wording in the "Rule of 1's" (above).

It's possible to insure *more* than $100,000 by creating several different joint accounts and trust accounts, as the following table shows. You may never have a million bucks at your disposal, but here's how the wealthy beat the system by insuring as much as $1.4 million for a family of four at the same institution.

A Family of Four with over a Million Bucks

Account Type	Accounts	Amount
Individual	Husband	$100,000
	Wife	$100,000
	Child 1	$100,000
	Child 2	$100,000
Joint Accounts	Husband and Wife	$100,000
	Husband and Child 1	$100,000
	Wife and Child 2	$100,000
	Child 1 and Child 2	$100,000
Trust Accounts	Husband and Wife	$100,000
	Wife and Husband	$100,000
	Husband and Child 1	$100,000
	Husband and Child 2	$100,000
	Wife and Child 1	$100,000
	Wife and Child 2	$100,000
TOTAL		**$1,400,000**

Here's how the $1.4 million coverage works:

◆ **Individual account.** Each family member opens an account in his or her own name. Funds are insured up to $100,000 per person at the same institution, regardless of the different branches they're opened at or the types of regular accounts.

◆ **Joint tenancy account.** Two members of the same family establish an account in both their names. In order to qualify for federal insurance, both family members must have equal drawing rights. If a husband and child set up a joint account, each must be able to withdraw half the money on deposit, even if the son or daughter is a child. The joint account works only once with the same two names. Switching the order won't make any difference.

◆ **Testamentary revocable trust.** This is a complex trust arrangement in which the account holder places funds in trust for a spouse, child, or grandchild *only*. Each beneficiary is insured separately.

However, there are all sorts of conditions placed on this type of trust. They vary according to state laws, and anyone considering establishing such a trust should see a lawyer, financial planner, accountant, or all three. Simply put, the trust is established for the beneficiary and the funds are payable upon the death of the account holder. However, that person can revoke the trust before he or she dies.

The Money Line

Both federal insurance agencies say that investors are covered up to $100,000 per person at the same institution in proportion to their holdings. For example, if a husband and wife have a joint account with $100,000 on deposit, they are each covered for $50,000. If the husband then sets up an identical account with one of his children, he is covered for an additional $50,000 for a total of $100,000. If the husband establishes a third account with another child, his share of the funds are not insured. Accountholders can have up to $100,000 in a variety of joint tenancy accounts and still be covered for up to the same amount by the FDIC.

How Much Money Can You Afford to Lose?

This question doesn't apply to federally insured banks, where you're protected, it only involves the gamble you take with uninsured investments. If, for example, a federally insured bank offers you a yield of 5 percent on a one-year $10,000 CD, you're guaranteed to earn $500 in a year. You'll get back $10,500 on your $10,000 investment. You can't say that about speculative investments such as stocks and bonds, although the gamble may pay off with earnings higher than what you'll earn from a bank.

For example, if, in 1924, you had invested $1,000 in the S&P 500 (a basket of 500 stocks that makes up the Standard & Poor's) and let it ride through the ups and downs of the stock market, you would have more than a half-million bucks today! Does that mean the stock market isn't risky? No, because the stock market could average a negative 10 percent return one year, and a positive 10 percent return the next. It just means that the longer your money is invested and the more diversified your investments are, the more you reduce your risk.

The following table shows how different types of investments performed against inflation over a 20-year period ending in 2003. Note, for example, that there was less volatility between the maximum and minimum return on government bonds than there was with stock investments.

Investments vs. Inflation

	Maximum	Minimum
Common stocks	34.1%	-13%
Long-term government bonds	12.5	4.9
Intermediate-term government bonds	10.1	2.9
Treasury bills	9.8	1.05
Inflation	6.1	1.6

How Long Can You Be Without the Money?

This is a critical decision lots of people skip over. If you're tempted to succumb to the razzle-dazzle of a stockbroker's pitch, or some super-high rate in a bank ad, before you plunk down your cash, remember this: You might need the money sooner than you think.

If you need your cash six months or a year down the road for an emergency or something else you hadn't planned for, what are you going to do? What if the investment rate picture and other financial factors change and you want to move your money to a higher-earning instrument? What do you do then? If you withdraw your funds early, you'll probably be charged a stiff penalty.

So Really ... How Safe Are Banks?

Compared with a couple of decades ago, most U.S. banks today are almost as strong as Fort Knox, thanks to ringing up record profits (often at your expense through low savings rates, high credit card rates, and stiff fees). Way back in the late '80s, as a result of mismanagement and bad loans, 1 bank in 120, and 1 thrift in 200, were going down the tubes. Then things got a whole lot better. There were 4 total failures in 2001, 11 in '02, 3 in '03 and only 3 midway through '04.

Recently, the failure rates were as low as 1 in 3,000. In fact, 9 out of every 10 banks in the country were given a top three-star safety rating by the respected independent research firm of Veribanc, Inc., Wakefield, Massachusetts. "Today," says Warren Heller,

Watch Your Wallet

Don't let yourself get lulled into a false sense of security! While it's true that very few banks fail any more, that's because the industry has been making money hand over fist through outrageous fees. The banking customer still pays in the end.

Veribanc's director of research, "so few institutions are having difficulties, those that are in trouble often can hide in anonymity."

But if you're the kind of person who'd rather be safe than sorry, call Veribanc at 1-800-837-4226 and, for $10, get a safety rating on any bank, savings bank, thrift, or credit union for $10 over the phone. A second outfit's rating costs only $5. You can also get more in-depth reports for $25 or $45, or a list of the top "Blue Ribbon" banks in the country for $35. [*Note: all prices are current*]

The Least You Need to Know

- FDIC-protected deposits in banks, and Treasury Securities and U.S. Savings Bonds, are guaranteed by the full faith and credit of the U.S. government.

- You could wind up in the poorhouse if your uninsured investments take an extra-bad turn for the worse.

- The higher the potential reward, the greater the risk.

- Treasury-only money funds pay double what banks pay you on the average Money Market Account.

- Interest on savings bonds may be tax-exempt if the proceeds are used to finance higher education.

- At all FDIC-insured banks and thrifts, your money is protected for up to $100,000 per person at the same institution.

Chapter 10

Savings and CD Accounts: Beating the Averages

In This Chapter

♦ How to know the pluses and minuses of savings accounts vs. CDs

♦ The secrets of shopping for the highest-paying FDIC-insured accounts—locally and out-of-state

♦ Key questions to ask before you open any type of account

♦ How to avoid paying fees and penalties that zap your hard-earned cash

After watching their Wall Street investments get clobbered following a dramatic eight-year rise, more Americans are realizing there's a way to invest—and not lose. The answer is those old-fashioned, FDIC-insured accounts at banks. Granted, they pay piddling returns (such as a measly $1/2$ percent on a passbook account and not much more than 2 or 3 percent on CDs) compared with what you were used to earning from stocks in the 1990s, but still, a gain is better than a loss, right?

Example: Using three different stock indexes, had you invested $10,000 at the start of 2001, by May you'd have lost $322 using the Dow Jones Index,

$119 down with the S&P 500, and a whopping $322 down with the NASDAQ Composite Index. On the other hand, you would have earned more than $60 from the average six-month bank CD. If you had shopped the *highest-paying* U.S. banks, the CD would have paid even more.

Yet banks are getting away with murder because millions of people are willing to settle for low yields. They don't know where to go to earn more, and still have the protection of FDIC insurance coverage. Many are unwilling to go through the hassle of changing banks even if it would help their pocketbook dramatically. Millions of folks, especially senior citizens, are still clinging to the old-fashioned savings habits they learned as children—plopping money into passbook accounts to "save for a rainy day" without worrying about low rates. The sad result is that today there's more money deposited in low-paying savings accounts than in 3 or 4 percent CDs!

This chapter shows you how to turn those piddling-interest instruments into cash cows by doing business with the safest, top-paying outfits. First, it explains how to earn more with the three basic types of savings accounts, and then it tells the steps you should take to get the highest yields with *CDs*. You learn the key questions to ask before you hand the bank a penny of your money.

Understanding Savings Account Basics

Should you get a passbook, Money Market Account (MMA) or a CD? The answer is simple. The first two accounts are liquid, which means you can add to your savings or withdraw funds at any time without getting socked with a penalty. Savings accounts also can act as temporary "garages," where you can park your funds while you're scouting around for a high-paying CD or other investment.

With a CD, you lock up your money for a specific period of time, usually anywhere from three months to five years. But if you withdraw funds early, you usually get hit with a penalty, although there are a few banks offering no-penalty CDs.

Savings accounts come in three flavors:

> **Passbooks.** The same old account that Ma and Pa lectured about when you were a youngster. You deposit your money, and the bank gives you a little book to record your transactions. The accounts by law paid 5 percent interest until 1986, but after that the average rate dropped steadily to just a tad above 1 percent.

> **Statement savings.** Walks, talks, and quacks exactly like a passbook, except there's no little book involved. Instead, the bank sends you a monthly statement

that shows all your transactions. This, of course, reduces the time you spend bothering a teller, which is precisely what the bank wants.

Money Market Accounts (MMA). These pay about 1 to 2 percent more than the other two accounts, and you're permitted to write a maximum of three checks a month (to parties other than yourself) on the account. That makes it handy for you to transfer enough money, once a month, from your MMA to your checking account to pay bills, as discussed in Chapter 8.

Certain Types of Accounts Pay More

CD yields have been beating the average MMA by as much as one to two full percentage points. The longer the CD term, the higher the yield and the more it tops what you can earn on an MMA.

Tiered MMAs Pay More for Larger Deposits

If you're lucky enough to have $25,000, $50,000, or $75,000 to deposit into an MMA, many banks will pay you even higher-than-average yields on what they call a "tiered" account. The more you deposit, the higher the yield. The rub is that generally you must open the account with at least $10,000, and, if your account balance ever sinks as low as $1,000, your yield may plummet to only 1 or 2 percent.

Beware of Fees, Right and Left

Nothing in life is free, especially savings accounts. All three kinds hit you with tariffs, as fees have been on an upswing throughout the entire banking industry. The following types of fees are common for the three types of savings accounts.

- A monthly or quarterly "maintenance fee," just for keeping your money in the bank. It will probably be between $10 and $20 a month.

- A special fee if your account balance falls below a certain minimum during the month. Figure about $15 or higher.

- An ATM fee every time you use an automatic teller that doesn't belong to your bank. Now there's also a "double-whammy" charge, because the other outfit whose ATM you use, slaps you with a fee, as well. These usually add up to $3 or more.

- On an MMA, you'll probably get charged $10 to $15 if you write more than three checks a month. Plus, some banks will charge a $15 to $25 penalty if you close your MMA account within, say, six months after opening it.

Shopping for Savings Accounts

Bankers are not dopes. The biggest reason they covet your basic savings and checking business is because these are their bread-and-butter, "core" accounts. Once you become a customer, you're also a prospect for buying CDs, bank mutual funds, personal loans, and mortgages. To bait the hook, the bank may offer you a "relationship package" deal that offers a slightly higher yield on your CD, plus maybe a no-fee credit card, if you maintain a combined balance of $20,000 or more for your accounts. The downside is that you'd probably do better by splitting the accounts among several different outfits.

The fact is, not enough consumers do a thorough job of shopping banks before they sign on the dotted line. They just stay at the same old place where they've been keeping their checking or savings. They don't check out what other outfits are offering, and they fail to compare the fees as well as the rates—preferably at a half-dozen institutions. In short, they're trading "comfort and convenience" for getting mugged by costly banks.

Here are some big secrets for earning more on your savings and CDs:

♦ In the same city, on the same day, the odds are 10-to-1 that you can find another bank that will beat your bank's MMA yield by one-half percent to a full percent or more. All you have to do is get on the phone and call around.

♦ Don't just shop local banks. Contact the top-paying FDIC-insured banks in other states that will offer double what your hometown institutions pay on MMAs. There's a free list of these banks on the Internet at www.bankrate.com, with their toll-free phone numbers. These FDIC banks are super-safe, and just as convenient to do business with as the bank down the street. Distance has nothing to do with FDIC insurance protection.

The Road to Riches

Don't forget to look into Internet banks. Instead of depositing your money with Tillie the Teller at your local branch, you handle your entire transaction online and by mail. The overhead of these institutions is a lot less than at a traditional bank, so they pass the savings on to the customer. Moreover, most Internet banks are FDIC-insured for the same $100,000 protection as brick-and-mortar institutions.

♦ Instead of parking all your CD money in one term, such as six months or one year, consider "laddering" your buys with different terms. It's protection against a rise or fall in rates. For example, say you have $10,000 to invest. You buy a six-month $5,000 CD, a one-year for $2,500 and a two-year for $2,500. When the six-month account matures, you roll the money into a two-year. Then do the same thing when the other accounts mature. The rule of thumb is:

Go short when rates are rising. When rates seem to have reached a peak, lock up a long-term CD. When rates have bottomed out, go with short-term CDs so that you can renew at a higher rate later on.

Key Questions to Ask Your Banker

Even though banks use confusing account names, such as "Master Passbook Account" and "Money Market Passbook," you can cut through the confusion by asking these questions:

- What are the rate (before *compounding*) and yield (after compounding)?

- Is the account tiered? That is, does it pay higher yields on larger balances? (This has become a big deal with MMAs.)

- What is the monthly maintenance fee?

- Is there an additional fee if I don't keep a certain minimum balance?

- Is there a fee if I close my account early?

- Is there a per-check fee on my MMA (three third-party checks are permitted per month)? Is there an additional charge if I *exceed* three checks a month?

- Is there more than one version of this account?

- Is the account federally insured?

Fiscal Facts _____

Compounding is simply interest added to interest. The more frequent the compounding (such as "daily" or "continuously") the better.

Higher-Paying Out-of-State Banks Are Just As Safe (or Safer) As the Bank Down the Block

If you don't check out higher-paying banks in other states, you're making a big mistake and losing money. Just because an institution is 1,000 or 2,000 miles away doesn't mean it's not 100 percent safe. The banks are not only FDIC-insured, they're also rated among the strongest in the nation. Most of them boast a top, three-star safety rating by the respected independent research firm of Veribanc, Inc., in Wakefield, Massachusetts. Veribanc uses FDIC data to verify each institution's financial health.

These institutions—especially banks that only do business on the Internet—will pay you more on an MMA than your local bank, and 1 or 2 percent higher on your CD.

Remember: No one has ever lost a dime in an FDIC-insured bank, thrift, or credit union, up to the $100,000 limit, regardless of where it is based.

Of course, the whole idea of going out of state to make more money will go over like a lead balloon with your local banker. He'll tell you it's not patriotic to pull money out of your community and hand it to some faraway outfit. But hey, aren't big banks gobbling up little banks in other states? And don't giant outfits like Citibank and Bank of America peddle credit cards across state lines? What's good for the goose ought to be okay for the gander, right?

How to Set Up Your MMA

These are the basic steps for investing in a high-yielding, federally insured MMA out of state:

1. Contact the institution by mail or by phone, to reach the person in charge of consumer deposit accounts. Some banks have a "national money desk," which handles inquiries from individuals outside the institution's local area.

2. Verify if the account is federally insured. Explain how much you want to invest and for how long.

3. Ask for the latest rate and yield on the account you are interested in, and how long the rate is good for. Some may be "introductory" deals where the rate plunges after a few weeks or months. Banks are apt to change their rates on a weekly basis or more frequently. Many change their rates on Tuesdays or Wednesdays.

4. Find out if the account is "tiered." That is, are there higher yields for larger deposits? Is the rate "indexed" to some other rate, such as Treasury securities?

5. Determine what all the fees are and how you can avoid them. Important: Get a copy of the bank's Fee Disclosure document and read all the fine print.

6. Ask when your deposit will begin earning interest and how many days after opening an MMA account you can withdraw funds.

7. Ask for an account-opening form and a pre-assigned account number.

8. Get the correct mailing address of the bank branch you are dealing with. The bank may have several locations.

9. Make your check payable to the institution—not to an individual—if you open the account by mail. Write "For deposit only" on the back of the check. For maximum protection, include your Social Security number.

10. If the institution doesn't provide a deposit form, attach a letter specifying how much you are depositing, the type of account, the pre-assigned account number, the check number, and the amount. Include your name, address, phone number, and Social Security number. Keep a copy of the letter.

11. Mail your letter and check to the correct bank branch.

More Savings Shopping Secrets to Know

Before you agree to open an account, check out the following tips:

◆ The time for you to wheel and deal is *before* you sign, not afterward. You may not know it, but banks now are willing to negotiate with customers a lot more than in the past. You can try maneuvering on everything from having certain fees waived, to asking for a cheaper credit card rate. Don't be bashful. Stand up and bark, and tell the bank what you want in exchange for your business. But don't tell it to an account representative or teller. Tell it to the branch manager or an officer.

◆ This is critical. Bank fees today are hammering every consumer to death. When you shop your half-dozen banks, get a copy of each outfit's "Fee Disclosure" document. Compare each fee—every one—with your own personal banking behavior. How many checks do you usually write per month? What average balance do you typically maintain? How often do you use an ATM? Then ask the banker, "Are you sure you've told me about all ways I can earn more interest, avoid fees, and save on my loans?" You're not being a pest; it's simply good business. The squeaky wheel always gets the grease.

◆ You need to read your contract *before* you sign anything. Also check the flyspeck footnotes at the very bottom of bank ads. This is *your* money we're talking about, not the bank's!

The Money Line

Banks are holding less and less of the consumer's money. Twenty-five years ago, households kept nearly 30 percent of their wealth in bank deposits, including CDs, but now it's down to about 13 percent.

Knowing Where the Money Is—In a 1 Percent Rut

Shockingly, Americans not only keep $1.3 trillion in low-paying savings accounts, but whenever Wall Street shudders a little bit, more of them run like lemmings to deposit even more of their funds in those 1 percent investments.

Watch Your Wallet

When buying a CD, decide for how long you can afford to sock money away without touching it. Early-withdrawal penalties can cost you three or six months' worth of interest.

The result is that today there's a lot more money in the three basic types of savings—passbooks, statement savings, and MMAs—than in small-denomination CDs.

Until recently, consumers put 56¢ of every savings dollar into small-denomination CDs and 44¢ into basic savings accounts such as MMAs and passbooks. But 10 years later, 62¢ of that dollar went to lower-paying savings accounts and only 38¢ to CDs. The following table spotlights this trend.

Where the Money Is—Annual Figures (in Billions of Dollars)

Date	CDs	MMAs and Passbooks
1989	$1,148.1	$893.7
1990	$1,171.0	$923.8
1991	$1,106.3	$1,045.2
1992	$866.2	$1,187.4
1993	$780.2	$1,219.4
1994	$814.6	$1,149.9
1995	$929.8	$1,134.7
1996	$946.0	$1,271.7
1997	$967.1	$1,397.5
1998	$960.0	$1,536.7
1999	$956.1	$1,736.2
2000	$1,046.2	$1,872.1

How much are American savers losing by keeping so much money in low-paying savings accounts? Plenty. Suppose that 1,000 people each keep $1,000 in an MMA paying 1 percent interest. That comes to a grand total of $10,000 in interest per year. Now let's assume those same 1,000 customers move their MMA accounts to other banks that offer 3 percent—something they could easily do. The interest increases to $30,000. If the customers decide instead to put their money into CD accounts paying 3 percent, the interest is still $30,000.

As you can see, CDs are definitely worth looking into. However, keeping a lot of money in a savings account might be the better strategy for emergencies if either of the following conditions apply:

♦ You might have to access the money suddenly for some reason, such as putting a new roof on the house or getting Junior a set of braces. There's no penalty for withdrawing funds from an MMA, as there is with a CD.

♦ The high-tier rate on an MMA is paying more than CDs are paying. That can happen if you have $20,000 or more to open an account. But on longer-term CDs such as five years, the CD yield could top the tiered-MMA yield.

So remember, ask lots of questions, shop around—locally, out of state, and on the Internet—and make your money work as hard as it can for you.

The Least You Need to Know

♦ Do business only with FDIC-insured institutions, anywhere in the country.

♦ Open short-term accounts of less than one year when rates seem to be rising; go longer when you perceive them dropping.

♦ Don't forget that basic savings accounts almost *always* pay less than CDs.

♦ Comparison shop for the best savings account deal; it can really pay off.

♦ Remember that some out-of-state, FDIC-insured institutions will pay you 1 to 2 percent more on CDs than your local bank.

Why Credit Unions May Be the Best Place to Park Your Money

In This Chapter

◆ Why credit unions are better deals than banks

◆ Why credit unions might lend you money when a bank won't

◆ Seven ways to quickly find a credit union that you can join

◆ How your credit union deposits are protected up to $100,000

◆ Why credit unions are the friendliest places around

There are more profitable places to keep your hard-earned cash than a low-paying bank that pays nearly zip in interest, charges horrendous fees, no longer knows you by name, and maybe charges $1 for you to talk to a live teller. One of the best spots is a credit union, which may be easier to join than you think. If you're a novice in the money world who's been wondering if a credit union is for you, this chapter explains the basics and how to get started.

The name of the game is to make your money grow the best way you can, without being hassled or disappointed by your institution. With a credit union, the pluses can be as long as your arm—starting with friendly people who often are as hospitable as your next-door neighbor.

How Credit Unions Work

There are 9,488 credit unions in the United States, according to Callahan & Associates, a Washington, D.C., industry analyst. What's more, because of federal legislation, credit unions are broadening their membership base, especially in communities, to make it far easier to join. A credit union is a cooperative financial institution owned and controlled by people like yourself who use its services. That's "cooperative," as in "working together." These people are called "members" instead of "customers," and their members all have something in common, such as where they work, live, or go to church. Now, if you merely live in a certain geographic area, you might be eligible to join. A credit union provides a safe, convenient place for its members to save money and get loans at cheaper rates. Moreover, every member can vote for the board of directors and the credit union's rules.

The Money Line

The first state to pass a credit union act was Massachusetts in 1909, but by 1935 there were 39 states with credit union laws, with 3,372 of them serving 641,800 members. Today there are more than 83 million members. Today, every state has a credit union league that coordinates the credit unions in its state. Also, more than 3,000 credit unions have their own websites.

Most people who join a credit union wish they'd done it years ago. Why? Because of credit unions' caring attitude toward their members, and the fact that their deals are better than a bank's. Credit unions' deposit rates are almost always higher, their loan rates are lower—as much as 3 to 4 percentage points below what a bank charges on credit cards. Plus, you won't run into the same blizzard of fees that you encounter at a bank.

Most important, credit unions are *not-for-profit*. They're simply made up of people who want to pool their money and make loans to each other. The idea goes back to nineteenth-century Europe, and believe it or not—unlike at a bank—a credit union member's *character* and *desire to repay a loan* are more important than his income or credit record. Some difference, eh? Banks and thrifts, on the other hand, are in business to make a profit because they're owned by stockholders who expect to make a healthy buck on their investments. So if your friendly banker keeps sticking his hands in your pockets, you know why.

The banking industry hates credit unions with a passion. It has mounted intensive lobby efforts in recent years to get Congress to pass laws to make credit union operations taxable, which they still are not as of this writing. But Congress voted the other way, making it even easier for credit unions to expand their membership bases—as bankers everywhere howled.

How to Join a Credit Union–It's Easy!

Credit unions are for everyone. If there's a credit union at XYZ Manufacturing Company, for instance, any employee of XYZ is eligible to join. But there's a good chance that somewhere in your area there's a credit union that will welcome you as a member. There are many ways you can find one, says the Credit Union National Association (CUNA). In the following list, CUNA gives suggestions on how to find a credit union:

1. **Call toll-free.** Call the Credit Union National Association (CUNA) at 1-800-358-5710 for the phone number of the credit union nearest you.

2. **Ask your boss.** Your company may sponsor a credit union, or may be a select employee group (SEG) that has access to a credit union. Many employers offer direct deposit of your payroll to your credit union.

3. **Poll your family.** Your spouse's employer may have a credit union. Many credit unions allow a member's entire family to also join, including cousins, uncles, and aunts. But some may limit membership to just the immediate family.

4. **Ask the neighbors**. Some credit unions have a "community" field of membership for folks living in a certain area.

5. **Read the Yellow Pages**. Credit unions rarely advertise, but a credit union ad in the phone book may tell you its field of membership. Or, they can steer you to a credit union that you can join.

6. **Check online.** There is an online database of credit unions at www.CUNA.org. Go to "consumer information" and then to "credit union locator."

7. **Contact your state's Credit Union League.** Get the phone number from CUNA.

One more thing: When you join a credit union, you're a member for life!

Other than the membership requirement, you can do just about anything at a credit union that you can do at a bank. You can open a checking account (which credit

Fiscal Facts _____

The terminology is different, but the services are similar: Credit unions call a savings account a **share account**, whereas the term for a checking account is a **share draft account**.

unions call a *share draft account*), a savings account (which they call a *share account*), or a CD, just like at a bank. On the loan side, you can get a mortgage, a new- or used-car loan (where the credit unions' low rates will beat the banks' pants off), a home equity loan or line of credit, or a credit card. And credit unions have ATMs just like those other guys. Also although credit unions focus mostly on consumer accounts, in early 2004 many have been lending money to small businesses, as well.

Because credit unions are genuinely interested in their members' welfare, many of them do a better job of educating you about money than banks do. Because of their cooperative nature, they tend to have strong ties to their communities. Most credit unions, for example, issue their own newsletter to members.

How Credit Unions Beat the Banks' Rates

The following table shows what credit unions were paying and charging, on average, compared with banks and thrifts in a recent nationwide survey by Bankrate.com. Except for mortgages, which many of them don't offer, credit unions offer a big edge for your pocketbook.

Comparison of Loan and Interest Rates

	30-Year Fixed-Rate Mortgage	New Car	Variable-Rate Credit Card	Money Market Account	One Year CD
Banks and Thrifts	5.83%	7.14%	13.13%	1.32%	.98%
Credit Unions	5.88%	5.84%	10.20%	2.82%	1.07%

Source: Bank Rate Monitor

Credit Unions Also Offer $100,000 Insurance Protection

Is your money safe at a credit union? Oh, yes. Your deposits are insured up to $100,000 per person by the National Credit Union Administration, an agency of the federal government, which insures the deposits of credit union members at all federal- and state-chartered credit unions nationwide. The $100,000 protection is similar to the $100,000-per-person coverage of bank deposits by the Federal Deposit Insurance Corporation.

The Road to Riches

You'll save a bundle on fees, penalties, and other charges by going through a credit union. Where banks may nick you as much as 10 percent for a cash advance, a credit union may only charge you 1.5 to 2 percent of the transaction amount. Plus, the majority of credit unions don't hit you with an annual fee on credit cards. And if you go over the credit limit on your card, the credit union cost is apt to be $5 vs. the $29 that many banks charge.

A Friendship, Not a Confrontation

Any downsides to a credit union? We can only think of one. Because credit unions are smaller, you won't find as many of their branches or ATMs in your local area. But their benefits far outweigh that relatively slight inconvenience. In fact, lots of credit union members we know swear they'd never do business anywhere else. Said one, "The difference is this. When I did business with a bank, and tried to borrow some money, some squinty-eyed loan officer sat across the desk from me, shaking his head and saying 'No.' Now, when I visit my credit union for the same reason, there's a person just like myself sitting at the same side of a table with me, helping to figure out how I can get the money I need at the cheapest possible cost. It's friendship, not a confrontation!"

Many Credit Unions Are Also Online

Banks, brokers, and insurance and finance companies aren't the only outfits that offer helpful advice for your money online. Many credit unions also have a presence. Today, four times as many credit unions have websites compared to four years ago. Just click on the keywords "credit union" and start from there. In fact, one of the best electronic calculators we've found to help you compare the cost of leasing vs. buying a new car, is at a credit union: www.forestparkfcu.org/alvb.html.

If you need fast emergency cash, one of the quickest ways is to request it online from your credit union. Credit unions also are a speedy way to get an auto loan electronically, plus, they have arrangements with web-based auto brokers and car dealers to make the whole process super-fast. By going through a credit union, you can save $2 off the $14.95 price of getting the history on any used car from Carfax (www.carfax.com). Now that you know the facts about credit unions, do some research into your local credit unions. When you find a credit union that you like, join it, and put your money to work for you, not your banker! Also, remember that although membership in a credit union is usually restricted to a special group or field of interest, chances are excellent that you can find a credit union that you can join.

The Least You Need to Know

- Credit unions are nonprofit, cooperative organizations that usually pay higher savings rates and charge lower loan rates than banks.

- Credit unions call their customers "members" and have a membership requirement, such as belonging to a certain organization or living in a particular geographic area, but you can easily find one that you're eligible to join.

- Credit unions have the same $100,000 federally insured deposit protection as FDIC-insured banks, so your money is safe.

- You'll probably find friendlier service at a credit union, because you'll be served by people who have the same interests at heart.

Part

Maximizing Your Dollar—Whether You Borrow or Save It

If you're up against the wall with personal debts or credit problems, or you just want to make the best possible mortgage or auto deal or even if you're feeling guilty for not having a plan in place when it comes to your paycheck, this section is for you!

This chapter explains how to protect your valuable credit rating at a time when the whole financial world is judging you by your credit score. It also tells you how to strengthen your credit to get the loan you need or how to prevent a financial crisis even if it's at your front door.

Don't borrow another dollar until you check out these tips to save on loans and protect and maximize your earning power—not to mention saving your skin at the credit bureau!

Chapter 12

How to Boost Your Credit Rating

- ♦ How much of your personal data credit agencies have
- ♦ Red flags creditors know to look for on your credit report
- ♦ How to obtain your credit score and a copy of your credit report
- ♦ Key questions to ask a credit counseling agency
- ♦ How to improve your chances of getting credit and removing errors from your credit record
- ♦ How to handle disputes

Three giant companies—Equifax, Experian, and Trans Union are credit bureaus that have personal credit information on just about every person in the United States.

Nobody ever told you how to get around this super-snooper system, but there are ways. People with bad credit? They get stung with extra-high interest rates by banks and finance companies that are making a killing from those "sub-prime" loans. Reports show even those with *good* credit can easily become victims of erroneous information that winds up on their report without their knowing it.

Shockingly, most consumers don't even bother to get a copy of their own credit report to look at and check for errors. They remain in the dark, never realizing how much negative stuff the credit agencies have dug up on them. The info can range from their date of birth to their income, payment habits, and the people they owe. Even worse, few people know the inside scoop on how credit reports work and what lenders look for.

This chapter goes inside the shadowy world of credit bureaus, explains how they "score" your credit history, and tells you what to avoid. You learn how to strengthen your credit file and greatly improve your chances of getting a loan.

Big Brother Is Watching You

You can forget about how "private" you think your personal financial life is. The odds are 450-million-to-1 that if you have a credit card, department store account, savings or checking account, auto loan, student loan, or mortgage, there's a computer file on you. Everything is in it—your job, how much money you make, where you've lived, and how you've paid your bills.

A little scary? You bet. Big Brother is watching you like you wouldn't believe. Its computers sit in a company you've maybe never heard of, run by people you've never met. All three big guns of the credit-agency business probably have the same information on your life.

The Money Line _____

The profile of the average American who's in debt counseling looks like this: 35 years old; 53.8 percent are female, 46.2 percent male; 46.2 percent are married; 41.6 percent own their own home; average annual gross income is $29,425; average total debt is $23,184; they have 10.1 average creditors; and are 78.8 percent in debt as a percentage of their annual income.

Almost 20 years ago, three outfits got together with a company named Fair, Isaac & Co., in San Rafael, California, and worked out a system to predict the probability of individual consumers paying—or not paying—their bills based on the characteristics in their credit report. Using this as a model (called FICO, after Fair, Isaac & Co. (www.fairisaac.com), each credit bureau came up with a credit "score" on each person. With a little weighting, juggling, and tweaking, they're able to compare any bureau's score against the others. It's sort of like working with three bathroom scales to get a comparable answer.

Getting Your Credit Score

Until the year 2000, you couldn't get your credit score. Fair, Isaac & Co. hid that information for all it was worth. Then, thanks to pressure from the Federal Trade Commission and consumer advocates, the gates opened up. Today, not only can you buy your credit score for a few bucks from Fair, Isaac & Co., the three major credit bureaus will sell it to you as well, along with your credit report.

What Goes into Your Score

The FICO score is designed to give lenders a fast way to accurately predict the risk involved if they give you a loan. The scores range from 350 to 850, with the average credit score 678 as of mid-2004. There are a slew of factors that go into making up each score, but the top five seem to be:

◆ Your previous delinquencies. Odds are that if you've been late in making payments before, you'll do it again. This accounts for about 35 percent of your score.

◆ How you've used your credit. If you've had a habit of maxing out your credit cards or have been close to doing it, it tells the lender you're a bigger risk than the guy who's been careful with his credit line. This accounts for 30 percent of your score.

◆ How long you've had credit. The person who's had it for a long time is a better risk than the person who's just gotten credit. This accounts for 15 percent of your score.

◆ How many times you've asked for credit. If you've made beaucoup applications for credit over a short period of time, it goes over like a lead balloon. This represents 10 percent of your score.

◆ Your credit mix. If you only carry unsecured credit cards, you're regarded as being riskier than the guy who takes out an installment loan and keeps making payments until the loan is paid off. By contrast, when you make credit card

Watch Your Wallet

Be careful to protect your credit rating—it affects more than you know. Not just potential creditors, but prospective employers and landlords; just about any *business* can file for a copy of your report and, for a mere fee of less than $10, know everything there is to know about your credit history.

payments, that only frees up more money to borrow. This accounts for 10 percent of your score.

Nowadays, your credit score can be the number one thing that causes a credit company to say "yes" or "no" to your loan application. Cold and heartless? Yes. But, getting accepted or turned down also can depend on whom you're doing business with. One typical minimum score to be approved for a loan is 620, based on the Fair, Isaac model. But, an auto dealer may finance your car if you score only 550, while a lender giving you an unsecured line of credit (you put up no collateral) may require something higher than 620. You can bet the auto dealer will charge you a higher-than-average interest rate.

The Money Line

While the FICO score is a big deal in the lending industry, especially for mortgages, each of the three major credit bureaus comes up with its own score on consumers, roughly patterned after the Fair, Isaac model. So don't be surprised if your score number is different with those guys. Equifax calls theirs a Beacon Score, Experian calls it an Experian/Fair, Isaac Risk Score, and Trans Union calls it an Empirica Score. But, some people simply call all of them FICO scores.

Smaller, regional credit bureaus supply personal credit data about you to any place you go for credit—from credit card companies and auto dealers to, yes, even the company that's considering you for a job. Whenever you apply for credit, those outfits feed your latest personal information into the Big Three's computers.

The Money Line

The Big Three agencies aren't the ones who finally decide whether you'll get a loan or be hired. They only "compile the data," as they say, and provide it to organizations that determine whether they'll extend credit to you. It could be the car dealer, department store, bank, or credit card issuer. And to confuse the issue, all those guys might evaluate your credit history differently. Little wonder the Big Three are a mystery to the average consumer, who knows zip about how the credit system operates.

Despite the fact that credit agencies have 450 million consumer credit reports on file, in one recent year only 9 million Americans bothered to peer into their own files to see the often gory information on their credit records. Of those, 25 percent discovered an error they eventually had corrected, according to the National Center for Financial Education, San Diego, California.

How to Get Your Credit Score and Credit Report

It's critical that every American consumer obtain a copy of his or her credit report at least once a year, for two important reasons: First, identity theft is rising dramatically across the United States. You could easily become victimized by some creep who steals your ID and runs up thousands of dollars in charges that you don't learn about until some collector tracks you down and demands payment. Second, studies by the U.S. Public Interest Research Group (PIRG) show that nearly one-third of all credit reports contain "serious errors" that could cause you to be denied credit in the future. PIRG further says 70 percent of the reports have "mistakes or errors of some kind," like wrong names, or they're missing positive information about you such as credit card and other loan accounts that were paid on time to prove your creditworthiness.

Before you grab a so-called "free" credit report offer that could wind up costing you as much as $70, know that you can order a report on your own from any of the three major credit bureaus—Equifax, Experian or Trans Union—for no more than $8. In six states the report is free. And, it won't cost you a dime if, within the past 60 days, you've been denied credit, insurance, or employment anywhere in the United States. You're also entitled to a free report once a year if you certify in writing that 1) you're unemployed but plan to look for a job within the next 60 days, 2) you're on welfare, or 3) you suspect there's inaccurate information in your report because of fraud.

The huge, dangerous downside to credit bureau business is that almost any Tom, Dick, or Harry can easily buy personal credit reports from the bureaus and use them to market their own products or pry into people's "private" credit histories.

Another Way to Do It

The best deal? Probably the no-kidding-it's-really-free online report from iPlace.com (www.iplace.com), owned by ConsumerInfo.com in Bristol, PA. All you do is give them your credit card number for authentication.

ConsumerInfo.com also promotes itself under the brand name Freecreditreport.com. You get a "free copy" of your report from one of the three credit bureaus, along with 30 days of the company's CreditCheck Monitoring Service.

Translation: When you sign up for a "free 30-day trial" as a CheckService member, you receive "unlimited free copies of your credit report," online monthly alerts to notify you of important changes in your credit file, a newsletter plus other services. Members get two encrypted passcodes to view their credit report online at any time. Then comes the hitch: If you don't notify ConsumerInfo.com within the 30 days that you don't want to continue the membership, an annual $69.95 fee is automatically charged against your credit card.

Another outfit, PrivacyGuard.com (www.privacyguard.com), owned by giant Cendant Corp. based in Virginia Beach, Va., dangles an offer of "three months for $1," for which you receive all three credit reports plus a quarterly Credit Alert. After the three months, the service costs $59.95 per year for unlimited access to your report including your spouse's credit history as well. Access to your driver's record is also included, and for an additional $8.50 paid to the Medical Information Bureau (which PrivacyGuard refunds) you can see your entire medical history file.

For $7.95 you can get a single credit report online in seconds from Qspace.com (www.qspace.com), which was purchased by ConsumerInfo.com, with access limited to 30 days. Or, for $29.95 the company will sell you a "comprehensive" report that combines your credit history from all three big credit bureaus.

If you do business with any of these outfits, be sure to check out the security of information you send them over the Internet. The sites mentioned here are well protected.

The cheapest route: If you want to save a few bucks by contacting the bureaus directly (their addresses are provided later in this section), be sure to order all three reports because the info may be different on each. For example, for $12.95 you can order Equifax credit reports online and also get your FICO credit score, computed by Fair, Isaac & Co. Without that credit score, the report costs $8.50 when ordered online. Remember to do this 60 to 90 days before you apply for any major credit. That will give you time to clean up any mess you discover on your report.

Here are the addresses and phone numbers of the Big Three credit agencies plus Fair, Isaac & Co., another credit reporting outfit to help provide you with your information:

> Experian (formerly TRW)
> PO Box 2104
> Allen, TX 75013-0949
> 1-800-682-7654
> website: www.experian.com
>
> Equifax
> PO Box 740241
> Atlanta, GA 30374-0241
> 1-800-685-1111
> website: www.equifax.com
>
> Trans Union Corporation
> 760 W. Sproul Road
> Springfield, PA 19064-0390
> 1-800-888-4213
> website: www.tuc.com

Fair, Isaac & Co.
200 Smith Ranch Road
San Rafael, CA 94903
415-472-2211
website: www.fairisaac.com

How to Read Your Credit Report

A credit report is basically divided into four sections:

- ◆ Identifying information
- ◆ Credit history
- ◆ Public records
- ◆ Inquiries

Among the errors you might spot: There might be two or three misspellings of your name or more than one Social Security number. The errors will stay on your report until you complain and correct them. (Imagine an identity thief 1,000 miles away having a ball running up charges in your name.) Other information includes your current and previous addresses, your date of birth, phone numbers, driver's license number, your employer, and your spouse's name. Each account shows the name of the creditor and the account number (which may be scrambled for security purposes). The entry will also include: When you opened the account; the kind of credit (for example, installment loan or credit card); whether the account is in your name alone or with someone else's); total amount of the loan—with high credit limit or highest balance on the card, how much you still owe, fixed monthly payment or minimum monthly amount, and the status of the account (paid, open, closed, or inactive); and how well you've paid.

The reports also have payment codes ranging from 1 to 9. An R1 or I1 on a report is an indication of good payment history on a revolving or installment account. Regarding the "public records" section, just hope it's completely blank. Otherwise, it could show

Watch Your Wallet

Be careful of how many lenders you shop when you're looking for a loan. Every time you apply to borrow, that fact can wind up in your credit report. And when lenders see all those inquiries when checking your report, it can scare the heck out of them. For one thing, it could cause them to hike your interest rate or hit you with stiffer fees.

you've had a problem. The "inquiries" section has two parts—one for "hard" inquiries that you initiated by filling out a credit application, and "soft" inquiries by companies that want to send out promotional information to pre-qualified people. (Yes, the credit bureaus sell their lists!)

> **The Money Line** _____
>
> Credit agencies look under every rock. They gather information on you from hundreds of thousands companies such as retailers, banks, finance companies, and credit card issuers. In turn, those companies feed monthly updates on consumers back to the Big Three. Examples of the information provided includes: names, old and current addresses, Social Security numbers, birth dates, employment information, and how people pay their bills. They also gather information from public records in state and county courts. But, this information is limited to tax liens, legal judgments, bankruptcies, and, in some states, child-support payments.

How "Predictable" Are You? The Big Three Think They Know

Credit agencies work with outside mathematical experts to develop what they call "predictive models"—computer programs that try to estimate your *future* credit behavior based on your *previous* behavior. Einstein would have trouble understanding these complicated computer whatchamacallits. They involve far-out terms such as "regression analysis" and "neural network"—concepts that are way above the heads of average people.

These programs can predict the probability of someone going bankrupt three, six, or nine months down the road, or they can determine the likelihood of a person stiffing his or her creditors by never paying bills over the next 24 months.

Making the Biggest Mistake of All: Not Starting Early

If you ask lenders about the biggest mistake consumers make with credit reports, they all agree on one thing: People don't bother to get their report in shape *before* they try to take out a loan. Instead, they waltz into the lender's office, fill out an application, and look like they've been run over by a truck when the loan gets rejected.

A little advance homework and spending $8 for a copy of their credit report could have avoided that mess.

Credit experts say that for …

◆ Mortgages, you should check your credit three to six months before you apply.

◆ Car loans, check your credit and get pre-approved by a bank or credit union before you step inside an auto dealer's showroom and get whisked into some loan guy's office.

◆ Credit cards, always review your credit report with a fine-tooth comb before you apply.

Look at it this way: If you don't do your homework and get turned down for a loan, that's one more black mark on your credit record!

Beware of Getting Scammed

Credit repair outfits that promise to cure your credit problems immediately are illegal, and if you're not careful you could wind up in prison. Credit repair scams—not to be confused with decent counseling organizations that help you rebuild your credit and get out of debt—number in the hundreds. They like to prey on folks who've filed a recent bankruptcy or have such lousy credit that no one will lend them a dime. Know two things right off the bat:

◆ These fly-by-night, rip-off artists can't do anything for you that you can't do for yourself.

◆ They'll probably charge you anywhere from $50 to several thousand dollars for something that you can get for free or just a few bucks.

How bad are their con games? "In many cases," says the Federal Trade Commission (FTC), "these outfits take your money and do little or nothing to improve your credit report. Often, they just vanish." Example: Jane and her husband, both immigrants from South America who moved to this country, ran up $20,000 in debt on five credit cards. A credit repair clinic "consolidated" their debt, reduced their total monthly payments to only $350 per month, and told the couple the bills would be paid off in four years instead of 20. Their payments go through the credit repair clinic—but lately Jane's been noticing late payment charges popping up on her monthly statements.

"Don't worry, we'll take care of it," is all the company will tell Jane and her husband. But they hadn't done so. It's not the first time a credit repair clinic has dragged its heels in forwarding a client's money to creditors—or not paid them at all. Follow these tips:

♦ Only three things can improve your credit record: Time, a conscientious effort on your part, and a debt repayment plan.

♦ Say "no" to any credit repair outfit that suggests you invent a "new" credit identity by applying for an Employer Identification Number (EIN)—which businesses use to report financial information to the IRS—to replace your Social Security number (SSN). The trick is called "file segregation." It's not only frowned on by the federal government, it's also a federal crime to obtain an EIN from the Internal Revenue Service under false pretenses. Plus, you could be prosecuted for mail or wire fraud.

♦ Beware of credit repair mechanics who ask you to fork out money for their services before they are provided. That's in violation of the Credit Repair Organizations Act, which requires those companies to tell you in writing about your legal rights. They're also supposed to give you a contract that spells out exactly what services they are to perform, how long it will take to get results, and the total cost. Even a "money-back guarantee" won't protect you if the company is shady.

The Money Line

The industry's acknowledged leader, CCCS (80 percent of the time) doesn't charge a fee to help people manage their debt and get out from under the clutches of credit card companies, banks, and finance outfits. For others, the average fee is only $10 to $20.

♦ Don't listen if a credit repair clinic suggests that you not contact a credit bureau directly, because "We do that for you." Horsefeathers. You can obtain your own copy of your credit report from any of the three major bureaus: Equifax (1-800-685-1111), Experian (1-888-397-3742), or Trans Union (1-800-888-4213). You can then correct any inaccurate information in writing, and dispute anything that you believe is in error.

"Why spend a lot of money for something that you can do yourself in 30 minutes?" credit counselors often exclaim to us. The nonprofit Consumer Credit Counseling Service, with 1,440 locations nationwide, is a good place to start repairing your credit. It will guide you in fixing your credit report, and, for little or no fee, negotiate with creditors and set up a payment plan you can afford. Call 1-800-388-2227 for the location nearest you, or for on-line counseling.

Look Out for Those "Debt Reduction" Offers

In another scam arena, what's the deal with those hundreds of "debt consolidation" and "free credit counseling" offers you keep seeing and hearing? Are they for real? Can they honestly help you? Answer: Some can, but beware. A lot of them are no more than "debt management mills" that lure you with a low-cost payment plan, and then scalp you for hundreds or thousands of dollars later on.

The "quick-fix" credit counseling business has exploded in the past few years, and with the new Bankruptcy Reform Act, which has made it harder for folks to wipe out all their debts—the boom has only begun. One Internet search engine, for example, now lists *123,000 different credit and debt counseling sites!*

The theory is that, by working with your creditors, a good counselor can usually negotiate with them to stop charging interest and fees on your accounts. It can also often reduce the amount you owe, and "re-age" the accounts to make them current. Collection agencies will get off your back after you've made an on-time payment or two. And, under many programs you'll be entirely out of debt within three to five years instead of the 10 to 20 years it would otherwise take you. You could save thousands of dollars.

How can you avoid getting scammed by the "debt mills"? First—we know some people will disagree with us—think twice before you let anybody lend you a dime under a "debt consolidation" loan because 80 percent of the time you'll only wind up more deeply in debt. Plus, you might pay an up front "processing fee" of $250 to $1,000, only to see the company disappear after they've received your cash.

Second, don't allow them to steer you toward bankruptcy unless it is positively the last resort. Some outfits merely charge a fee and shove you to a bankruptcy lawyer. Know that no matter how panicked you might be, a decent counselor may be able to help you avoid that credit-ruining nightmare. (One foolish guy we know—he must've had a death wish—voluntarily chose bankruptcy when he had debts of only $8,000 and could have easily worked out a repayment plan.)

Most important, do your homework before you sign up with anyone. These are the most critical questions to ask up front, advises National Foundation for Consumer Credit's president and CEO, Durant Abernathy:

- Is yours a not-for-profit organization?

- Where does your funding come from? (In CCCS's case, creditors bankroll most of the operation, but so what? CCCS has more clout than you do in renegotiating debt downward, plus, wouldn't you rather have the creditors pay for the counseling than you?)

The Money Line

Under federal law, if you're turned down for a job due to your credit report, the employer must notify you of your right to get a copy of your credit report for free from the credit agency. The credit agency must notify you automatically that the employer accessed your credit file if it contains any derogatory public information about you (such as bankruptcies, liens, and judgments).

- Are you accredited by any outside agencies? Which ones?

- What professional financial training does your staff have? Are your counselors certified, and if so, by whom?

- How will you disburse my funds to creditors? How often? How will you insure protection of my money?

- What'll be my total costs—fees, charges, everything?

- Will you work with my creditors even if they don't support your organization?

- How are funds collected?

- Can I get counseling in-person or over the phone, whichever I prefer?

- How will working with you impact my personal credit rating?

The Road to Riches
Lesson #1 in credit reports is, don't trust the information in your personal credit file, and don't expect anybody besides yourself to correct it.

- Can I retain access to my credit card if I need it for credit purposes?

- Can I enroll in a debt management repayment plan to educate myself?

- What other changes in my personal financial lifestyle will I have to make to successfully get out of debt?

In other words, know who you're doing business with before you grab one of those tempting deals over the television or Internet. Anyone can pretend to do a "quick fix" without the right game plan to retire debt. But you don't want to get trapped by a scam that's little more than a gimmick to help fund a loan to drive you more deeply into hock.

Don't Worry, The Bad Stuff Comes Off ... Eventually

Fortunately, under the Fair Credit Reporting Act of 1971, negative information on your report can't hang around forever. By law, the agencies are *supposed to* wipe off any bankruptcy data 10 years after it was entered. They're also *supposed to* erase any tax liens, lawsuits, judgments, or accounts put up for collection after seven years.

But don't assume that will happen, or that everything on your report is accurate. The agencies, like every company, are working with the human factor. A data clerk can easily hit the wrong computer key when he or she enters your information. He may have misread something on your credit application back at Bubba's Auto Emporium.

Here's another unpleasant possibility. As has been charged by Congressional committees investigating how the credit reporting services operate, an agency could just plumb forget about eradicating your negative information when it's supposed to. It's happened thousands of times.

Learning the Three Cs Are Just an Old-Fashioned Pipe Dream

There was a time when you could go into a bank, and the banker—who was your friend and neighbor—had known you since you were in pigtails or knickers. He'd okay your loan with no credit check or other hassle. You can kiss those days goodbye. Banking has become big business, and big business today doesn't want to take any risks. You and your habits are now impersonal numbers in a Big Three computer. Oh, sure, banks still insist that they lend money the old-fashioned way—on the basis of what they call the "Three Cs":

- ◆ **Character.** It may not have anything to do with what kind of person you really are. More than likely, admit the credit agencies, it means how long you've lived at the same address and worked at the same company.

- ◆ **Capacity.** How much debt can you afford, based on your present income? The lender looks at your living expenses, current financial obligations, and the payments that your new loan would require.

- ◆ **Credit.** How long have you had credit accounts such as credit cards, mortgages, and personal loans? What is the credit limit you're allowed on each one? How close are you to those limits now? Have you made your payments on time?

Sometimes lenders use a different third "C"—collateral—meaning, "How much security can you put up, so in case you don't pay us back, we can grab your stocks and bonds or Aunt Agatha's jewels?"

Nobody's perfect, and lenders know that. But, if you've had a car repossessed, or another lender has given up trying to collect on what you owe, the Three Cs have probably gone down the tubes in your case.

Determining If You're Good, Bad, or Gray

Lenders have a habit of lumping you into one of three ranges: "good," "bad," and "gray." The lender's computers make the first cut. The top scores are considered "good," and these customers are automatically approved for a loan. The "gray" scores are for people who score somewhere in the middle of the range. These are personally reviewed on an individual basis. The "bad" group might just as well have leprosy. But, occasionally the lender may move a person into the "gray" group to give him or her "an extra chance."

An example of a person who would immediately be lumped in the "bad" category is someone who has had charge-offs in the past. Charge-offs are loans that creditors eventually have to wipe off their books because they've never been paid. "If we see someone who has had charge-offs greater than $300 in the last four years, we just immediately decline it," explained one credit agency executive. "I don't want anyone in my office spending any more effort on that one."

If you've been habitually 30, 60, or 90 days late in making your payments, you could be hurting your credit record even more. All late payments are bad, but 90 days is worse than 30, as you might guess. Credit card companies are a little looser when you don't pay on time, because after all, they *want* you to go past the due date so they can charge you interest on your balance!

The "Sub-Prime" Revolution: Low Scores Get Loans

The biggest new trend in credit reports and the loan business are sub-prime loans, made to people with less-than-great credit, who pay higher rates to borrow. By using Fair Isaac's technology and messaging all the data that credit bureaus collect, sub-prime lenders believe they've figured out which low-score consumers are still likely to pay back their loans.

Instead of charging a sub-prime customer 5.5 percent to finance a new car, he might pay 8 or 9 percent. Ditto for mortgages. The home loan might be 9 to 11 percent instead of 6 percent. But, the difference in total interest cost can be tens of thousands of dollars over the life of the loan!

No wonder banks and finance companies are falling over themselves to buy up sub-prime lending companies. One Florida thrift institution we know now engages in this business almost entirely, for mortgages. It has scores of credit representatives doing nothing all day but phoning all slow-paying accounts and goosing them to get their payments in ASAP. In the lending business, they call these institutions "bottom-feeders."

It's Thumbs Down in Most Cases

The most closely guarded secret of all? The lenders' approval ratio. It's the percentage of applicants who get approved or disapproved for their loans. Sources at the Big Three agencies give this picture:

- If a credit card issuer sends a mailing to consumers that says they have "pre-approved" status for credit, the odds are nine out of 10 they'll actually be approved. But, if the card company somehow finds out that the person's credit has "deteriorated" lately, it may conclude, "Hey, this person is not as good as we thought he or she was." Result? The person gets approved, all right, but the creditor may bust his credit limit from $5,000 down to $200 to $500. He also may pay a higher rate of interest on the money he borrows.

- The person who just picks up a credit application at a store, and then fills it out and mails it in, has a two out of 10 chance of getting approved.

- The person who applies for a Gold Credit Card (with a $5,000 credit line and other perks) has a four out of 10 chance of being okayed.

- New car loan applicants also have a four out of 10 possibility of approval.

For a plain-vanilla credit card, credit scorers used to look for someone with an annual income of at least $12,000. Now, some have dropped the requirement to as low as $8,000. To obtain a Gold Credit Card, a person needs an income of about $30,000.

Why are the minimums falling? Because of fierce competition for customers. The credit card pie is only *so* big, and more and more outfits want a piece of it. To cover their higher risks, creditors may charge a higher interest rate (plus special fees) and monitor these new customers once a month. Another reason for easier credit is that the percentage of delinquencies (people who fall behind in their payments) is decreasing.

The Money Line

Certain inquiries don't show up on your credit report. Examples include inquiries made by you to monitor your report for accuracy or to obtain a copy for your records, or inquiries made by companies who want to send you an unsolicited credit offer through the mail.

You carry one credit card, but in the past three months you've applied for two more, and are now in the process of also trying to borrow money to finance Junior's college education. You've also contacted a few companies about changing jobs.

That makes six new inquiries on your credit report in a very short time. What happens? The two credit card companies check you out at one of the Big Three credit agencies and count four inquiries besides their own. Alarm bells ring in their minds. They figure that all those inquiries mean you're about to plunge into big debt. They look like red flags to a bull. Whammo! You get turned down.

Guarding Against Mix-Ups

When Congress was considering the Credit Repair Reform Act which, unfortunately, died on the Senate floor, it found that many credit reports contained errors, as mentioned earlier. Yet, according to the U.S. Public Interest Research Group (PIRG), consumers often can't reach a live person at the credit bureaus to request copies of their reports. One PIRG rep tells us the situation is "a ticking time bomb."

Many of the errors undoubtedly were the credit agencies' fault, but there are tons of horror stories created by consumers themselves. You can prevent errors and mix-ups on your credit report by following these simple tips:

♦ Always use the same name. If your full name is Jeremy C. Bullwhistle III, don't write "J. C. Bullwhistle" or "Jeremy Bullwhistle" (without the "C"). Don't use "Jerry," or your last name without the three Roman numerals after it. The reason for this is that you don't want inconsistencies appearing on the report. You could get tagged with the bad credit of Jerry Bullwhistle–the-Credit-Card-Maniac who lives 2,000 miles away. You'd be amazed at how many folks commit that simple mistake and wind up spending months or years fighting the credit agencies to prove they're the *real* Jeremy Bullwhistle III.

♦ Always use your Social Security number. You've got the only one like it in the world. This will help you prevent your name from being confused with folks with the same name.

♦ Always list your home addresses for the past five years. It will help you in the future if you move.

How to Handle Disputes

Let's say you check your credit report and you spot a $1,000 dispute with Max's Clothing Store from three years ago. You don't know anybody named Max, and the last time you bought a suit was five years ago.

The bad news is that it can sometimes take weeks or months of letters and phone calls to correct the report. But, the good news is that you can do it if you follow these steps carefully, remembering to *always* keep a file copy of anything you send to somebody else.

1. If you think Max's Clothing Store is responsible for the error, send Max's a letter by certified mail, asking that it send a written statement to all three credit bureaus, telling them it was a mistake.

2. Write each of the three credit bureaus a certified letter, and enclose a copy of the letter you sent to Max's, to make sure the store followed through on the changes. Give the bureau all the details; describe the mistake and include your full name with your middle name, address, date of birth, and Social Security number. Note whether you're a junior or senior or have three Roman numerals after your name.

3. Make photocopies of any documents that you think support your claims.

4. Include a copy of your birth certificate if you believe your name was mixed up with someone else's.

Under the Fair Credit Reporting Act, a credit bureau usually has 30 days to resolve the problem. If you feel the bureau is dragging its feet or not handling your situation fairly, contact the attorney general of your state or the Federal Trade Com-mission in Washington, D.C. at 202-FTC-HELP. Although the FTC can't act as your lawyer in private disputes, information about your experiences and concerns is vital to them. Send your questions or complaints to Consumer Response Center– FCRA, Federal Trade Commission, Washington, D.C. 20580. Remember that a bankruptcy remains on your credit report for 10 years, while other negative infor-mation such as a judgment or lien stays on for 7 years.

The Road to Riches

In case you find an error on your credit report or wish to dispute a creditor's charges, you are entitled to submit a 100-words-or-less statement to each credit bureau, explaining the situation. By law they must insert this into your report, so that anyone inquiring about you can see your side of the story. Be sure to send your statement by certified mail and keep a copy.

Protecting Yourself from Fraud

Americans lose more than $2 billion a year to credit-card-fraud artists. And according to a September 2003 survey by the Federal Trade Commission, there are 27.3 million Americans who have been victims of identity theft in the last five years, including 9.91 million people or 4.6 percent of the population in the last year alone.

Experian suggests following these tips to protect yourself against fraud:

- Sign your new cards as soon as they arrive.

- Treat your cards like money. Keep them in a safe place.

- Shred anything with your account number on it before throwing it away.

- Don't give your card number over the phone unless *you* initiate the call.

- Don't write your card number on a postcard or on the outside of an envelope.

- Remember to get your card and receipt immediately after every transaction, and double-check to be sure they're yours.

- Notify your card issuers at once if your billing statement is incorrect or your credit cards are lost or stolen.

Helping Hands

Struggling under a heavy personal debt load? Also contact the following sources for helpful information on consumer credit and how you can strengthen your credit report:

Bankcard Holders of America
524 Branch Drive
Salem, VA 24153
703-389-5445

The Banker's Secret Bulletin
PO Box 78
Elizaville, NY 12523
1-800-255-0899

National Center for Financial Education
PO Box 34070
San Diego, CA 92163
415-567-5290

Consumer Federation of America
1424 16th Street N.W., Suite 604
Washington, D.C. 20036
202-387-6121

Maintaining Good Credit

The key to maintaining good credit is to follow a few simple rules:

- ◆ **Pay your bills on time.** Almost all lenders will look at whether you're on time or late with your bills. Most lenders are lenient and will tolerate a maximum of 30 days late. If you are currently behind on your accounts, catch up before you apply. This is how you can make the grade to get credit. You have to fit the profile of the people who pay their bills on time.

- ◆ **Don't be too close to your credit limits.** Typically, lenders will compare your credit card balances to the total amount of credit you have available. The more cards you have close to the limit, the more of a risk you are to lenders.

- ◆ **Cancel any credit cards that you don't use.** If you already have five or six major credit cards (even if they have zero balances), you will have a tough time getting additional credit. Why? Because lenders will think that you already have more than enough.

- ◆ **Get a copy of your credit report and correct any errors on an annual basis.**

- ◆ **Find out how many inquiries there are on your credit report.** The more inquiries there are, the less likely you are to get the credit you're seeking.

The Money Line

People who have recently applied for a lot of credit are less likely to keep up with their payments on a timely basis. If you have five or more inquiries in the past six to eight months, wait a few months before you apply for credit again.

Knowing Other Ways to Strengthen Your Credit

If your credit score is low, or you haven't established a credit history, you can do a couple of things to build up your profile.

- ◆ Apply for a gasoline credit card or department store card, which are relatively easy to get, and *always pay your bills on time.*

- Take out a secured credit card from one of the hundreds of banks that offer them. See Chapter 13 for information on these cards, but if you get one, *be sure to pay the bill on time!*

- Wait approximately 6 to 12 months to apply for additional credit. By then your good payment behavior on those accounts will start showing up on your credit report, and you'll have a much better chance at further credit.

A good credit rating creates countless opportunities. Don't let a bad credit history get between you and your dreams.

The Least You Need to Know

- Know that most of your financial information—your salary, bank accounts, credit cards, and loan information—is stored in computers at the Experian, Equifax, and Trans Union credit agencies, as well as at FICO.

- Improve your credit report by paying your bills on time, cutting down the number of credit cards you carry, not living up to your credit limit, and paying off your outstanding debts.

- Don't apply for credit at too many places. All those inquiries will show up on your report and scare creditors away.

- Review your credit report annually to check it for mistakes; you may also want to obtain a copy before applying for a loan to make sure it's accurate.

- Be sure to dispute any errors on your credit report.

The Right Credit Card for You

In This Chapter

- ◆ A crash course on the credit card jungle
- ◆ How to find the card that fits your budget to a T—including one that will cost you *nothing*
- ◆ How to beat banks that are raising all their fees and charges
- ◆ How to stay out of the debt (and bankruptcy) trap with credit cards
- ◆ Where to get a card even if you have bad credit
- ◆ How debit cards can wipe out your bad credit card habits and save you thousands of dollars

There's no bigger rip-off than credit cards, and the odds are stacked against you not getting hurt by them. High interest rates have hardly budged in twenty years. Banks and other issuers have jacked up their already-ridiculous fees even higher. And there are new fees in addition to the old ones. As the number of personal bankruptcies soars past 1.3 million annually, banks try to make it harder for people to go bankrupt—but at the very same time they fill mailboxes with offers of easy credit for people already drowning in debt. In short, banks are getting away with murder—and you're their patsy, as credit card profits get bigger and bigger. You must now gain control of this ugly situation for yourself, or face the possibility of being taken for a bigger and bigger ride.

Shockingly, one out of every four cardholders has no idea of what interest rate they're paying on their plastic.

The stakes are enormous. Consumer credit card debt has soared to a record $1.6 trillion. In the past decade our personal income has risen by 72 percent while personal debt has leaped 123 percent and is still growing. In short, credit cards are the No. 1 poison pill. At the same time, card issuers have made it harder and harder to escape falling into debt, as they pile on the fees. Last year the industry took in $43 billion in fee income, up from $39 billion in 2002, according to R.K. Hammer Investment Bankers. Fees accounted for 35 percent of industry income last year, up from 18 percent six years ago. This chapter is a crash course in everything that's wrong with credit cards and how to escape their debt threat. You'll learn how and where to shop for cheaper rates, how to avoid those insane fees and charges, which type of credit card fits you to a T, why promoters' card tricks really aren't what you think they are, and how to see through the freebies and perks that banks keep dangling before your eyeballs. Your pocketbook and your debt picture will be saved!

Credit Cards: Personal Debt Enemy #1

Engrave this on your mind. Credit cards are the main reason so many Americans are up to their ears in debt, and why the bankruptcy rate is so high. The banks, of course, will refute this, but if you want to confirm it, ask any bankruptcy attorney what caused his clients' problems in the first place. The lawyers can even describe how more low-income senior citizens have turned to charging groceries on their credit cards in order to survive.

 Watch Your Wallet

Over-limit fees are up 17 percent over three years. The top issuers now charge $33.50, industry-tracker CardWeb.com says. Some now charge the fee if a cardholder is over the limit any day during the cycle, instead of just on the last day.

A big business? Oh, yes. According to the National Foundation for Credit Counseling, the average U.S. household with at least one credit card carried a card balance of $8,500 in the year 2003, compared with only $2,985 in 1990. Total bankcard debt reached $425 billion, and unused credit lines (the additional amount consumers could charge on their cards) was another $1.8 trillion. There are more than 475 million cards in circulation and in one recent year alone, credit card issuers made $60 billion in interest charges.

Yet the card issuers' greed keeps growing, as cardholders keep getting slapped by a slew of new card fees, deceptive interest-rate practices, and especially higher charges to customers whose card behavior is not the greatest.

Can't Live with 'Em, Can't Live Without 'Em

Notice how more credit card offers have been bombarding you lately? Card companies send out more than 3 billion offers a year to consumers. Some folks with household incomes of $50,000 or more report they get two or more dozen direct mail pitches a year. Why? Credit cards represent enormous profits for banks. They sock you with rates averaging more than 14 percent while paying puny interest of 0.98 percent on checking and 1 or 2 percent on savings. In short, they have found a golden goose.

Yet Americans continue to be hooked on plastic, plain and simple, because of its convenience. We simply run to the mall, whip out our credit cards and say, "Charge it!" No money leaves our wallets. That's a good feeling—temporarily. Then later, when the bill comes in with all the charges and interest, it's pay-up time. Sure, the bank will let you get away with a teensy minimum payment, but that's how they make their money, by keeping you in debt forever. And, if you're late with your monthly payments—by as little as one day—you pay a big $25 to $35 penalty and wind up with an ugly mark on your credit record that'll haunt you for years. Plus late payments may cause your card issuer to jack up your interest rate by several percentage points!

It's time to take the bull by the horns, dear friend, and get rid of the debt monster!

Why Cards Keep You in Perpetual Debt

You can make purchases with your credit card up to a certain dollar limit decided by the card issuer. That's your maximum credit line, determined by your credit history. As you use the card, you're constantly borrowing against your limit and repaying the money. Say your credit limit is $1,000 and you buy a garment for $100, or take a $100 cash advance against the card. You have $900 left. When you repay the $100 (plus the interest charges), you again have $1,000 in available credit. That's called a "revolving" credit account, similar to a home equity line of credit (see Chapter 16).

Okay, say that you're a "revolver," a person who doesn't pay off his monthly balance, but instead "rolls" part of the bill over to the next month. Nearly seven out of 10 cardholders do this, and the average amount they roll over every month is more than $4,000.

Let's set it straight one more time. Banks and other credit card outfits *want* you to do this. They make their profits by making it easy for you to finance your balance. If you paid off your bill every month, they wouldn't make nearly as much money.

How expensive can a credit card get? Take the case of a cardholder with a balance of $2,500 who pays 18.5 percent interest. If he or she made only a minimum monthly payment of 2 percent of the unpaid balance, which many card issuers allow, it would take more than 30 years to pay the card off. Even worse, the total interest would come to $6,500. All for a $2,500 loan!

Credit Cards: Just Try *Not* Having One

Skip credit cards entirely? Just try it. Today a credit card is almost as important as a birth certificate. You need plastic to rent a car, buy an airline ticket, reserve a hotel room, order from a mail-order catalog or TV shopping network, or rent movies. A woman we know moved into a new town and tried to deposit $20,000 in a bank. She showed her driver's license and voter's registration card, but the bank insisted on seeing a credit card before they'd accept her as a new customer. She didn't have one, so they declined her business!

Credit cards definitely have a place in your personal financial life, although we know lots of wise people, especially older folks, who make a habit of paying cash, who aren't plagued by one cent of debt. The key to avoiding credit card trouble is to be smart about how you use credit, *before* you even apply for a card! Make up your mind that you're going to be disciplined; you're too smart to fall into that plastic trap! Here are some tips:

- Figure how much credit card debt you can afford to pay back in full each month. *Then, don't charge a dime over that amount!*

- Don't fall for banks' come-on card deals. Read all the fine print in their hustle literature. Is the rate fixed or variable? Will a low-ball introductory rate jump to a higher rate in six months? What's the grace period (the number of days to pay of the balance before the interest charges kick in)? What's the annual fee? The late-payment fee? The fee for going over your credit line? For cash advances? The average Joe foolishly doesn't take a few minutes to examine all that tiny print.

- Watch out for deceptive language. Many outfits offer you a "pre-approved" card, but they may reject you if you're unemployed or don't have an adequate income. Many promise a credit line "up to $100,000," but are more apt to offer $5,000 after reviewing the application. In other words, the promises in their literature don't amount to a hill of beans.

◆ Limit your number of credit cards to one or two—no more. Not only will this help keep your debt down, it will help your credit profile overall. Lenders monitor what your total possible debt could be if you ran up all your cards to the limit, and could get so scared they'll deny you for a loan.

◆ Tell your bank you're considering moving your accounts to a different institution if you feel your card rate is too high (say, above 14 percent) or if your fees are grotesque. Believe it or not, they might cut the rate and lower or waive some fees right on the spot.

CAUTION   Watch Your Wallet

One good way to slash your credit card debt is to transfer the balance from a high-rate card to one offering a lower rate. But, you must study these deals carefully in advance.

An outfit may tempt you with a low-ball introductory rate of, say, 2.9 percent, good for a few months. But read the fine print: In many cases, that low rate may only apply to the amount you transfer from your old issuer, not to new purchases with the new card. There's usually a "balance transfer fee" of 3 percent—but we've seen some that cost $50 to $80. Even worse, if you pay late once on the new card, the issuer could jack up your rate to anywhere from 15 to 25 percent.

And did you know that …

◆ In effect, your card is free if you pay off your balance each month and pay no annual fee?

◆ You can cut your card costs nearly in half if you have good credit?

◆ You can even get a card if you've had credit problems or haven't had a chance to build up a credit record of your own? (See "Secured Cards for Those with Bad (or No) Credit," later in this chapter.)

Credit Cards: Different Types

The main types of credit cards are …

◆ Fixed-rate cards.

◆ Variable-rate cards.

◆ Gold cards.

- ◆ Secured cards.

- ◆ Cards with gimmicks, such as cash rebates and air miles.

The sections that follow explain each of these types in more detail. Besides the standard cards issued by banks, thrifts, and credit unions, consumers may qualify for an American Express card—provided their financial condition is eligible for a minimum credit line of $5,000. You pay no interest rate with an American Express card because the balance is due in full each month (except for the Optima card). The annual fee is $75. American Express makes its money from these fees, and from merchants and other businesses that accept the cards. The merchants pay them a small percentage of any amount charged on the card.

> **Watch Your Wallet**
>
> Although credit card issuers make it tougher for people to qualify for a low-rate credit card, at the same time, many have offered higher spending limits to existing customers. Some bank executives deny this, but the overriding evidence is that more and more easy credit has been pushed on consumers.

Retail credit cards (such as those issued by department stores) are also big business, but their interest rates tend to be higher than the rates banks charge on their standard cards. We've seen many stores slap customers with rates as high as 21 percent, which is almost as bad as paying juice money to a loan shark when you're only earning 4 percent or 5 percent on your CDs.

Remember: No matter what credit card you use, your payment record on the card is going to wind up on your personal credit report, which can be accessed by any bank or company to which you apply for credit.

Fixed-Rate Cards

This is your ordinary, everyday, plain credit card. The interest rate is *fixed* at a certain percentage, but typically with 15 days' notice the card issuer can still raise your rate. In most states, the customer has the right to stop using the card and pay off the balance in full at the old rate. Whatever you buy, that's the percent interest you'll pay on the purchase. This type of credit card has become an ugly duckling because the average rate has stubbornly remained at about 14 percent, according to the newsletter *Bankrate.com*. In cities such as San Francisco, the rate is even higher an astronomical 19.5 percent!

> **The Road to Riches**
>
> Here are several credit card industry resources to help you find the right credit card:
>
> www.bankrate.com
>
> www.cardweb.com
>
> www.creditcardgoodies.com

To avoid paying these high fixed rates, shop the best card deals nationwide. You'll find rates as low as 9 percent. Locating a cheaper out-of-state card is a perfectly safe and smart thing to do. After all, most big card issuers are national anyway. The only catch is that the lower the card rate, the more difficult it is for people to get their credit approved. Nine-percent issuers tend to want only squeaky-clean credit records, so standards may apply. But, if your credit is good, give it a shot!

It may be necessary to switch banks to get a better deal on your credit card. If so, fine. The new bank may give you a special "balance-transfer" check to pay off your balance at the old bank. The balance then will show up on your new card account at the outfit to which you switched your business—or you simply pay off your old balance and open a new account at another bank. Either way, cut your old credit card in half and enclose it with your check and a letter to the old bank. Advise them you are closing your account (give the number) and keep a copy of the letter.

> **CAUTION**
>
> **Watch Your Wallet**
>
> Just because the Federal Reserve keeps cutting its key rates doesn't mean that variable card rates will follow. For example, the Fed cut key rates five times in 2003, but variable-rate cards all of a sudden stopped dropping. Why? Those cards have a "floor" below which the rates won't fall. Translation: You lose.

Variable-Rate Cards

Choosing a variable-rate credit card can cost you less in the long run. With this type of credit card, your interest rate changes according to an index used by the bank. Often, the rate is tied to the bank's prime rate plus six to nine percentage points. For example, if the prime is 5 percent the variable rate on your credit card would probably be in the 13 percent range. But there's a "rate floor," which many variable-rate issuers refuse to go below, regardless of the prime-rate-indexed formula. More than 70 percent of all credit cards now are variable-rate.

Remember that your introductory rate on a variable-rate card can be as low as 0 percent to 9.9 percent. Six or more months later it will jump to the fully-indexed rate, which today averages 10.20 percent.

Variable-rate cards are great when the prime rate is low, as it was in the early 1990s when the prime stood at only 6 percent. Then, the average

> **The Road to Riches**
>
> "What credit card extras do I *really* need, or could do without?" That's the key question you should ask before you consider a Gold, Platinum, or Titanium card. Some, for instance, will offer credit card life insurance along with the card, when you may find that term life insurance is a better deal. In many cases, all you need is a standard card, period.

variable rate was only 12 percent. But, when rates start rising, variable-rate plastic becomes less and less attractive.

Gold, Platinum, and Titanium Cards

The secret to shopping for Gold cards lies in their perks, such as emergency road-side service, buyer protection plans, and cash back if you spend thousands of dollars. All too often, though, cardholders are tempted to choose Gold cards as a "status" symbol. The only thing a Gold card *can* promise you is a higher credit limit—and sometimes expensive annual fees. Gold card applicants require a stronger credit record, and the cards come with mandatory benefits such as $150,000 travel-accident insurance.

In recent years, card issuers, catering to a strong economy, have also brought out upscale Platinum and Titanium cards. If you put them under a microscope, they offer many of the same features as Gold cards, plus a few more. But just as with standard cards, you're going to have your pocket picked if you don't pay close attention to the fine print. Here's a good example of why.

First USA offers a Visa Platinum credit card with introductory rates as low as 0 percent. The "fixed" part of the rate deal only lasts for six billing cycles when the rate rises to a 9.9 percent variable rate. For cash advances, the rate is 19.9 percent. There is no annual fee, a credit line of $5,000 to $100,000, a 30 percent discount on a slew of different products and services, auto rental insurance, a $1 million travel accident policy, and a 20-to-25-day grace period.

The shocker is that First USA's rate soars to 19.99 percent if the cardholder makes two late payments within a six-month period, and to 22.99 percent if there are two consecutive late payments in such a period. In other words, a late payer with a $3,000 balance would pay about $393 in extra interest on an annual basis!

![CAUTION] **Watch Your Wallet** _____

In the late 1990s, card issuers began stinging cardholders who really paid their monthly bills on time, but got hit by $29 late-payment fees. What happened? Issuers sat on the on-time payments for a few days before they were posted. Consumers launched class-action suits, which cost the companies millions of dollars. You can prevent this manhandling by sending your payments via U.S. Post Office Priority Mail (it costs $3.50) and, for 40 cents extra, request "Delivery Confirmation" which shows the date and time when your payment was received.

Secured Cards for Those with Bad (or No) Credit

There are more than 400 issuers of *secured* credit cards for folks with a poor credit history or no history at all. Anyone who's been hanging his head because he lost his card during bad financial times now has new hope.

A secured card works like this: You typically keep $200 to $500 on deposit with the bank. It issues you a card with which you can make purchases for up to your deposit amount. More and more institutions also pay you a small amount of interest on your deposit, such as 2 to 4 percent.

The interest rate you pay on a secured card is a little stiff, typically above 15 percent, but it's temporarily worth it for you to start rebuilding your credit. Banks used to charge an application fee of $20 to $40 on secured cards, but that's fading as competition heats up.

Why the boom in secured cards? Because banks have discovered a huge, new market of people with damaged credit, young people applying for a card for the first time, divorced people who don't have their own personal credit records, and new workers, including immigrants.

> **The Road to Riches**
>
> Don't jump at the first secured card offer that comes along, no matter how plastic-hungry you are. With so many banks beating the bushes for business, you should shop these cards as aggressively as you would a standard credit card.

Who can get a secured card? Almost everybody, with a few exceptions. Requirements vary. Many card issuers will accept those with bad payment records; a few will even take customers with bankruptcies that are at least 6 to 12 months old. Others insist that you be employed for one year or have no excessive credit card debt or federal tax liens. Income requirements and opening deposits vary. As of mid-2004, several secured card issuers include:

- Amalgamated Bank of Chicago, offering a rate of 9.25 percent with no application fee, an account-opening deposit between $5,000 to $10,000, and an annual fee of $50;

- Merrick Bank, offering a rate of 14.70 percent with a deposit of $300 to $3,000, and an annual fee of $36;

- Washington Mutual Bank, offering a rate of 15.55 percent, a minimum deposit of $300, and an annual fee of $35.

Is a secured card for you? The answer is "yes," if your credit needs repair and you don't mind paying the high interest. If you mind your manners and make your monthly payments on time, this will be a plus on your credit record. Six to 12 months later, you might be able to ask the bank to increase your credit limit, or apply for a standard card. For example, Key Federal Savings Bank allows you to apply for their unsecured credit card if you have maintained a good track record on your secured card for 24 months.

Credit cards with bells and whistles are popping up all over, as every card outfit and its brother tries to get a piece of the credit card pie. The main gimmicks are discounts on merchandise and services, promises of cash rebates, and free airline miles. The more you use a particular card, the more rebates and freebies you get. These can range from discounts on new cars to free air travel and cut-rate hotel rooms.

Watch Your Wallet

Beware of third-party outfits that "guarantee" to get you a secured credit card or "fix your credit" for a fee. The company may be a fly-by-night scam, and besides, you can easily handle your card application by yourself and deal directly with the bank. You do not need a third party to do this for you.

That all sounds groovy, but in reality these card issuers have been cutting back on their deals because the market has been saturated and some outfits have lost money. Cutbacks have been in the form of offering a lower dollar value of the freebies and perks, and reducing the time period for which the offers are good. Once, these deals were so liberal that the General Motors Gold card enabled customers to earn up to $7,000 toward the purchase of a new GM vehicle. Now, on its GM MasterCard, the maximum is $3,500 over seven years.

When choosing this type of card, ask yourself two questions:

♦ Could I get a better deal with another card that offers a lower interest rate and lower fees?

♦ Do I really need the "free" merchandise, discounts and whatever? If the card gives me points toward buying a Chevrolet sedan, but I'm in the market for a Ford pickup, it doesn't make much sense.

If you're not satisfied with the incentives, don't be afraid to ask the issuer for a better deal. The name of the game today with card issuers is, *negotiate!*

The offers have lots of different twists, the most popular being money-back gimmicks that rebate a percentage of your purchases. For example, Citibank Driver's Edge for Visa and MasterCard, Sioux Falls, South Dakota, 1-800-967-8500, rebates up to 2 percent toward the purchase or lease of any new or used vehicle, regardless of make or model. That's up to a total of $500. Expiration is three or five years, depending on the rebate program. Amoco Visa, 1-800-858-3299, offers up to 3 percent rebate on

Amoco purchases, and 2 percent on non-Amoco purchases, toward gasoline, credited automatically to the monthly statement. The Golf Card from American Express gives one point for every eligible dollar. Points may be redeemed for advance tee time reservations, golf equipment, clothing, and instructions.

As with any credit card, it's not the gifts and pizzazz that count, it's what you wind up with in your pocket. Compare the bottom-line costs—after the rebates.

Frequent-Flyer Miles

Most major airlines are tied in with at least one big bank. Read all the small print carefully. Note the exclusions and restrictions, such as blackout dates, when you can't fly, and the limitations on miles and the expiration dates. Some cards offer bonus miles when you sign up, and many businesses, such as rental car companies, hotels and phone companies will bait you with frequent-flyer miles. A few banks, such as First USA in Wilmington, Delaware, 1-800-945-2023, offer three different cards with free miles from United Airlines, British Airways, or Southwest Airlines. Be sure to figure the real bottom-line cost of these programs versus what a nonrebate card would cost you.

How Debit Cards Work

Debit cards, discussed in Chapter 8 are growing more than three times as fast as credit cards. In the race to create a paperless banking system, nearly 9.5 million families now use debit cards instead of checks at supermarkets alone. That's resulted in 250 million fewer checks a year being written just to buy groceries.

It's estimated that 60 million debit cards are now in use and that transaction volume will soar to $32 billion by 2006, up from only $6 billion eight years ago.

The Money Line

VISA debit cards hit the market in 1989. In June 1993, VISA re-named its card the VISA Check Card.

The pluses are enormous:

♦ A debit card frees you from carrying cash or a checkbook. You don't have to give your home or work phone number, or other personal information, to Tillie the sales girl at the department store as you do when you pay by check. She simply swipes the card through the same keypad machine she uses for credit cards, you sign a receipt, and you're on your way.

◆ Anyone can get a debit card, unless, of course, they've been rejected for a checking account by their bank. The cards—which have been referred to as "an ATM card with clout"—are issued through a financial institution either by Visa Check Card or MasterCard's MasterMoney card. You can use them just like a credit card, provided you have enough funds on deposit or enjoy overdraft protection, which is a good idea.

◆ Unlike an ATM card, you don't have to punch in a PIN number when you pay your tab at DeCesare's Restaurant or at Marv's Discount Warehouse. Supermarkets may require your PIN code, and you can also use your debit card with its special PIN at an ATM machine to withdraw cash.

◆ Debit cards are accepted by all merchants who take Visa or MasterCard credit cards. The only hang-up is that although you can use the card to pay a car rental bill, you'll need a credit card to actually drive the auto off the lot. And many hotels, while allowing you to pay by debit card, won't let you use it to make a reservation.

◆ It's an excellent way to live within your means and avoid disgusting 18 to 24 percent credit card interest rates.

However, there are downsides to debit cards as well:

◆ There's less protection if your card is stolen. A thief who grabs your debit card or PIN number could drain your account overnight, which is why some banks set daily limits on total dollar transactions for your safety. Keeping all your receipts is a must because they reveal your debit card number, which is all the thief needs.

◆ Debit card issuers may not intervene in the event of a dispute between you and a merchant, the way they will for a credit card transaction. And there are no "stop payment" orders. But, as with credit cards, you may dispute unauthorized charges or other mistakes within 60 days. Try contacting the card issuer anyway if you can't resolve the problem with the store.

◆ You'd better record each transaction in your checkbook, lest you wind up bouncing checks.

So call your bank and ask about their debit card programs. If your bank doesn't offer them, then it's time to start looking for a new bank.

Ouch: Those Fees Hurt!

Okay, you've got the types of cards down pat. Now you need to know the key cost factors you could be hit with. The three main ones are interest rate, annual fee, and grace period. The kind of card you want depends on the way you pay off your credit card bills. If, as we said earlier, you're a "revolver," you want a credit card with a very low interest rate. If you pay your balance off in full every month, you want a card with no annual fee. This card will cost you nothing.

Watch Your Wallet

To save on credit card fees make sure you know what fees are associated with your credit cards, make sure your payment is in the mail well in advance of the due date (at least 2 weeks), have your payment taken out of your checking or savings if there's no fee, or pay it off and use it only for emergencies. Some stores will also let you make payments at the store rather than requiring you to mail a payment. They don't seem too keen on letting people know about this, so you'll have to ask to see if you can make a payment at the store.

Remember, if you don't pay off the full balance, interest keeps accumulating on the unpaid amount. The meter begins ticking the moment you buy something with the card or more likely, the day the card issuer bills you for what you owe.

The interest could keep you in bondage forever if you don't use your noodle. For instance, says Bankcard Holders of America, it would take *eight years and eight months* to pay off a $1,000 balance at 16.5 percent if you only pay the minimum payment every month. (The minimum is normally only 2 percent of the amount owed.) You'd wind up paying $766 interest on your $1,000 loan. But you could pay off the debt in *three years* and pay *$500 less* in interest just by adding an extra $10 a month to your payment.

You pay the annual fee just to have the right to have the card for one year. The fee is usually $20 to $55, but many banks charge no fee at all. If you're the meticulous type and always pay

The Road to Riches

Double-check the rates and fees on your credit cards. The rate may have gone up over the past year if you're carrying a variable-rate card that is tied to some index. If your rate today is 16 to 19 percent, you're being taken to the cleaners. Also, you might have missed the fine print on a bank notice, stating that the card's annual fee has been raised. The most you should pay is about $30.

your monthly card balance in full, you should carry a no-annual-fee card and nothing else. The card will cost you nothing. It will be like having a free card.

The grace period is the number of days you have to pay off all new purchases without being hit by a finance charge. The usual grace period is 20 to 25 days. Typically, if you don't pay off your entire bill, all new purchases get clobbered by finance charges immediately.

For example, two brothers, Eenie and Meenie, both carry credit cards with an 18 percent rate. Each has a $1,000 balance on his card, on which there's no annual fee. Eenie pays off the entire $1,000 before the 20-day grace period is up. The card costs him zero. But Meenie only makes the minimum payment, $20, and gets charged 18 percent interest per year on the remaining $980. If you can't pay off your credit card entirely, always be sure to pay at least the minimum payment on your card before the grace period expires. Late payments will go over like a lead balloon at the next place you apply for credit. You'll probably get rejected.

Other niggling card costs:

◆ **Late fees.** You'll usually be nicked with a flat $29 to $35 charge, or two or three percent of your outstanding balance, if you don't make at least a minimum payment by the due date shown on the bill. Many banks have been raising their late fees even higher, charging even if your payment is one day late. Tip: Allow 7 to 10 days for your payment to reach the card company.

Watch Your Wallet

One way to protect yourself from getting hit by late-payment fees is to pay your bills online. Just about every major bank now offers online payment service, with a typical cost of about $5 per month. Some may offer an introductory free trial offer for several months.

◆ **Cash advances.** You can borrow money against the card, but the interest rate you pay for this type of transaction is apt to be higher. It's not uncommon for your regular rate to be, say 15 percent, but the cash advance rate to be as much as 24 percent. Plus, there's usually no grace period and you might have to pay a small fee. Usually, the cost of a cash advance is expressed as a percentage of the dollar amount advanced, or a flat dollar figure, whichever is higher. There also might be a dollar minimum that may be advanced.

◆ **Inactivity fee.** Some banks will nick you $15 to $25 if you don't charge anything on your credit card for six months. If you close your account, you might be charged another $25. Sound ridiculous? It is.

◆ **Over-limit fee.** These are going up, too, as banks penalize you up to $25 for exceeding your credit line by as little as $1.

Meanwhile, grace periods are getting shorter, reducing the number of days you have before the interest rate meter starts clicking on your card balance. When you put all these charges and tough new rules together, if you get the impression that card issuers are now really slamming it to the little guy, *you're right!*

The Biggest Secret of All: Watch Your Habits!

Americans are up to their ears in debt, and credit cards got them there, no matter what stories the banking industry tells you. Bad card habits have caused divorces, bankruptcies, lost dreams, and emotional wreckage. You can avoid the credit trap by following these simple rules:

- Know your credit limit based on your income, amount of current debt, and credit history. A rule of thumb is that your total monthly debt should not exceed 38 percent of your monthly income. For a review on managing your debt, check out Chapter 2.

- Carry only the number of cards you need, even though you haven't used up your credit line. Creditors look at how much you're potentially able to go into debt, based on your total lines of credit, when they review your record.

- Don't apply for more than one card at a time. Some creditors may think you're going to charge like mad and take off for Brazil.

- Consider joining a credit union to take advantage of their lower interest rates.

- Remember that a bad credit record will dog you for years. Nothing can screw up your life faster than going overboard with credit cards. Your card payment record will shadow you in everything you do, including buying a home (or renting), getting a job, and opening a checking account.

- Pay against your balance ASAP. *Don't be late—don't let bills hang around!* Every day you wait is going to cost you more in interest.

- Contact your card issuer immediately—and put everything in writing—if you can't make your payments on time or if you want to dispute a charge.

- Don't get fooled when card issuers lower your minimum payments. It only makes it easier for you to stay in debt, and increases the total interest you'll pay. This is a tar pit if ever there was one.

- Contact one of the personal-credit counseling organizations such as Consumer Credit Counseling Services, 1-800-388-CCCS, if you run into severe financial problems. They've helped millions of people, and can probably help you, at no charge or for a small fee.

Although it would be a lot easier if we just did away with credit cards altogether, there's no question about it: They're here to stay. So the next best thing to do is to choose your card with care and avoid falling into the many credit card traps that are set for you.

The Least You Need to Know

- Credit cards are the number-one reason why more than 1 million people file bankruptcy each year.

- Banks are raising *all* their card fees—from late-payment and over-limit fees to cash advances.

- Never be late with a payment. It will cost you dearly!

- The three most important things to shop are the interest rate, annual fee, and grace period.

- People with bad credit will pay a higher rate, but you can get a secured credit card no matter how terrible your credit is.

- Cards that offer rebates, cash rewards, and free air miles are a bummer unless you really need those services, and provided they'll honestly save you money.

Chapter 14

To Lease or Not to Lease

In This Chapter

- ◆ Determining the differences between leasing and buying
- ◆ Avoiding the biggest rip-offs of all
- ◆ Finding out what your old car—and new car—are really worth and getting the top price
- ◆ Why you should never show any emotion when you buy
- ◆ Why dealer financing can rip your wallet apart
- ◆ The most critical points to remember before you close a deal

Getting a car is probably the second-biggest money deal you'll ever make, right after a house. But, should you lease or buy? *That's* the $64,000 question. Leases have become the rage as car prices keep rising, because the monthly payments are less and you can turn the car in for a new one in three or four years. Yet very few people know the behind-the-scenes tricks to negotiating the right lease or obtaining the best outright buy. The average Joe never learns how he's being taken for a ride by nervy salespeople, or how he could have easily saved hundreds—perhaps thousands—of dollars. Meanwhile, dealers keep using crafty showroom and backroom tactics to drive up the cost of your car, from verbal gimmicks to trapping you with charges on things you don't need.

Whether you know it or not, the way you handle yourself with the salesperson—what you say and what you don't say—has everything to do with whether or not you'll get scammed. Your costs can be inflated without you ever knowing it. In particular, the average buyer knows zilch about the numbers behind a leasing deal, and that's where this chapter will help you. Although leasing today may appear to be the cheapest way to get behind the wheel, it's loaded with hidden mathematical schemes. You'll learn how to compare the bottom-line costs of a lease versus a purchase, the key questions to ask, and how to prevent the dealer from robbing you blind. The chapter exposes many of the dealer's biggest tricks, to enable you to come out ahead when you wheel and deal for your new wheels.

Knowing the Biggest Rip-Offs

When you go into a store to buy a television set or washing machine, they tell you the price and maybe the cost of an optional service contract. And that's about it, right? Not so with a new car. Auto dealers are the add-on champions of all time. Besides the financing rip-offs, which we'll discuss a little later, the list includes …

◆ Invoices and stickers that could have been created by somebody in the back room, not the manufacturer.

◆ An outrageous delivery charge. Should the cost of hauling the car from Detroit be included in your price?

◆ The dealer's "setup and preparation" charge. What did they do besides a wash and vacuum? After all, the car didn't arrive in bits and pieces from the manufacturer, did it?

> **Watch Your Wallet** _____
>
> You probably can't do much to avoid setup-and-prep charges, but there are other ways you can foil a dealer's adding to the price. For one thing, the window sticker on most new cars shows an "MSRP" price (Manufacturer's Statement of Retail Price) at the bottom. That's what the carmaker has determined to be the optimum retail price for the options on the sticker. You won't be able to escape the delivery (freight) charge on the MSRP, but the dealer's charge for setup-and-prep is a tip that the dealer has that much more room to discount the selling price.

◆ A whole bunch of options—a power sun roof, for example, or power seats—all priced sky-high.

♦ Dealer maintenance, which you can buy cheaper somewhere else.

♦ Extended warranty plans that they scare you into buying because "Nick, the mechanic, does work at $70 an hour."

♦ Dealer interest rates that have been booted up higher than what you could get from a bank.

♦ Vehicle undercoating. Forget it. You don't need to spend the extra couple hundred bucks. Do you think manufacturers are stupid enough to build new cars that rust out overnight?

♦ Credit life insurance. You're not required to buy it, and you shouldn't. Insurance experts have pointed out that of every $1 people spend on this scam, only 40¢ is paid out in the form of claims. Most people are already covered by life insurance policies or other assets if the borrower dies.

♦ Trade-ins. The dealer promises to lower your monthly payment if you trade in Old Betsy. But, he's already figured how much it will cost him to spruce up the car and how much he can sell it for at auction. He knows exactly how much money he has to play with to get your business. He'll take his cost of that old clunker out of your hide one way or another.

The Road to Riches

Dealers make money from the manufacturer that not even their salespeople know about. One is a "dealer holdback" that doesn't appear on the invoice. It may be 2 to 3 percent of the MSRP; so on a $25,000 car, the dealer would get up to $750 back from the manufacturer. Also, there may be special dealer "incentives" from the manufacturer that don't go through the salesperson. To wheel and deal on *these* incentives you'll have to talk directly to the sales manager or another higher-up.

You don't need all the extras the salesperson will try to load on you. They only increase the debt you'll have to finance, and boost the salesperson's commission. Even so, consider options carefully, and make your own decisions. You may wish to include certain attractive options if you plan to sell the car a few years later. Reason: Today many options—for example, power windows, cruise control, and a CD player—have become almost-standard equipment that your future buyer will expect when he or she buys the car from you.

Negotiate the Rate, Not Just the Price

There's an old belief that you're always better off financing through a bank instead of a dealership because dealers tack 1 or 2 percent onto the rate. That's not necessarily true anymore. Because one particular dealer may place a big slug of business with the same institution, it may offer the dealer a cheaper rate than you could get on your own.

Fiscal Facts

The best deal available these days is zero-percent financing, which is free money. Auto manufacturers are willing to make such loans to boost sales of certain new models. If you borrow $20,000 for 4 years, you'll save $2,546 in interest over borrowing the same money at 6 percent from a bank.

You can do even better than that. Let's say you could afford to pay cash for that new car. You'd be smarter to take the free loan and invest the cash in CDs. In this instance, you'd keep $5,000 at hand to make payments the first year and open $5,000 CDs of 1, 2, and 3 years. As each CD matured, you'd make payments with the principal and pocket the interest. If those CDs paid an average of 3 percent, you'd earn a total of $900 in interest.

Yet many car buyers still foolishly focus only on the sticker prices when they visit dealership showrooms. Why? Because there's something triumphant and emotionally satisfying about whacking the car price down by a couple of thousand bucks, when you really should be working on the dealer's most vulnerable spot—financing.

How About Those "Manufacturer Rebate" Deals?

The buzzword now, more than ever, is "rebate." Manufacturers are offering buyers incentives to clear out dealers' inventories, with few of the rebates applying to next year's models. If they do, the typical rebate is apt to be $500 instead of $1,500, but most likely the incentive on next year's line will be low rate, not rebate.

The Road to Riches

On the Internet, check the authoritative www.edmunds.com site for information on everything about cars, from rebates to dealer invoices, reviews, rebates, financing and road tests. For more information on rebates, visit Kelley Blue Book (www.kbb.com). For comparisons on what it will cost you to finance at different rates and terms, Yahoo's auto-rebate listings have simple to use calculators that tell you whether it's cheaper to lease or buy.

After you've done all the haggling on the car's selling price—remember that the manufacturer may offer the dealer a behind-the-scenes incentive of up to $250 per car that you never see, which gives you room to wheel and deal—the question is: What should you do with your rebate money? Most buyers apply it to their down payment and lower their monthly finance cost.

However, don't expect many dealers to offer you *both* the rebate plus a low interest rate. They'll tell you it's an "either/or" proposition. You can take advantage of either option but not both. Generally, if you grab the rebate you'll pay a much higher interest rate, ranging anywhere from 6.9 to 9.5 percent, depending on your credit history. This could wind up costing you more than $1,000 in extra finance charges.

Suppose you and the dealer settle on a $20,000 price with a down payment of 10 percent, or $2,000. That means you'll finance the other $18 grand. Assuming the finance rate is 3.9 percent for 48 months, which is about par for the course with auto manufacturers, your monthly payment will be $404.30. If you were also able to apply the $1,500 rebate to the down payment—which most dealers won't let you do—the monthly figure would drop to $370.61. However, if you stick the rebate money in your pocket and go with traditional financing at, say, the current 8.5 percent average, your monthly payment shoots up to $444.

Determining If You Should Buy or Lease

Leasing has been the rage in recent years, growing to almost one third of all new car deals. But car dealers admit that leasing is nothing more than renting with an option to buy. You keep the car for two, three, or four years, then you either buy the vehicle or turn in the keys, period.

If you finance, on the other hand, you're en route to owning the car.

Fiscal Facts

Credit unions are offering auto loans that work like a lease. Basically, they enable you to get a better car with lower monthly payments. You don't have to put any money down or make any security deposit, and, unlike with a regular lease, you don't have to pay a disposal fee when you turn the vehicle in. You have four options at the end of the program: (1) Return the car to the credit union and the balance is paid off; (2) Sell the car and pay off the loan balance; (3) Trade the car in and pay off the balance; and (4) Keep the auto and pay off or refinance the balance.

Know How a Lease Works

In a nutshell, leasing is just like buying a car except that you pay only a portion of the principal with your monthly payments. When the lease expires, you can do one of two things:

♦ **Walk away from the car and owe nothing.** That's called a closed-end lease. It's outlawed in some states, but it's the most popular type of lease nationwide.

Fiscal Facts

The **residual value** of a leased car is the lessor's calculation of the value of the car at the end of the lease period. When your lease period is up, this becomes the **buyout price,** or what you would have to pay in order to own the car outright.

Closed-end leases are based on the concept that the number of miles you drive annually is fairly predictable (12,000 miles per year is typical), that the vehicle will not be driven in rough or abusive conditions, and that its value at the end of the lease (the residual) is therefore somewhat predictable.

♦ **Consider buying the car.** That's an open-end lease. Your monthly payments may be lower, but you could wind up on the short end of the stick, as you're about to find out.

At the beginning of the lease, the dealer figures out how much your car will probably be worth at the end of the lease, say, in three or four years. That's called the *residual value*—what the dealer thinks the street price of the car might be at that time. When the lease is up, you can buy the car for the residual value, or *buyout price.*

Some dealers figure the residual value in two or three years, instead of four or five. That tips the scales in their favor. Why? Because a car can depreciate by 10 percent the moment you drive it home, and maybe by another 20 percent two or three years later. The younger the car, the higher the residual value. If you get a three-year lease and the dealer has figured the value after two years, you'll have to spend more than you should to buy the car when the lease expires.

Look at the Bottom Line

Let's say you're deciding between leasing or financing a $27,000 vehicle, but don't have the $5,400 down payment (20 percent) to go the financing route. Under a three-year lease, the dealer will typically want—up front—the first month's payment of, say, $450 plus $50 in taxes as well as another $450 as a refundable security deposit. That makes a total cash deposit of $950. Assume the lease is for four years, and the residual value is $15,000. If you finance the car loan instead of leasing, you'll be borrowing

$21,600 for four years after making your $5,400 down payment. Assume you pay 6 percent in taxes up front, and that your interest rate is 6 percent. Your monthly payment will be $507. So far, the lease gets the slight nod. But, how will your wallet really make out in the long run?

With the straight loan deal, in four years you'll own the car outright after paying a total of $2,749 in interest, and 21,600 on the principal. Had you leased, you'd probably make a $450-per-month payment and could simply turn the car in after four years and say good-bye. You wouldn't own a dime's worth of the vehicle and would still need new wheels. To buy the leased car, you would have to pay the dealer the $15,000 residual value.

But, suppose the street value of the car has declined to only $13,000? You'd be out the $2,000 difference, because you could probably buy a similar car for $13,000. It would only be a good deal *if* the residual value were *less* than the street price. In that case, you'd be foolish not to pay the residual value and keep the car. You could sell it at a profit and use the money as a down payment on another set of wheels.

Watch Your Wallet

Dealers may talk you into a lease by using language that sounds like you're purchasing the car instead of leasing it. For example, one Detroit automaker instructs its dealer sales staff to never use words like lease, interest rate, and residual when they chat with you in a showroom. Instead, they're instructed to use words such as buying, equity, and guaranteed future value. And, you have the option to trade or sell after a couple of years.

The key to getting the best deal on a lease is to do your homework. Check out these sources before and after you lease:

◆ You can get an excellent checklist and brochure on auto-leasing tips by sending a check or money order for $1.50 to Consumer Task Force for Automotive Issues, Reality Checklist, PO Box 7648, Atlanta, GA 30357-0648.

◆ What's your leased car worth now? Click onto the Internet at www.edmunds.com/edweb/.

◆ Go to the library and look up the market value of your car in the *National Automobile Dealers Association Used Car Guide*.

◆ Check the classified ads in your local paper to determine your car's value.

Don't Touch That Pen Until You Read This

Before you sign any lease, go over these points as though your life depended on them:

◆ Lease for no more than three years. That's the most you want to get stuck with if something unforeseen happens.

◆ Know that dealers are pushing shorter and shorter leases, such as two years. One reason: Their warranties from manufacturers to cover any possible problems with cars may only be for that long.

◆ Realize that if you turn the car in before the lease expires, the dealer will sock you with an early termination charge of $250 to $500. Insist that the charge be calculated by the level yield method, which means the dealer only recovers his charges for services and depreciation—no more.

Say you lose your job and can no longer make the payments. When you turn the car in, that's called voluntary early termination. You'll still be responsible for all remaining monthly payments, plus the preset residual value. In that case, the total due could be twice the value of the car!

◆ Calculate how many miles a year you drive. If you've exceeded that estimated mileage when the lease ends, such as 12,000 to 15,000 miles a year, the dealer will hit you with an extra-cents-per-mile charge. Be honest up front. If they tack on a higher mileage cost at the beginning, it will probably be *less* than what you would be charged when the lease is up.

◆ Determine if the lease requires higher insurance limits. Insurance is your responsibility, not the dealer's.

◆ Find out what the dealer means by "normal wear and tear." If, when the car is turned in, it's dented and dinged all over, and the seat cushions are ripped and torn, it's gonna cost you.

◆ Keep documents to prove that the car maintenance was done by a reputable outfit; you may have to produce these when you turn in the car.

◆ Check all the fees and payments under the lease. According to the "Truth in Leasing Law," you have a right to see them.

◆ Negotiate. Dealers can wheel and deal on leases just as on a sale.

◆ Check to see whether you are restricted from taking the car to another state if there's a chance you might move. Some dealers are finicky about this.

♦ Watch your timing. If you're financing an auto, you want to take advantage of "close-out pricing" toward the end of a model year, such as in June. But, this can boomerang on a lease because the dealer has built a full year's depreciation—a loss in value—into the first-year cost. Result: Between July and October when next year's models come out, you might be charged that one year of depreciation in three monthly payments.

If you lease your car for four years or more, and you drive more than 15,000 miles a year, you're going to end up paying through the nose.

Reason: Heavier driving can run the mileage up to 80,000 miles or thereabouts at the end of four years, about the time the car starts to show wear and tear and mechanical problems. Most lessors allow 15,000 miles per year and charge 12 cents to 15 cents per mile thereafter. The driver with 80,000 miles on the speedometer would have to cough up $3,000, or even more if the vehicle is in dinged-up condition.

> **The Road to Riches**
>
> If you only drive, say, 10,000 or 12,000 miles a year, ask for a better lease deal. Example: A dealer may normally base the car's residual value on 57 percent of the manufacturer's stated retail price. Under a low-miles program, he might boost the residual value to 60 percent of the MSRP, which would reduce your monthly payment.

Used Cars: Buying Right and Selling Right

A new car depreciates the moment it is driven off the dealer's lot. The amount of depreciation can vary, but we've heard of as much as 20 to 30 percent in the first year.

When you finance a used car, expect to pay an interest rate of 2 to 3 percentage points above the rate you pay on a new car. If a new car costs 9.5 percent to finance, chances are, a used car will cost 7 to 9 percent in the same town. (If your credit is really bad, prepare to get hit with a rate that may be 15 to 18 percent or higher.)

One good source of information on what a used car is worth is the National Automobile Dealers Association's *Official Used Car Guide*. It covers domestic and imported cars and small trucks. On the pages of the guide you'll find three columns of numbers for each auto make and model:

> **Watch Your Wallet**
>
> Some auto finance experts advise not to lease a car longer than 36 months because you may wind up paying for repairs on a car you don't own. If the transmission or brake system, goes out, it can cost you hundreds or thousands of dollars. Incidentally, fall is the best time to cut a cheaper leasing deal, just before the new models arrive.

- ◆ **Trade-In value.** Shows what the car is worth in trade at the dealer—*if* the vehicle is in tip-top condition in both appearance and mechanics.

- ◆ **Loan value.** Normally determines how much a bank will lend you to finance the car.

- ◆ **Retail value.** Tells you what price the car will fetch in the marketplace, whether you sell it to someone or buy it from the dealer. The value assumes the car is in great shape. If it isn't, the value will be less.

Also try the excellent price guides on used and new cars offered by Edmunds on the Internet at www.edmunds.com/edweb/. The site is loaded with prices, tips on buying and leasing, and gives you a great peek at all the incentives and rebates dealers work with to make a bundle off you.

How to Get Top Price When You Trade In or Sell a Used Car

First, look at the vehicle you're trying to trade or sell. Ask yourself, "Would I buy this car if someone offered it to me?" If not, invest a few bucks at an auto detail shop, a complete car wash (including wax), and a mechanic if necessary. On many used autos, this couple-hundred dollars of investment could bring an extra $500 to $1,000 in the selling price or trade-in value.

On a trade, the new car dealer is saying to himself, "Let's see, if I accept this clunker against the price I'm going to try to get from this customer on a new car, there's some fixin' I'm gonna have to do. Like new carpets, a couple of tires, wash and wax, maybe an engine tune-up and other stuff." The dealer figures he'll sell your slightly renovated car for, say, $5,000 at an automobile auction; he offers you $4,000 for Old Betsy. He spends $300 to get it in shape, and pockets the $700 difference.

Now you know rule number one when you trade your car in on a new one: Do some preliminary shopping around *before* you let a dealer know that you have a used car to trade. Consumer experts differ on whether you should tip to the dealer that you have a trade-in *before* you negotiate for your car, but in this book, we're suggesting that you wheel and deal on Old Betsy first—after you've done some homework.

So you get Old Betsy polished and super-cleaned before you show up. You check out its real value on the Internet at www.edmunds.com/edweb/. The dealer's salesman at first will try to low-ball you and steal the car—guaranteed. He'll try to maneuver you up and down and inside out by working the old car numbers against the new car numbers, but you can't let him do that. Cut a clean deal first for Old Betsy based on what it's really worth. Better still, sell the car yourself. (Dealers know that many consumers don't know how to do this.) Otherwise, the dealer might try to grab your old $5,000-value car for $2,500.

Then, test drive the new car. If you like it, negotiate the new-car price at a discount off the dealer's sticker price. That "price" is nothing more than packaged smoke. It means absolutely zip, and it won't give you a clue about the dealer's true cost or the hidden incentives he secretly gets back from the manufacturer when he sells the car (which we discuss later in this chapter). Some dealers tell us that this discounted price may be at least between $1,000 and $1,500 less than what the sticker price shows. The sticker price is called the Manufacturer's Suggested Retail Price, or MRSP, in the trade. Don't expect a big discount if there is an industry shortage of a particular model. In that case, the discount will be less.

Negotiate each and every one of the options and extras you want for the new car. Don't just accept whatever numbers the salesman throws at you. You should wheel and deal on these items the same way you haggled on the price of the car. At least the dealer will know you're no idiot.

Only after that should you get into the financing subject—never before.

Keep in mind that the dealer's goal is probably to make a profit of 8 to 10 percent on the vehicle, but you really want to chew him down to 2 to 5 percent over his cost. (The first thing you should have said to the salesperson in the showroom was, "I'm a serious buyer and I'm ready to buy today.") Don't get emotional over any new car you see; that's suicide. Take another person with you to keep the haggling better balanced. Remember, you're on the dealer's turf and the cards are heavily stacked against you. Every trick you can use will make it a more level playing field.

You always ask the questions, *not* the salesman. Ignore whatever documents the sales guy shows you during his spiel. Don't even look at them. Those papers don't count until after the deal is cut. Take a pencil and a notepad with you to help you with your own figuring.

Ignore the salesman's pet comments and shrewd language such as "What do I have to do to get you into this car?" or when he says, "You're wasting my time because you're not serious," or "This is my last offer." You just say, "When I get the answers to all my questions I'll tell you whether I'm interested." Period.

Repeat: Stifle Those Emotions When You Shop!

Follow these rules whenever you are buying a new or used vehicle:

- ◆ Don't get excited about the vehicle. The salesperson can read you like a book. If he or she senses you're falling in love with that little two-seater with the stick shift and double carburetor, it's going to cost you.

- Don't be anxious to close the deal on the same day. And, don't be afraid or let any of the salesman's guilt-trip ploys get to you. No matter what little threat the salesman makes, you can always walk out and come back later!

- Shop at least one other dealer who offers the same car. Dealers know from experience you're going to do this and that's what will give you clout in negotiating the cheapest price.

- Bargain on a lease just like you would if you were buying. Car shoppers make a big mistake by being too easy on the dealer when they lease a car instead of buying it.

Getting the Best Financing

Competition in the new car market is so ferocious that many dealers earn more of their living from the finance charges than from the profit they make off their autos. This section explains how you can avoid the pitfalls and walk out with the best deal.

Should You Avoid Dealer Financing?

There are two schools of thought about dealer financing. The old school believes that you should avoid dealer financing altogether because you'll save 1 to 2 percent right off the bat. The newer school, mentioned earlier, has learned that, because of increased competition, the dealer may offer an interest rate cheaper than the bank's. Either way, don't even think about going to an independent finance company where the rates are even higher—unless, of course, your credit is so shot that there's no other way out. Also many dealers love to charge higher rates to poor credit risks.

One strategy is to go to a bank or thrift institution and obtain a pre-approved loan for the amount you plan to finance. Better yet, join a credit union if you're not already a member. Credit unions are big in car loans, and their interest rates always beat what banks charge.

Credit Unions Offer the Cheapest Rates

It's less expensive to finance a new car through a credit union than through a bank or thrift. Besides offering cheaper rates, a credit union will provide you with information on the dealer's *real* cost of the car. A credit union also often arranges special mass car sales with local dealers who guarantee credit union members special low rates.

When you walk into the dealer's showroom armed with a pre-approved loan, you'll have enormous clout for two reasons. First, the dealer knows you're a red-hot, live prospect—and he won't let you out the door until he gives you his best deal. Second, he won't try to flim-flam you with his own financing (which may be more costly), because you already have a cheaper deal in your pocket. A nice position to be in!

Get a Simple Interest Loan

With a simple interest loan, you'll be paying interest only on the remaining amount of the loan. How come? As you make your payments month after month, you'll be steadily paring down what you still owe on that original $20,000 borrowed for four years. Say you make 10 monthly payments of $470. At 6 percent interest, your first payment of $470 is on the whole $20,000. Of the $470, $100 is interest and the other $370 reduces the principal you still owe to $19,630.

After the tenth payment, you will have whittled the principal down to $16,219. But your monthly payment will stay the same. Here's why: When the bank sets up your simple interest loan, it figures a flat amount of how much total interest you'll pay on the $20,000 you're borrowing. You can arrange your payments so that they'll still be $470 every month. That's easier for you, because you wouldn't want to start out with a gigantic payment and have it get smaller every month. You might not be able to afford the payment in the early months.

> **Example:** On a four-year (48-month) loan, the total interest comes to $2,546. Divide 48 payments into $2,546 and you get a monthly interest payment of $53. The bank gets its $20,000 back, plus the $2,546 interest. You can budget for a steady monthly payment figure.

Watch Your Wallet

Simple interest loans are commonly offered by banks and credit unions, whereas many finance companies charge higher interest through front-end loans. If a finance company does offer a simple interest loan, it will probably be at higher interest rates than you'd pay at a bank. If you have a poor credit history, the rate could shoot up even higher.

What you should avoid is a "front-end installment loan." Unlike the simple interest example you just read, with the installment loan *you pay interest every month on the original $20,000 you borrowed.* In this case, your total interest cost would work out to $4,800, or $2,254 more than with the simple interest loan. Your monthly payment would be $517 instead of $470. Better that money goes into *your* pocket instead of the dealer's (or the bank's).

Other Financing Secrets You Should Know

The following tips will help you stay focused on the bottom line when you buy a car:

- **Don't slide into the low payment mentality.** This is where many folks never learn. Car dealers are no idiots. They know the average person is more concerned about being able to afford their monthly payments than they are about the total cost of the loan. So what do dealers—and banks—often do? Suggest you stretch the loan term to five years instead of three. They say it will "make it easier on you." Humbug. All lower monthly payments do is jack up your financing cost.

  For example, a $20,000 loan financed through a bank at 6 percent for three years comes to $608 a month, with a total interest cost of $1,904. But over five years, though the monthly payment drops to $387, your interest cost jumps to $3,199. Not much of a deal, huh?

- **Make as big a down payment as you can.** Generally, you'll be required to make a down payment of 10 to 20 percent when you buy a new car, although we've seen credit unions finance 100 percent of the price. Some banks will do that, too, but only on luxury models. Why a bigger down payment? Because the more you put down, the lower your interest rate is apt to be.

- **Check out manufacturer financing carefully.** Boy, are they enticing—those car dealer ads with low-ball financing and the promise that you can drive the car home by five o'clock! Car manufacturers have captive finance companies to help their dealers wheel and deal. They desperately want your business and they'll turn cartwheels to get it—including a super-low interest rate and same-day credit approval, even on Sundays.

  This type of financing used to have several downsides. First, the low-ball rate only applied to certain models, like that little convertible with the purple stripes and no trim. Other regular models may have cost more to finance. Second, if you did get the dealer's low manufacturer rate, the dealer may have taken it out of your hide by charging you more for the car. Third, manufacturer financing was less apt to give you a simple interest loan.

  But lately, because of enormous competition and the world economy, U.S. and foreign manufacturers have been pushing low-rate deals right and left. On some models, for instance, Detroit's Big Three automakers not only were offering cash rebates of more than $2,000, they also had low financing 0% for up 60 months. And the deals covered a broad list of models.

◆ **Stay away from variable-rate loans.** Most car loan rates are fixed—that is, you're charged the same interest during the entire loan term. Some car financing rates are variable—meaning the rate can go up or down, depending on which direction all bank rates are going. If rates rise, as they did in 1994, your car loan rate could go up by as much as 2 to 3 percentage points in a year.

If that happens, the bank may make it "easier" for you by keeping your monthly payment the same, but stretching the term of your loan. Result: Your 48-month loan could turn into a 50-month loan. You wind up paying a bigger finance cost.

◆ **Take advantage of car rebates.** If Bubba's Auto Showroom says the manufacturer has a special $1,000 "rebate" offer, you may want to grab it—that is, *if* the rebate applies to the exact auto you want. Here's why:

Say you're working with that same $15,000 example at 9 percent bank interest for four years. The loan payment is $373 per month. The total cost of the car is $17,917.On the other hand, if you take the $1,000 rebate and apply it to your down payment, you'll reduce your monthly payment to $348. The total cost of the loan will be cut to $16,723.

◆ **Never give the dealer your SSN until after you've settled on all the interest rates, fees, and conditions.** If he runs your credit history through a computer system beforehand, it can affect the deal he offers you. A buyer with A-1 credit might get an 8 percent rate on a used car, while folks with spotty credit records might pay 10.5 percent.

◆ **Check whether you can pay off your loan early.** Some lenders will let you do it, others won't. So before you sign for a loan, ask if you can pre-pay the loan without a penalty. Are there any extra fees or charges? If a pre-pay is okay, be sure to note on your payment checks how much is going toward reducing the principal and how much is going toward the interest. This way you'll have proof if the dealer or the bank ever challenges you.

Fiscal Facts

Some lenders have a complicated little gizmo built into the way they calculate your payments. It's called the **Rule of 78s.** It's complicated as heck—and depends on state law—but it simply means that most of your early payments are going only toward the interest, not the principal. In that case, you won't save very much by paying off the loan in advance.

◆ **Get a tax deduction on the car by hocking your house.** It's a little bit risky, but lots of people do it. You can no longer get a tax deduction on a straight car loan—the IRS did away with that in 1990—but you can get one by borrowing against your home. How? By opening a home equity line of credit. First, you figure how much of your home you own—what the house is worth, minus what you owe on your mortgage. Banks, thrifts, and credit unions will usually lend you up to 75 or 80 percent of that amount (see Chapter 18, for more on this).

For example, if your home's appraised value is $250,000 and you owe $100,000 on the mortgage, your equity in the house is $150,000. If the bank lends you 80 percent of that $150,000, the amount of the principal is $120,000.

If the interest rate on the home equity loan is less than the rate on a car loan, you'll save on your financing costs. Plus, if you're in, say, the 28 percent tax bracket, you'll save money compared to the taxes you'd pay on a straight auto loan. Reason: The IRS allows you to deduct the interest expense.

Watch Your Wallet

Banks like home equity loans because they're protected by holding a lien on your house. *This means that if you can't meet the payments, the bank could take your home,* never mind the car.

Because buying or leasing an auto is probably the second biggest transaction you'll ever make (after your home), it's important to do your homework and negotiate the deal carefully. Car dealers are loaded with behind-the-scenes tricks and rip-offs that can zoom your cost sky-high. Most important, figure the real difference in the bottom line between buying and leasing.

The Least You Need to Know

- Haggle on a leasing deal just as you would if you were buying the car.

- Go in prepared to buy, but volunteer very little information. You—not the salesman—should ask the questions. Car salesmen can read you like a book.

- Just say no to vehicle undercoating, credit life insurance, extended warranties, and other unnecessary charges.

- Get the deal on your trade-in done first before you begin discussing a deal on a new car. Then get the dealer's discounted price before you start haggling.

- Always shop the same vehicle at more than one dealership.

- Get pre-approved for a loan through a bank or credit union before going to the dealer. You'll save money on interest rates by not financing through the dealer, *and* you'll have more negotiating power because you have the money in hand.

Chapter 15

Mortgage Shopping: Let's Make a Deal

- ◆ How to decide which kind of mortgage is best for you

- ◆ How to determine how much house can you afford

- ◆ The key differences between fixed rates and ARMs

- ◆ How the right mortgage can save you *tens of thousands of dollars*

- ◆ Where to get cheap government-backed financing with only 3 percent down

- ◆ How to decide what's more important—rates or points

Hey, where do you think mortgage rates are going?" That's one of the most frequently-asked questions in the world of personal finance. Rate guessing—knowing when, or when not to, make your move on a new mortgage loan or a refinancing—has turned into a giant crapshoot. No one knows for sure where the numbers will be in one week, a month, or a year from now. The average homebuyer is bedazzled by the interest rate jungle, different types of mortgages, and a list of fees as long as your arm. Yet a mortgage loan is probably the single biggest chunk of money you'll ever have to borrow and pay back. It's for the number-one asset you'll ever own—your house. Dollar-wise, you're talking about an investment that will probably cost you $300,000 to $400,000 over your lifetime. But, if you don't buy your mortgage wisely, it could easily cost you tens of thousands of dollars more!

This chapter explains the tricky, complicated mortgage process in simple language. It tells you step-by-step what to watch out for, what kind of mortgage will fit your personal money situation like a glove, and when it's time to grab the right interest rate. You'll learn how to strengthen your credit record so your loan application will be approved, and how to get into a new home with little or no cash down even if you're a first-time buyer. On top of that, you'll learn super-easy ways of tackling mortgage math, and short-cut ways to shop for the best deal.

Learning the ABCs of How Mortgages Work

A mortgage is nothing more than a loan. If you don't have the money to pay all cash for a house, a mortgage lender may loan you up to 95 percent of its appraised value. You deposit the rest up front as a down payment. The lender holds a lien on your home until you fully repay what you borrow—meaning that if you default on your payments, the lender can take the house.

We're not talking about small change in mortgage loans, folks; we're talking hundreds of thousands of dollars. That's the total tab of a 30-year mortgage when you add up the amount you borrow plus the huge interest you'll pay on the loan.

The key to getting the right mortgage is learning which type of loan will fit your present and future budget to a T. There are two major types of standard "conventional loans" (as opposed to government-insured loans, also discussed in this chapter).

They are fixed-rate and adjustable-rate mortgage (ARM) loans. Trying to compare the two appears complicated, but it isn't. You can do it. Just keep asking yourself this one basic question: How will each mortgage gimmick impact my pocketbook, today and several years from now? The answers will come to you, as mortgage lenders knock themselves out trying to get your business.

Mortgage-ese You Should Know

The mortgage process is chock-full of confusing terminology. The following definitions should help clarify things a bit:

◆ **Annual Percentage Rate (APR).** Interest rate reflecting the first-year rate, including certain points and credit costs.

◆ **Appraisal.** A professional estimate of what a house is worth, based on its style, appearance, construction quality, improvements, usefulness, and the comparable value of nearby properties.

◆ **Caps.** The maximum amount a mortgage rate can change annually or over the life of the loan on a one-year adjustable. For example, if the caps are 2 percent annual and 6 percent life of loan, a mortgage whose first-year rate is 8 percent could rise to no more than 10 percent the second year and 14 percent over the entire term.

◆ **Closing.** The final settlement of the transfer of property. It involves the buyer's signing of the mortgage and mortgage note, and a change of title to the home.

◆ **Closing costs.** Fees and other charges paid by the buyer and seller at closing.

◆ **Conventional mortgage.** A mortgage *not* insured by the government (such as an FHA or VA loan).

◆ **Deed.** The document that transfers the title from the seller to the buyer.

◆ **Down payment.** The buyer's payment to the seller at closing. The payment is based on a percentage of the purchase price required by the buyer's mortgage loan.

◆ **Earnest money.** Money paid by the buyer to the seller at the time an offer to purchase the home is presented.

◆ **First mortgage.** A mortgage that is a first lien on the property pledged as a security.

◆ **Loan-to-value ratio.** Proportion of a home's value on which a lender will issue a loan.

◆ **Mortgagee.** The lending party under the terms of the mortgage.

◆ **Mortgage note.** A signed promise to repay a mortgage loan in regular, monthly payments under pre-agreed terms and conditions.

◆ **Offer to purchase.** A legally-binding, written contract that declares how much a buyer will pay for the property, provided certain conditions are met.

◆ **One-year adjustable.** Mortgage whose annual rate changes yearly. The rate is usually based on the movements of a published *index* plus a specific margin, chosen by the lender.

> **The Road to Riches**
>
> Always compare APRs—with the points included—when you shop, so that you're comparing the total costs of mortgages that offer the same interest rate.

♦ **PITI.** Principal, interest, taxes, and insurance—the four main parts of a monthly mortgage payment.

Fiscal Facts

An **index** is a known benchmark used by a lender to set its mortgage rate on a variable-rate (as opposed to a fixed-rate) loan. The lender adjusts the homeowner's rate when the index goes up or down. When the index rises, the interest rate increases; when the index declines, the rate is adjusted downward.

♦ **Points.** One point equals 1 percent, or one one-hundredth, of the total mortgage amount.

♦ **Qualify.** To meet a lender's mortgage-approval requirements.

♦ **Sub-prime loan.** A loan made at higher interest rates to less creditworthy individuals.

♦ **Title.** The right of ownership and possession of a property.

♦ **Title insurance.** A policy that protects a buyer against errors, omissions, or defects in the title.

♦ **Up-front charges.** What you are charged at the beginning of the home buying process, such as the fee for an appraisal of the property.

$64,000 Question: Should You Get a Fixed-Rate or an ARM?

Here's the difference: A fixed rate is typically for 30 years or 15 years. It locks in your interest rate—and your monthly payments—for the entire life of the loan. You don't have to worry about the payment suddenly shooting up. The rate is carved in stone.

An adjustable rate (ARM) starts out lower than a fixed rate with lower monthly payments, but is usually only good for the first year of the loan. Then the lender hikes the rate and payment based on the index it uses. It can increase the rate again and again, up to a maximum of 5 or 6 percent over the starting rate, according to how often the index changes.

Which rate is for you?

Suppose you borrow $100,000 at 7 percent interest. The $100,000 is called your principal. With a 30-year term, your monthly payment would be $665, and your total interest cost over all 30 years would be $139,511. But suppose that instead of a 30-year loan, you took one for 15 years at 6.75 percent. The monthly payment on the 15-year loan would be higher—$899—but the total interest over 15 years would be sensationally less—$61,789. You'd save a whopping $77,722 with the 15-year loan!

But hold on. A 15-year loan is a good option for middle-age and older buyers who can afford the higher monthly payment. It will save you a ton of money in interest, and it builds up your equity a lot faster. The disadvantage is that there's less tax-deductible interest on a 15-year loan. Plus, people with low incomes probably won't qualify as borrowers because their budgets can't handle the stiffer payments.

A 30-year fixed-rate loan has its advantages, too. It's a good investment when interest rates are low. Also, there may be considerable tax benefits, especially in the early years. Your payment stays the same even if rates rise, regardless of inflation. The one disadvantage is that your equity builds up more slowly with a 30-year loan. Here's an example, based upon a $100,000 loan:

How Much You Can Save with a 15-Year Fixed Rate, Assuming the Rate Is the Same

	30-year	15-year
APR	5.625%	5.625%
Monthly payment (principal and interest)	$575.66	$823.73
Paid after 15 years	$30,117.03	$99,999.54
Total interest paid	$107,237.60	$48,271.40
Interest saved		$58,966.20

ARMs' Initial Payments Are Lower but Could Shoot Up Later

Suppose someone lends you $1 today. He charges you a dime in interest this year, but next year he starts working with a different formula that could increase your interest to 15 cents in the second year, 20 cents in the third year, and so on, until it gets up to 80 cents or a maximum of a dollar. That's sort of how adjustable-rate mortgages (ARMs) work. You start out paying cheap interest, but later, the rate can skyrocket.

The only thing ARM rates have in common with fixed-rate mortgages is that they're both usually for 30 years. But, unlike a fixed-rate mortgage, the ARM interest rate can adjust periodically—typically every year or six months. The adjustment is based on which index the lender ties its ARM rate to. The rate can go up or down according to the index—and so does your monthly payment. But, your

The Road to Riches

One index may change more often or more slowly than another index, and that can affect how long it takes the lender to change your ARM rate—and your monthly payment.

indexed rate may not start showing up until the second year of your loan, after the first adjustment.

What kind of mathematical nonsense is this? Lenders discount their first-year ARM rate as a low-rate ploy to get you in the door. As a result, their introductory ARM rate looks mighty good to you—it's probably $\frac{1}{2}$ to 1 percent or more, less than the interest on a fixed-rate. So far, so good. But, at the beginning of the second year, as we just explained, the ARM rate jumps to the index rate plus a margin (for example, markup) that the lender tacks onto the index. This produces your indexed rate. If the index continues to rise, your ARM rate keeps going up as well. But, if the index goes down, the ARM could fall, too.

The ARM indexes that lenders use have complicated names that consumers aren't aware of. But, don't let it throw you. The main thing is, by knowing the lender is basing your ARM rate on a publicly-known index, it's better than having an index that the bank secretly concocted in its kitchen.

Here are the most common ARM indices.

♦ **The 1-Year Treasury Bill Index.** This index is for ARMs whose rates generally change once a year. The lender will notify you of your new rate 30 to 45 days before it takes effect.

♦ **The 11th District Cost of Funds.** This gets its name from the Federal Home Loan Bank's 11th District which is based in San Francisco, but whose index is used by lenders nationwide. It's used mostly for ARM rates that are adjusted monthly. Your new rate is usually determined by the index value 30 to 90 days before the next rate change.

♦ **LIBOR—the London InterBank Offered Rate.** This is the most volatile index; it can jump up or down more frequently, with no set pattern as to how often (as opposed to huge and up and down movements annually or every six months, for example). When mortgage rates are bouncing up and down erratically, lenders like the LIBOR index, because it protects them against getting clobbered by a rate jump in one fell swoop.

Every ARM Wears a "Cap"

Just because the lender can change your ARM rate whenever his index changes, it doesn't mean he or she can keep increasing your rate forever. There's a limit to how high the rate can go: This limit is called a "cap." There are really two caps on every ARM loan: A 2 percent cap per year, which means the rate can only rise by 2 percent in any given year, and a 6 percent cap over the life of the loan. If, for example, your ARM loan started out at 5.5 percent, it can never go higher than 11.5 percent.

But that's pretty scary, considering the fact that if your lender raises the rate by 2 percent a year, in four years' time you could be at the 11.5 percent level—when fixed rates might be only 7, 8, or 9 percent. That's why ARMs are best for people who plan to move within four years, or for younger, first-time home buyers who may be short of cash for a few years.

Watch Your Wallet

Beware of negative amortization! This is the ugliest of all types of mortgages, and it is usually found on adjustable-rate loans. Negative amortization is a little confusing, but basically it works like this: When you make a monthly payment, you may not get all of your interest, or any of your principal, credited against your loan because of the mathematical formula the lender uses.

Some Mortgages Are Cheaper in the Early Years

Several options for mortgages are 3/1, 5/1 and 7/1 mortgages, where you lock in a fixed rate for five or seven years, then switch to whatever ARM rate exists at that time, plus a cap. While the starting rate will be a tad above the standard ARM, it's nevertheless lower than that on a 30-year fixed. That makes these loans ideal for folks who don't plan to remain in their home for many years, or who expect their future income to grow.

For example, one big lender was charging 6.25 percent on a 30-year fixed-rate mortgage, and on the same day had a 5 percent first-year introductory rate on its ARM loan. At the same time, it had a 5.5 percent rate for new homebuyers taking out a 5/1 or 7/1 loan. But for people who wanted to refinance their present mortgage, it charged 5.625 percent for a 5/1 refinance and 5.75 percent for a 7/1 refinancing.

Maybe You Need a 5/25 or a 7/23

These are a couple more flexible mortgages that might fit your financial situation. They're very similar to the 5/1 and 7/1 plans just outlined, with a minor variation.

Say you can only afford a low monthly payment, and don't plan to stay in the home for more than a few years. Let's suppose interest rates are rising, and you prefer to lock into a fixed rate instead of gambling with an ARM rate that could increase by 2 percentage points a year. A 5/25 or 7/23 mortgage may be for you.

With these loans, you take out a 30-year mortgage for which you pay a fixed rate for the first five or seven years. At the end of either term, your rate adjusts to a new fixed rate (which may be higher) for the remaining 25 or 23 years. Some lenders offer customers an option to convert to an ARM mortgage after five or seven years. Either way, these types of "balloon" mortgages, as they're called, are good for first-time homebuyers with more income ahead.

Cheap Government-Agency Financing

Can't afford a big down payment and four-figure closing costs? There are ways to get into a new home through government-agency programs that are ideal for new, young families and folks who don't have a lot of cash.

One reason lenders are pushing these types of programs is this: The federal government is clamping down on lenders—especially banks—if they fail to help provide affordable housing for low and middle-income families. They've set aside billions of dollars for these efforts—and in hundreds of cities across America, local governments have come up with "free money" for down payments and closing costs. Some of the deals are the following:

◆ **Fannie Mae "Flexible 97" Program.** The Fannie Mae Flexible 97SM program is designed for borrowers with very good credit who either need or want to make a minimal down payment. It is available nationwide and charges a market rate for a 30-year fixed-rate mortgage, but has a minimum 3 percent down payment. That money can come from a confirmed gift or a family loan, whereas under other low-down-payment programs, the 3 percent must be your own cash. Also with Flexible 97, the seller can contribute up to 3 percent of the total mortgage amount toward your closing costs. In other words, if the costs were $3,000 on a $100,000 loan, you wouldn't have to put up any closing money. So if the down payment were a gift from Uncle Joe, you'd get into the house without having to use any of your own cash. Plus the program has a loan ceiling of $227,150, and there's no limit on maximum household income. For details, call Fannie Mae at 1-800-732-6643.

◆ **Federal Housing Administration (FHA) Loans.** The federal government doesn't actually *lend* the money for these loans; rather, it insures, or guarantees, the loan for the lender under several different mortgage programs. The down payment may be only 3 percent or less, and the fixed rate is lower than what you'd pay for a conventional 30-year loan. But, the big news is that ARMs are back in the FHA program. The downside is that the credit limit on how much you can borrow is limited by the median home prices in different areas. The loan term can be from 15 to 30 years.

◆ **Veteran's Administration (VA) loans.** These loans are also federally insured or guaranteed, with no down payment and have some of the same features as with an FHA loan. Borrowers must have current or previous military service. Loans may be for a 30-year or 15-year fixed-rate, or a 30-year ARM, and 100 percent financing is available. Rates are in the same ballpark as FHA loans.

◆ **Community Home Buyer's Program (CHB).** This may be the cheapest deal of all. Lately, there's been a new thrust toward 100 percent financing, but traditionally the CHB down payment requirement has been only 5 percent, with 2 percent of that allowable as a gift from family or friends. The 2 percent doesn't show up on your credit report, so it doesn't count as a debt you owe. Plus you don't need cash reserves to cover two months' worth of mortgage payments (normally you need them with other low-income loans).

How to Know When Fixed or ARM Rates Are Best

Timing is everything when you choose a mortgage. When interest rates are low, more homebuyers choose a fixed-rate because it locks in their monthly payment for 15 or 30 years. When fixed rates start approaching 10 percent, more people tend to shift to ARMs because the low introductory rates are then typically 2 to 3 percentage points below a fixed-rate.

For example, when the average fixed rate was 6.8 percent nationwide a few years ago, and the ARM rate was 4 percent, almost all homebuyers chose the fixed rate. Buyers avoided ARM rates because, despite the cheap 4 percent financing, the rate could rise to as high as 10 percent (6 percentage points above the starting rate). But a few months later, the fixed rate had climbed to 9.1 percent and the ARM was at 6.8 percent. Then the reverse happened; most consumers began choosing ARM mortgages instead.

Rates Can Go Up ... and Down ... and Up

If you studied all the changes in mortgage rates over the past 10 years, the picture would look like a roller coaster. For example, ARM rates averaged 8.17 percent in 1990, then dropped to 4.43 percent in 1993 and 6.18 percent in '94. But by 2001 they were down to 6 percent and in 2004 had dipped to 3.8 percent. Similarly, 30-year fixed rates topped out at 10.01 percent in 1990, fell to 7.18 percent in '93, then to 8.99 percent in '94. By mid-2004 they had fallen to 5.7 percent.

To understand how an ARM might work, let's look at this example. Pretend that the average fixed rate is 7 percent, but in the first year, the average introductory ARM rate is only 5.5 percent. You choose the ARM because it's cheaper. Your monthly payment on a $100,000 mortgage would be $567.79 in the first year. But, in the second year, the lender starts to set your new rate based on an index such as the one-year Treasury bill. Say the index is 5.2 percent. The lender adds its margin, typically 2.75 percentage points. That increases your rate to 7.95 percent (5.2 + 2.75), but because of the 2-percent-cap-per-year, your new rate can't go any higher than 7.5 percent. That's the maximum rate you pay in the second year, so your monthly payment increases to $696.21.

In year three, let's assume the index has now gone up to 5.4 percent. Add the 2.75 percent margin again, and your ARM rate becomes 8.15 percent (5.4 + 2.75). Because that rate is below the 2-percent-per-year cap maximum, your new rate stays at the 8.15 percent level. Your monthly payment jumps to $739.36 in the third year.

Play out that same scenario through the fourth year. The lender hikes your rate again, to a new index of, say, 5.6 percent plus 2.75 percent, or 8.35 percent. That becomes your new rate because it's within the 2-percent-cap limit, and payments rise to $752.57 this year. At this point, four years after you took out your ARM loan, which type of mortgage would have been the better deal—the ARM or a fixed-rate? Obviously the fixed rate. The following table shows you why.

ARM Costs Can Rise

	ARM	**Fixed Rate (7%)**
First year	$5,466	$6,968
Second year	$7,365	$6,894
Third year	$7,925	$6,816
Fourth year	$8,038	$6,731
Total interest cost, first 4 years	$28,794	$27,409

Of course, ARM rates can go down as well as up, depending on what happens to the index. The indexes that ARM rates are tied to will change periodically. The higher the index, the higher your ARM rate (based on a formula the lender uses). In strong economic times, and during periods of inflation, the index will probably rise. During a recession, such as the one between 1990 and 1993, the index will fall. (Remember: An index is only a benchmark that the lender uses to figure the ARM rate you are charged.)

Worst-case scenario: If the fourth-year ARM rate in the example we gave stayed at 8.35 percent for the remaining 27 years, you'd wind up paying a total of $167,776 in interest over the life of the loan—*plus* the $100,000 principal you owe. By comparison, had you grabbed the 30-year 7 percent fixed rate at the beginning, you'd pay a total of $139,508—a savings of $28,268.

Calculating What It's Gonna Cost

Except for low down-payment government programs (described in this chapter), you'll probably make a down payment of between 5 and 20 percent on that little house with the picket fence. You'll also have closing costs that run 2 to 5 percent of the amount borrowed. And you'll be forking over money for not-so-incidental things such as moving, new-house fix-ups, and any outside legal fees attached to the purchase.

That's a lot of cash outflow. So it's not wise to plunk down *all* your money into a down payment. There's a better way around it. To budget for the house, you should ask yourself these questions:

- How much house can I really afford?

- How low do I want my monthly payment to be?

- How long do I plan to stay in the house?

Watch Your Wallet

Be forewarned: Lenders provide you with a "good faith estimate" of the total costs of a mortgage loan at the time you apply, but the real final cost can be a lot more than the "estimate." There's no federal law that forces these guys to make the estimate 100 percent accurate.

- How much out-of-pocket is required for incidentals to move into the house and stay there over the next three to six months?

Don't forget, you also need to take rates, points, APR, fees, and closing costs into consideration when figuring out how much your mortgage is really going to cost you.

Identify Which You Should Watch Most—Rates or Points

There's another little animal in the mortgage jungle that directly affects the cost of your loan. It's *points*. A point is one one-hundredth of your loan amount. On a $100,000 loan, each point is $1,000. Lenders charge points to cover the costs of completing a mortgage application and to earn income. The buyer pays the points at closing, for example, when buyer and seller sit down together and close the sale. If a $100,000 mortgage comes with three points, that's $3,000.

"Which is more important, rates or points?" It depends on your situation. The *rate* is probably the key because it determines your monthly payment of principal and interest. But points can directly influence the rate you pay, even though the two are completely different things.

Points come into play when the lender determines how much of a monthly payment you can afford. Because that payment is influenced by the interest rate, one way to bring the rate (and your payment) down is to increase the number of points. Many lenders have five or more rates-and-points combinations; some may have a dozen. For example, a lender that quotes a rate of 8 percent with no points might also have quotes of 7.5 percent with one point, 7.2 percent with two points, and 6.8 percent with three points.

Remember: Nothing is for nothing in this world. If the lender offers "zero points," it's going to make up for it in another way, such as with a higher rate or bigger fees.

As you can see, rates and points move in opposite directions. The higher the rate, the lower the points, and vice versa. If you want to lower your monthly payment, you can "buy down" the rate by paying more points. The lower rate can also reduce your interest expenses. On $100,000 borrowed at 7.5 percent for 30 years, the monthly payment would be $699. Over the first five years of the loan, total interest would be $3,121. If you lowered the rate to 7.2 percent by paying more points, the monthly payment would drop to $679 and total interest for five years would decrease to $2,994. Besides having the lower payment, the lower rate would save you $127 in interest, but the benefit would apply only to the first five years.

> **The Road to Riches**
>
> The longer you plan to stay in your house, the more you should pay points in exchange for a lower interest rate.

If you don't have a lot of ready cash or aren't planning to stay in the house for more than five years, taking fewer points and a higher interest rate would probably be the better strategy.

Understand That "APR" Tells You the Real Cost

What's an APR? It stands for Annual Percentage Rate, a complicated term that throws almost any mortgage shopper for a loop. An APR is simply a percentage number that includes the rate plus certain fees and charges, It helps you compare apples with apples when you try to stack two loan offers side by side to decide which one is the better deal. The Consumer Credit Protection Act requires that lenders disclose their APRs.

The APR is almost always higher than the rate, but it reflects *the real cost of your loan on a yearly basis.* That creates a more level playing field for you to judge all the different mortgage deals. For one thing, the APR includes the points *and* many of the fees you're charged on your loans. Starting to get the idea?

Suppose (as in the following table) that Megabuck Bank offers a 30-year fixed-rate loan at 6 percent. Friendly Federal's rate is only 5.5 percent. That makes Friendly's offer the better deal, right? Maybe not. You could pay three points for Friendly's loan, compared with only one point at Megabuck. Plus, Friendly might have forgotten to tell you about other fees, such as mortgage insurance premiums, prepaid interest, and its cost of originating the mortgage. That could total a few thousand bucks. On the surface, it *looks* like Friendly Federal has a cheaper mortgage based on the rate alone. But, when all the costs are figured into the APR, the cheaper mortgage is Megabuck's.

The Money Line

If you can afford a higher rate with higher monthly payments, some lenders may offer you a no-points deal.

The Lowest Rate May Not Be Your Best Deal

	Megabuck Bank	Friendly Federal
Rate	6%	5.5%
Interest	$7,194.60	$6,813.48
Points (based on a $100,000 30-year mortgage)	$1,000.00 (1 point)	$3,000.00 (3 points)
Closing costs	$500.00	$2,500.00
Total cost in first year of mortgage	$8,694.60	$12,313.48

Learn the Up-Front Fees and Closing Costs

Besides the cost items that go into your monthly payment, there are other costs on the front end and back end of a mortgage loan. Ideally, you want to do business with an outfit that doesn't rook you at either end. Most lenders will charge you up-front fees; others may not charge anything at all to get your business. Beware of lenders who load on extra costs like photos, document charges, notary, and so forth. These can run into hundreds of dollars.

The Road to Riches

When you shop, always ask lenders for their APRs on fixed-rate loans vs. ARMs, and compare those with other lenders' APRs in the area.

Typically you should only pay for …

- **Up-front fees.** Appraisal and credit report.

- **Closing costs.** Points, recording fees, documentary stamps, mortgage insurance, document preparation, and inspection.

Remember that you must have enough cash for closing costs, which have to be paid when the final papers are signed. Most lenders will provide you with a "good faith" estimate of these costs in advance. Make sure you get it in writing. Typically, closing costs run between 2 and 6 percent of the loan amount.

Finding the Cheapest Mortgage the Quick, Easy Way

Okay, so now you know all the major costs of getting a mortgage, but you're probably thinking, "How am I going to remember all this stuff? I feel like I'm drowning in an ocean of rates, points, formulas, and other mathematical gobbledygook. There's gotta be an easier way!"

There is. Try this simple solution. It works like a charm, and there's probably no better way to shop a mortgage, even if you have three college degrees in math. First, pick out a half dozen or more of the lenders in your area that seem to be offering the best combination of rates and points.

Second, assume you'll be in your new house for five years—which is about the average length of time most families stay. (Five years also happens to be the magic cut-off point for deciding between a fixed-rate and an ARM, remember?)

Then ask each lender to tell you—*in dollars and cents, not percent*—the following:

- Total up-front fees *and* charges on the types of loans you'd consider.

- Total interest charges (not counting the principal) for the first five years.

- Total closing costs, including points.

Got that? Three dollar items, from each lender. Then add up the total cost of the mortgage—those three items—for the first five years at each lender, and compare the various deals. Voila! You immediately see who offers the best deal! When you shop for the lowest mortgage cost among several different lenders, add up the three main cost areas (shown in the following table, "The Mortgage Shopping List") for each lender, and compare. Be sure each lender covers *all* the costs. Don't let them get away with saying, "Then, of course, there are certain other fees and charges." You want them all—now—period.

Tip for the cyber crowd: Two good places to find the latest mortgage rates, and calculators that help you figure what different loans will cost you, can be found on the Internet at www.bankrate.com, and www.interest.com/calculators.html. Other top-rated websites are:

- www.indymacbank.com

- www.LoansDirect.com

- www.mortgagebot.com

- www.Countrywide.com

- www.e-loan.com

Online Mortgages—The Big New Game in Town

The online mortgage business is exploding—from less than $500 million in 1998 to more than $40 billion in 2004. Some sites make their own loans, while others work with multiple lenders. Major players also include www.quickenmortgage.com and www.iown.com. But going online for a loan isn't as simple as getting a generic rate quote. You must obtain rate and other information that's specific to *you*, such as your geographic location and your credit history.

How it works: The lender wires your mortgage funds to a local title company, to be paid at closing—just like with regular mortgages. Bad credit record? No problem. Online lenders have special "sub-prime" lending facilities to accommodate risky borrowers, although at higher rates. Some Internet mortgage peddlers don't stop at new and refinanced mortgages. e-loan.com will also finance your car, cash out your home's equity, and let you apply for a credit card. quickenmortgage.com enables you to check the latest home listings, market by market across the United States, and will even direct you to home improvement companies that will repair your downspouts and remodel your kitchen.

The Money Line

By the year 2003, of the $1.4 trillion in money borrowed for a mortgage, nearly 20 percent originated on the Internet, up 19 percent since 1998. *Source: Forrester Research.*

To get lenders to bid against each other for your business, it's possible to submit loan applications to two outfits at the same time. This may enable you to get a lower rate and lower fees, but when the lenders discover what you're doing, don't be surprised if they give you poorer service.

The Money Line

Lenders are super-hungry for business. With mortgage rates at 40-year historical lows, the increase in the number of homebuyers has created a dog-eat-dog competition. As a result, many lenders waive fees, reduce their down payment requirements, discount their financing costs (for example, a $250 cash bonus applied to closing costs), approve loans for buyers with risky credit records, and often permit buyers to lock in their rate 30 days *before* closing instead of *at* closing.

Those Ugly Closing Costs

There is more to mortgages than the rate and how many years to borrow for. There are nasty, hidden fees—by the ton—that can put a big crimp in your pocketbook. The worst and most confusing are closing costs, the money you shell out when the loan becomes final. A recent bankrate.com survey shows that, on a $125,000 mortgage loan, you'll get nicked anywhere from $2,500 to $6,250, depending on the lender. For example, of the lender and broker fees, the cost for "administration" averages $413, but can range from the lowest, $45, to the highest, $725. That's a heckuva difference! Third-party fees, such as those for an appraisal, roam anywhere from $175 to $375, the average being $269. And when you get down to "government fees," for stuff like city, county, and state tax stamps, and/or intangible tax, the average is $558, but the highest can be $1,425 and the lowest, $50.

The time to investigate closing fees is well *before* you close on the house, not the last minute when the papers are signed. The key to not getting ripped off is to educate yourself in advance.

Determining Who Lends the Money

Lenders fall into one of three categories:

◆ **Financial Institutions, such as banks, thrifts, and credit unions.** Sometimes the institution offers the loan, sometimes it's a mortgage company owned by the institution. You can't tell the difference offhand in most cases; it's more a technicality than a real difference anyway. For example, if your bank directs you to a loan office somewhere else, you'll probably be dealing with a mortgage company owned by the bank. Provided the lender is legally licensed by the state, it doesn't make any difference anyway, because most lenders sell off their mortgages to a secondary market.

◆ **Mortgage companies.** The term may be loosely applied to an organization that specializes only in mortgages, or to a bank or thrift that has an affiliated mortgage company (hence the term "mortgage banker"). Mortgage companies can be big national outfits such as Countrywide Mortgage or Norwest, or small homegrown lenders. They make the same loans that banks make. Size isn't important, especially if you're getting a standard 30-year loan.

◆ **Mortgage brokers.** They're like mortgage bankers (although they are not connected with financial institutions), but they can be part of a national loan company. But there's an important distinction: *Brokers don't actually fund mortgage loans.* Instead, they put borrowers and lenders together. They call on a number of loan sources to arrange the best possible match. Brokers can be a great help if you've had past credit problems because they can locate lenders who will be more flexible than others.

Remember: No matter how charming the broker is, he or she is representing the seller of the mortgage, not the buyer. That's where they make their money. Because the lender and the broker sometimes split some of the fees you're charged on a mortgage, it shouldn't cost you any more to borrow through a broker.

The Road to Riches

Doing business at a bank where you have a checking account or another loan can be an advantage. Why? You may be able to apply at the same branch where people already know you. Plus, because you have the other accounts, the bank may discount your mortgage rate by (say) $1/4$ of a percentage point if you agree to have your monthly payments debited automatically from checking.

Should you choose one over the other? Not unless you have a special circumstance. If a bank will give you a better break because you're already a customer, that's good. If a mortgage banker will cut its rate to get your business, that's fine. And, if a broker can get you a loan when others have turned you down, that's even better.

No matter whom you do business with, you should always shop around for the best possible lender. When you talk to a bank or mortgage company, ask for references from other customers. In the case of mortgage brokers, talk to lenders the broker uses regularly. Those are your best references, nobody else.

How to Play the Mortgage "Lock-In" Game

Unpredictable mortgage rates can drive homebuyers batty. They nervously watch rates dance up and down, week after week. But knowing exactly when to lock in their rate is like a cross between playing Blind Man's Bluff and Las Vegas craps. Even the "experts" can't tell you how high or low rates will be a week or a month from today. So what do you do if you want the best possible rate on the day you're supposed to close?

If you believe rates will drop between now and the closing date, skip, postpone, or shorten the lock-in because you might cut a better deal later. If you think rates are going up, tell the lender you want to lock in the current, lower rate for a certain number of days (such as 30, 60, or 90). But it will cost you something in return.

As part of the game, the lender may tempt you with different rates and points for different lock-in periods. For an extra half-point or so, you might be guaranteed the current rate for a set number of days. For every $100,000 borrowed, that would cost the borrower $500. (Remember: A point is one one-hundredth of the loan amount.)

Watch Your Wallet

Be careful. Some lenders lock you in the day you apply for a loan. Others start the clock the day you receive your credit approval.

You say you'd rather gamble and save the $500? Consider what happened to a couple we know. Their builder promised them their new home would be ready in 45 days. So they skipped paying the $500 to lock in a lower rate for 60 days. Guess what. The builder didn't finish the house for 90 days. Meanwhile, mortgage rates climbed by more than a $1/2$ percent. That added thousands of dollars to the couple's total mortgage cost.

When you play the lock-in game, follow these rules:

◆ Lock in immediately when rates are rising. When they're falling, stall for as long as you can.

◆ Learn the lock-in choices and how much each one costs. In general, the longer the lock-in period, the higher the points. You may discover that the lender won't lock in the rate.

◆ Make sure the lock-in period is spelled out in a document provided by the lender. You will likely be required to sign this sheet. The document should explain what would happen to your rate if the lock-in expires before you close on the house purchase.

What happens when the lock-in expires? Your rate should then float up or down to the current rate at closing. Sometimes, if rates have fallen, you'll pay the original rate that was in effect when you applied for your loan. If rates have risen, you'll pay the new, higher rate.

The Road to Riches
Beware of lenders who drag their heels in processing your loan.
Bear down on your loan officer. You don't have to be a pest, but you should keep on top of your application. Call in regularly with questions about your loan status. Find out if the appraisal has been ordered, completed, and reviewed. Ask the loan officer if he or she needs any additional information from you. The appraisal could be mistakenly routed to someone else. A couple of phone calls can get things back on track. Each step of the way, note in writing what the lender tells you. Keep a complete record; give the loan officer a report each time you talk. That way the lender will know you're ahead of the game.

Paying Through the Nose in the Early Years

The way lenders calculate the payback on your mortgage loan, you get socked with tons of interest in the early years of the loan. Very little of your monthly payment amounts go toward your principal. It's not until the later years that your monthly payments begin to reduce the principal substantially.

Assuming a rising interest rate environment, let's say you borrow $100,000 for 30 years at a 7 percent fixed rate, with a monthly payment of $665. In the first five years, the picture looks like this:

The First Five Years of a Mortgage ($100,000 at 7 Percent for 30 Years)

Year	Principal Still Owed	Interest You've Paid	Principal You've Paid
1	$99,984	$1,016	$6,968
2	$97,895	$1,089	$6,894
3	$96,727	$1,168	$6,816
4	$95,475	$1,252	$6,731
5	$94,132	$1,343	$6,641

In other words, after five years of the 30-year loan, you've reduced your $100,000 principal by only $5,868 ($100,000 − $94,132), but have paid a total interest of $34,050 (the sum of the five numbers in the column headed "Interest You've Paid")! Yet you've been making a monthly payment of $665 all along.

The Road to Riches
The way the math works out, the higher the interest rate, the greater the amount of your early payments that go toward interest. Conversely, the lower the interest rate, the less the amount of early payments that go toward interest.

But as the loan gets older, more and more of your monthly payment will start being applied toward the principal, and less toward the interest. Use the example in the preceding table. Although it's not shown, by the time you get to the twentieth year, about the same amount will go toward the principal and the interest. In your final (thirtieth) year of the mortgage, you will have paid off the original $100,000 loan and paid a whopping $139,511 in interest. Your total payments for principal and interest will be an astronomical $239,511!

Paying Faster May Not Pay

There's something called a "biweekly mortgage" which can cut your costs dramatically—for a fee. Under this plan, you make twice-a-month payments instead of only monthly payments. That adds up to 26 biweekly payments a year, the equivalent of one extra month's payment a year. Eight of the 10 biggest mortgage lenders now offer the plan. But, in exchange for the opportunity to pay off your mortgage faster, you'll be charged an up front fee of about $300 plus a small biweekly administration fee. Some financial analysts protest that this is "unconscionable" because a) people shouldn't be charged for increasing their monthly payment, and b) most of the savings come far in the future, as inflation also takes its toll. Paying off your mortgage on a biweekly basis instead of monthly can save you a bundle. On a 7 percent, $100,000 loan of 30 years, for example, you'd save a total of $23,716 over the life of the mortgage.

The Road to Riches
You might consider getting a "prepayment penalty mortgage," offered by lenders who will reduce your interest rate if you promise not to pay off your loan balance in the first few years of the loan.

Others claim the way to go is to prepay your mortgage, say, by adding $50 to $100 to each monthly payment. It can save tens of thousands of dollars. Here's how: Say you have a $150,000, 30-year fixed-rate mortgage at 7.5 percent. If you pay $50 extra per month, you'll finish paying off the mortgage four years early, saving almost $40,000 in interest. Conceivably, after your tax deduction on the loan is figured in, the real cost of the loan will probably be less than 5 percent. On the other hand, if you were able to get a 15 percent return on your money from the stock market, it wouldn't pay you to dust off your mortgage early.

Identifying the Right Time to Refinance—You Could Save Thousands of $$$$$

Think seriously about refinancing your current mortgage when the new rate is at least 1 percentage point below the old rate. The opportunity exists when mortgage rates begin dropping in the shadow of a weakening economy. This enables millions of homeowners to reduce their monthly payment, slash thousands of dollars off the total cost of their loan, and even arrange "cash-out" refinancing if they want to pocket some extra money from the refinance. That's when you see long lines of homeowners crowding lenders' offices to fill out refinance applications.

How much can you save? Say you took out a $100,000 30-year mortgage two years ago when the average was 8.5 percent. Now your bank is offering 7.25 percent for a 30-year, with fees and charges—including points and closing costs—of about $2,500. This will reduce your monthly payment from $768.91 to $682.18 and shave $31,230 from the total interest cost over the life of the loan.

When you divide the cost ($2,500) by the amount you'll save each month ($86.73), it will take about 29 months to break even. After that, it's all gravy.

You'll save even more if you obtained your loan in the 1990s when the typical rate was 10.5 percent. On the same $100K loan for 30 years, the monthly savings work out to $232.56, total interest is slashed by $145,580, and you break even in only 20 months.

> **Tip #1:** "Tailored rates" are being used and help keep the rate you'll pay lower based on your credit score. The lender starts using your credit score to determine how good a risk you are. The higher the score, the lower the rate.

> **Tip #2:** The key to whether or not you should refinance depends on how long you plan to remain in your home. Generally, a refinance isn't worth it unless you plan to stay at least four or five years. If you are there less time than that, you could come out on the short end.

Watch Your Wallet _____

To protect themselves from homebuyers who default on their mortgages, lenders insist the buyer take out Private Mortgage Insurance (PMI) if they have less than 20 percent equity in the home. PMI normally adds between $20 and $100 to the monthly payment, or as much as $1,200 a year. But crafty lenders often didn't tell homeowners when their equity hit 20 percent, and PMI continued on and on.

Now by federal law, the lender must discontinue charging for PMI when the owner's equity reaches either 22 percent of either the original purchase price or the appraisal value at closing, whichever is lower.

Putting the Tax Savings in Your Pocket

The one bright side to the staggering cost of a mortgage is that you can deduct certain items on your personal tax returns. That will effectively reduce the cost of your mortgage. For the deductions, you should obtain the help of a professional tax consultant, who can also bring you up to date on the Taxpayers Relief Act of 1997. For one thing, it liberalized the tax benefits for people who had to sell their homes after living in them for less than two years.

The main tax deductions are …

♦ The interest costs that you pay per year on the loan.

♦ The points you pay at closing, but only in the year in which the loan is made.

♦ Your (the buyer's) prorated portion of items such as property taxes and other statements that are finalized at closing.

♦ State and local taxes that are associated with the loan.

Using the example from the preceding table (a 30-year, $100,000 loan at a 7 percent interest rate), assume you are in the 28 percent federal tax bracket. The following table shows you what you can deduct from your federal tax returns over the first five years.

What Uncle Sam Will Let You Deduct (28 Percent Tax Bracket— $100,000 at 7 Percent)

Year	Annual Interest Payment	Tax Savings Per Year	Your Net Cost After Deduction
1	$6,968	$1,951	$5,017
2	$6,895	$1,931	$4,964
3	$6,816	$1,908	$4,908
4	$6,732	$1,885	$4,847
5	$6,641	$1,859	$4,782

If you also deducted state and local taxes from these numbers, you'd be able to save even more. It gets a little complicated, but again, let's assume you're in the 28 percent federal tax bracket. When you factor in state and local taxes of 6 percent on top of the federal tax deduction, the formula comes out to a total deduction of 32.32 percent.

Your total payment in the first year, for the example in the table titled "What Uncle Sam Will Let You Deduct," is $7,984. Of that, $6,968 is interest. Multiply 32.32 percent by $6,968 and you arrive at a tax deduction of $2,252 for federal, state, and local taxes in the first year.

The Point Is, Points Add Up!

When they shop mortgages, many homebuyers look only at the interest rate, and forget to figure in the points as part of their total cost.

The true annual percentage rate (APR) on a loan should include the points as well as the rate. On the same type of loan, the greater the number of points, the higher the APR. Check out the following table to see how the points you pay can affect your APR on a $100,000 fixed-rate loan at 7 percent for 15 or 30 years.

What a 7 Percent Loan Really Costs

Points	APR (15 Years)	APR (30 Years)
1	7.16%	7.10%
2	7.33%	7.20%
3	7.49%	7.30%
4	7.66%	7.41%
5	7.83%	7.52%

With Reverse Mortgages, the House Is Paying You!

Did you know there's a way for folks age 62 and older to convert the equity in their homes to cash for anything they want? And, that none of the money has to be paid back until the homeowner moves or dies and leaves the home to their estate?

It's called a reverse mortgage, and it works just the opposite of a regular mortgage. Instead of taking out a loan and making monthly payments to pay back the principal and interest, the house pays the homeowner. He or she can get the money in the form of a lump sum, a line of credit, or monthly payments—all nontaxable, according to experts. It's a perfect way for elderly folks to get some badly-needed cash for medical bills and other living expenses.

Reverse mortgages have been around since the 1980s, but they've been slow to catch on for a couple of reasons. First, Americans have been brought up to believe that it's best to "own your home free and clear." Second, reverse mortgages are somewhat complicated. Today there are only about 150,000 reverse mortgages on the books, but analysts believe that in the next several years as many as one million senior homeowners will take advantage of such loans. Reason: Seniors' attitudes are changing. Instead of believing that they must leave their home to their heirs, increasingly they're concluding that their children can take care of themselves.

The mortgages are different than a straight home equity loan or line of credit. With home equity, the applicant must meet certain income and credit requirements, begin monthly payments immediately, and the home must have a first mortgage on it. Also, there's no restriction on the age of the borrower. By contrast, to get a reverse mortgage you must be 62 years or older, your home must be free and clear of debt or nearly so, and the house must be free of any tax liens. Some types of reverse mortgages allow fixed monthly payments to you for a specific period of time, or a combination of payments and a line of credit. The interest rate is usually an adjustable rate that changes monthly or yearly, but the amount of the payment doesn't change.

The size of the mortgage that someone can get depends on the type of mortgage, the person's age, the current interest rate, and the value of the house. The older the person, the larger the monthly payment or line of credit they can get. That's because the lender uses projected life expectancies to calculate the mortgage amount. One big thing in the homeowner's favor is that their income and credit record don't matter when they apply for a reverse mortgage. Their medical history makes no difference, and no one is going to make them submit to a doctor's check-up.

The lender is protected, no matter what. If the person moves, the lender gets paid back from proceeds from the sale of the house, or by their family or estate.

In general, the borrower can't be forced to sell their home to pay a reverse mortgage as long as they occupy the house, even if its value falls below the total amount of the monthly payments. To make sure that seniors understand the ins and outs of reverse mortgages, some lenders require that the borrower attend a personal counseling session—offered by banks, thrifts, and other lenders—before they can apply for a loan.

Basically, there are only three major players involved in reverse mortgage programs, and only several dozen lenders with whom they work:

- U.S. Department of Housing and Urban Development (HUD), whose program is called Home Equity Conversion Mortgage (HECM).

- Fannie Mae, a government-chartered corporation that buys mortgages from banks and mortgage companies, which offers a Home Keeper reverse mortgage.

- A private company, Financial Freedom Senior Funding Corp, in Irvine, California, which offers its program through affiliate lenders in a limited number of western states.

You can find out more about reverse mortgages at www.reversemortgage.org, a site maintained by the National Reverse Mortgage Lenders Association in Washington, D.C. Then go to HUD's website at www.reverse.org, which even includes calculators where you can figure how much cash you could get from a reverse mortgage and what it will cost. Lastly, call HECM at 1-800-247-6553 for a free copy of *Reverse Mortgages for Beginners*.

Buying a house is stressful, but you can make the process easier and get the best deal possible on your mortgage or refinancing by planning ahead and knowing all of your options.

The Least You Need to Know

- A fixed-rate is best when interest rates are low; ARMs are generally a better deal if you don't have extra money to cover a big down payment and high closing costs, or if you only plan to remain in the house for less than four years.

- The easy way to shop for the best mortgage is to ask a half-dozen different lenders for the total *dollar costs* of their up front charges, finance cost over the first five years, and closing costs including points. Then add those three numbers for each lender.

- The Annual Percentage Rate (APR) is a good way to compare mortgage deals, apples to apples, because it includes fees and charges in addition to the rate.

◆ You can really negotiate better rates and fees with many lenders, particularly if your loan is preapproved.

◆ You should make sure your credit is in order at least six months before you apply for a mortgage.

◆ Reverse mortgages are a great way for senior citizens to easily get cash out of their home on a steady basis, to help them with living expenses.

Chapter 16

How You Can Win—Or Lose—with Home Equity Borrowing

In This Chapter

- ◆ How home equity loans can consolidate debts at cheaper rates
- ◆ Which type of home equity loan is best for you
- ◆ Why you should beware of low rate offers
- ◆ Tricks and traps your lender won't tell you
- ◆ How to figure the real cost of your loan
- ◆ How to be aware of scam operators pushing home equity

You see their commercials by the hundreds on TV. They advertise a "quick, easy way to get rid of your credit card debt" by borrowing money against your house. They're called home equity loans—which are like second mortgages—and home equity lines of credit, which work like a credit card. In the latter case, thousands of dollars are put into a reserve account that you can tap into whenever you want.

Looks good, sounds good. After all, an average 6.8 percent home equity rate beats the pants off those 18 and 19 percent credit card rates—plus, the interest on most home equity loans is tax-deductible. Yet the average borrower is in hock to the tune of $30,000 on these kinds of loans.

Little wonder that home equity is the banks' hottest product these days. Over the past decade, when home equity loans amounted to $34 billion, the figure skyrocketed to $500 billion just four years ago. In fact, up to four million Americans a year now take out a home equity loan to pay off 100 percent of what they owe on credit cards. Why not? After all, it looks like the greatest deal that ever came down the pike, because the interest rate on these loans is much less than it is on credit cards. Getting their hands on a slug of fast cash could sure help many debt-riddled consumers out of their jam. But there are dangers and traps galore. This chapter explains what they are, and guides you so you won't trip up and make the biggest mistake of your life.

> **The Road to Riches**
>
> Get your credit record in order before you apply for a home equity loan or line of credit. Despite the fact that the bank will hold a piece of your house until you repay the loan, it's still going to be nosey about your income, other debts, job, credit payment history, and so on.

Home Equity in a Nutshell: Your Nest Egg Is on the Line

With a home equity loan, you're putting the biggest asset of your life—your house—on the line by borrowing against the amount of equity you have in the home. The bank either gives you one lump sum of money (a "closed-end" term loan), or it sets the money aside for you in a reserve account (called a home equity line of credit that you can use at any time. You may access the funds by credit card, check, ATM, or even by phone. Your interest rate will be cheap—only 6 percent on average, versus the 18 percent or higher that your credit cards are probably costing you. But unlike borrowing with a credit card or taking out an auto loan, you'll be able to deduct 100 percent of the home equity interest from your taxes, up to $100,000. But you have to pay the money back. If you don't, the bank can foreclose on your house. What you've really done with a home equity loan is hock the farm. Hence, for the unsuspecting home owner, the loan can be a time bomb that one day could explode in their face. Instead of having one big debt (your credit cards), you could wind up with two giant debts (the cards plus your house). So before you jump at this kind of borrowing, you mustn't just think about the big benefits, but also of the possibly terrible consequences.

"The problem," says Cara Smith, housing specialist with Consumer Credit Counseling Service in Fort Worth, Texas. "is that about 60 percent of all home equity borrowers don't cut up their credit cards and close other lines of credit when they get their home equity loan. They go right on charging with their cards and wind up way over their heads in debt."

The Money Line

How do borrowers use their equity money? It breaks down like this: Debt consolidation, 40 percent; home improvement, 29 percent; automobile, 7 percent; education, 6 percent; major purchase, 3 percent; business expense, 2 percent; medical, tax payment, and vacation, 1 percent each; and other or "don't know," 10 percent.

Source: McIntire School of Commerce—University of Virginia

Experts suggest that before you go on a home-equity binge, you should first speak with your professional tax advisor. They advise to shop at least three lenders, make sure you understand every nickel and dime of costs, know everything that's included in the annual percentage rate instead of just noticing the advertised rate, and to be leery of introductory "teaser" rates that soar after the loan is only six or nine months old. Some home equity promotions, particularly from California lenders, have been nothing more than "flim-flams," reported one credit counselor.

Why Banks Love Home Equity Loans

Home equity lines of credit (HELOCs, for short) are the banks' darlings because they're collateralized loans. In case you default, the institution has something of value, your house. Also HELOCs are bigger loans than, say, the piddling $3,000 loan on which the bank makes less money. It takes a lot of those little loan customers to equal what a bank can make off a single home equity customer. Plus these borrowers tend to be more upscale than people with lower incomes who don't own a home.

No wonder every time you turn your head you see a bank hustling HELOCs. Because competition among banks and finance companies is so fierce, they're all wheeling and dealing to get your business. Many are even waiving up-front fees and closing costs.

How a Home Equity Loan Works

Say you still owe $25,000 on your mortgage, and appraisers figure that the market value of the house is $125,000. Subtract what you owe from what the house is worth to get your equity; in this case $100,000. That's your "loan-to-value" figure, or LTV. Let's say that Famous Finance Company offers to lend you up to 80 percent of that amount. Get the calculator out. Wow! That means you can get your hands on as much as $80,000!

Think that's impressive? The plot gets thicker: Now lenders are offering loans of up to 125 percent of the value of your home! In other words, on a $200,000 house with a $175,000 first mortgage, you'd get a $75,000 equity loan. (Your two loans would total $250,000, which is 125 percent of what the house is worth.) Hopefully you're not foolish enough to borrow that much without being sure you can pay the money back, because you'll be, as they say in the trade, "upside down" (owing more than the house is worth). Unless you have a steady source of income, the two payments could strangle you.

What does Famous Finance require from you before it hands over the money? Some collateral, such as a lien that gives the bank ownership of your house in case you default. That's right. If you can't pay the bank back, it can grab the home that you busted your hump for all your life. Welcome to the dangerous, fast-growing world of home equity borrowing.

> **The Road to Riches**
>
> What's better—refinancing or home equity? Better check. It might be cheaper to get a home equity loan or line of credit than refinancing your present mortgage and also taking out some cash. For one thing, the closing costs on home equity may be cheaper, plus, there's an outside chance the interest rate might be lower, as well. Do some shopping and compare.

Type A and Type B

Your friends at Famous Finance will lend you the money one of two ways: A *home equity loan* or a *home equity line of credit*. If you take a plain home equity loan, it will usually lend you at least 80 or 90 percent of your equity in your house; or, in some cases, as much as the 125 percent LTV we mentioned earlier. You get the money all at once and make fixed monthly payments, just like paying back a second mortgage. Just be aware that if you opt for an LTV, you could wind up with more debt than the house is worth.

But if you take a home equity line of credit, Famous Finance will give you a credit line in the same amount, which works like a revolving credit card account. As you pay back the amount, you're rebuilding the credit line so you can keep borrowing from it.

In effect, the credit line works like a giant credit card. You access the amount you need, whenever you need it, simply by using your credit card, writing a check against the account, or getting the money from an ATM. Typically, a home equity line is for 5 to 15 years, versus a standard mortgage loan of 30 or 15 years. By having access to the money when you need it, you don't have to keep going back to the bank and re-applying for loans.

The big downside is that with either type of home equity loan, you're not only robbing your nest egg, you're also swapping short-term debt for long-term debt.

How One Family Blew It

Here's a lesson on how *not* to handle your financial life after you take out a home equity loan. It's the sad, painful story of Tom and Marla:

> They bought a home a few years ago for $100,000 with 5 percent down. They borrowed $95,000 at 7.5 percent for a monthly payment of $654. Their mortgage balance was $93,180. The home value had appreciated by 5 percent per year to $110,000, and the equity in their home grew to $17,000.
>
> The couple bought a new car three years ago, for which they financed $18,000 at 8 percent for a monthly payment of $440. The loan balance had subsequently been reduced to $14,000. Tom and Marla carried a credit card balance of $8,000, at 18 percent, for an annual interest cost of $1,440 ($120 per month plus paying off 2 percent of the balance every month, for a total of $280 per month).
>
> They needed $5,000 per year for the next four years for their child's college education. At this point, their monthly obligations, counting a $416 college payment, came to $1,800, against total monthly family income of $4,167 ($50,000 a year). Tom contacted a finance company that agreed to give them a 125 percent loan, which amounted to $42,000. That reduced their monthly payment on debts to $440, a drop of about $700 from the earlier figure of $1,136.
>
> But now, two years later:

- The balance on the home equity loan is $39,320.

- Credit card balances are back up to $5,000, with a minimum monthly payment of 2 percent of the balance plus interest at 18 percent, for a total of $175.

- Total family debt has risen to $44,000, and monthly payments other than the mortgage have increased to $615 from $440.

◆ The only good news is that, counting the mortgage payment, total monthly payments are $1,280, which is *less* than the $1,800 per month the family was paying before. But the family is *now more in debt than before they got the home equity loan!*

How Another Family Got Hit by a Balloon

You think Tom and Marla's case is bad? Check what happened to another couple, Jim and Jane. They borrowed $20,000 via a home equity loan for five years at 8 percent interest. They can't afford a $600 per month payment, so what does the bank do? It offers them a balloon payment deal.

Watch Your Wallet

Some banks hide in small print the fact that they have a "base rate" on variable-rate loans. This sets a floor below which your rate will never go, regardless of what happens. For example, if the base rate is 7 percent and the bank's prime rate plunges so low that your loan rate should be 5 percent, you'll still pay the floor rate of 7 percent!

All Jim and Jane have to do is pay the interest on the loan every month; they don't have to pay on the principal (the $20,000) until the very end of the five years. Then, BOOM! They must pay the $20,000 all at once—just like a balloon being inflated. But suppose they can't come up with the $20 grand? They'll lose their home to the bank. Goodbye American dream!

On a $20,000 loan, at 10 percent interest for five years, the loan will cost them a staggering $10,000 if they only pay back the interest over that period. They'll still owe the $20,000 principal after the five years are up. In other words, they'll have to pay back $30,000.

Right at this moment, millions of consumers who've taken out home equity loans are caught in that trap. They're like time bombs waiting to go off. Assuming their credit is still okay five years from now, Jim and Jane could roll the first loan over into a new loan at the same bank. But that would only cost them more interest on top of the outrageous $10,000 in interest they've already paid.

However, balloon payments aren't a threat if you plan to sell your house before the loan matures. You could pay the loan off with the proceeds from the sale.

The Interest Adds Up

A home equity line of credit is a revolving account. Money goes out, money comes in; that's how the account revolves.

Your monthly payment is generally 2 percent of the total P&I (principal and interest) you owe. If the amount you borrow over a year (P) is $5,000 and your interest rate

(I) is 10 percent, the interest is $500. Therefore, the total P&I is $5,500. Two percent of that is $110, so that would be your monthly payment.

Fixed vs. Variable Rates, and the "Introductory" Teaser Rate Come-On

The interest rate you pay is critical because it could knock your wallet for a loop. With a fixed rate, you lock in your cost over the full life of the loan. The rate won't ever change and you'll know your costs in advance. With a variable rate, the rate can go up or down according to whatever "index" the bank ties the rate to.

Most home equity lines charge a variable rate that's based on the bank's prime rate plus anywhere from 1 to 3 percentage points. If the prime is 6 percent and the rate is prime plus 2 percent, then you'll pay an indexed rate of 8 percent.

Now, here's where the sneaky ploy comes in:

> Just about every bank in the land uses artificially low introductory "teaser" rates to get you in the door. For example, Megabuck Bank might feature a giant 7 percent rate in a newspaper ad or in the bank's lobby. However, the fine print at the bottom of the ad says, "Seven percent introductory rate is only good for the first six months, after which the rate will revert to Megabuck's prime rate in effect at that time, plus 2 percentage points." Translation: If you take this loan at 7 percent on July 1, next January 1 your real home equity loan rate will jump to 9 percent. Big difference? You bet. The interest cost on a $10,000 loan could increase by a couple hundred dollars.

> **The Road to Riches**
>
> Never borrow on home equity without finding out for how long the rate is good and what the real rate will be after the introductory period.

> **The Road to Riches**
>
> If you're not sure about your future job security, it might be better to get a home equity loan or line of credit now, while you still qualify. Then, if you get laid off, you'll be better able to pay off high-rate credit cards. Chapter 18 can also help you set up a financial emergency plan in case of job loss.

Keep these tips in mind when playing the rate game:

◆ Realize that, often, the more money you borrow, the lower your starting rate will be.

◆ Avoid variable-rate loans or lines at all costs when interest rates are rising. Get a fixed-rate loan instead. That will tell you your cost from Day One until the loan is paid off. But when rates are falling or you don't think they'll rise soon, you should go with the variable rate.

The Road to Riches

If you opened a home equity loan several years ago and interest rates have declined in the meantime, try to renegotiate a lower rate with your lender.

The Money Line

Some experts believe you should get a regular home equity loan instead of a line of credit because your payments will be locked in when you sign for the loan. The rate will be carved in stone, as opposed to fluctuating payments on an equity line, which depends on how much credit you use.

- Stay away from variable rates when you borrow for a longer term, such as 10 or 15 years.

- Understand that you can keep your monthly payment budget intact in a rising-rate environment by asking the bank to stretch the number of months to repay the money or by asking the bank to lower the payment, or both. However, remember that the longer you have the loan, the more interest you'll pay.

- If you're considering a variable rate, tell them you want to be able to switch to the future current fixed rate in the event that interest rates start shooting up. Some lenders will allow you to convert to a fixed rate once or twice during the loan term without paying any extra fees.

- Most variable rates have a cap (a maximum amount, or ceiling) that the rate can rise to. Be sure to ask what that is.

Pros and Cons of Home Equity Loans

Taking out a home equity loan isn't all bad. Consider these advantages:

- It's cheap. Six percent beats 18 percent credit card rates any day. Plus, you can try to negotiate an even cheaper rate with the lender.

- The interest can be 100 percent tax-deductible for up to $100,000.

- It's a fast way to get your hands on a good sum of cash to consolidate your debts at a lower cost, or for urgent big-ticket items such medical bills and tuition. For example, if you owe $5,000 on credit cards at 18 percent interest, and you take out a $5,000 home equity loan at 6 percent to pay them off, you've chopped your financing cost by more than half.

- You can pay back only the interest on the loan for several years or until it matures (such as in 10 years). Banks are flexible on this, but there's a built-in booby trap, as you'll discover in this chapter.

Before you dash off to the bank to get your home equity loan, keep in mind that a home equity loan isn't for frivolous folks. It's for disciplined people who will use the money wisely (not for vacations, second honeymoons, or a wild spending spree in Las Vegas). In other words, the rabbit should not go near the lettuce. You should not take out such a loan unless you are 100 percent certain you will be able to repay it on time.

There are some downsides of this type of loan:

- It reduces or eliminates your equity in your home.

- Your total cost over the life of the loan can be expensive.

- The amount you owe on the loan stays the same even if the value of your house depreciates.

- The bank can grab your house if you don't pay back the money on time. That's called a foreclosure. In fact, if you use home equity loan proceeds to buy a car and don't make the payments, they may take the house instead of the car.

- The biggest danger is that borrowers won't discipline their spending habits after paying off their debts, and get in over their heads all over again.

> **The Road to Riches**
>
> If you only need a small amount of cash for two or three years, a home equity loan probably isn't the answer. You'll be better off with a regular short-term, fixed-rate loan.

They Make It S-o-o-o-o Easy

Banks keep giving you more ways to access the money in your home equity credit line. Besides issuing you a bunch of checks to tap into the cash, some let you use your credit card or let you access the credit line by telephone or an ATM. Why?

Those cunning outfits don't make a dime off you unless you actually *use* the cash available in your account. That's why many of them charge an "inactivity fee" if you don't touch any of the money within a year's time. The fee could be anywhere from $50 to $150. (When was the last time anyone ever billed you for doing nothing?)

Other banks require that you borrow a minimum, such as $300 each time you draw on the equity line. Others will insist that you take an initial cash advance when you first set up the line to get your debt rolling—a foxy move on the bank's part.

Right at this moment, millions of consumers who've taken out home equity loans are caught in that trap. The loans are like time bombs waiting to go off. However, balloon payments aren't a threat if you plan to sell your house before the loan matures. You could pay the loan off with the proceeds from the sale. Whatever strategy you use, always figure out the final bottom-line cost in dollars and cents, not percent.

Fee-Fi-Fo-Fum ... but Mostly Scads of Fees

Fees range all over the lot, regardless of whether you're getting a straight home equity loan (a lump sum all at once) or a home equity line of credit so you can write checks for what you need.

But it all boils down to this: The bank or finance company charges you what it wants to charge you, and the numbers vary greatly. We've heard of closing costs, alone, running from $150 to $1,000. Some lenders will waive points (a point is one-hundredth of the total loan amount, or $10 for every $1,000 you borrow). Others will charge between one and three points.

On the straight home equity loan, fees could total a few thousand dollars for credit checks, appraisal fees, legal fees, title insurance, and closing costs when the loan is finalized. Always ask the bank these three questions before you take out the loan:

- What are my up-front fees and charges, including property appraisal, application fee, closing costs, points, annual maintenance fee, transaction fee, cancellation fee, and "inactivity fee" (in case you don't use your credit line within, say, six months)?

- What is my total financing cost (the dollar amount on the loan)? *Tip:* Some lenders will agree to lower your interest rate by $1/4$ to $1/2$ of a percent if you make your payments electronically instead of by mail.

- Will the lender agree to waive closing costs or any of the fees?

Get those amounts in dollars and cents, not percent. Then sit down and ask yourself questions like: For how long will I need the money? How will I be able to pay off the loan? How much can I handle in monthly payments? After getting the loan, can I fight off the temptation to run up my credit card bills? (Incidentally, most lenders won't let you borrow on home equity if your monthly payments exceed 28 percent of your gross monthly income.)

We know a couple who thought they were breezing through a home equity loan, only to discover that their total fees (not even including the interest) came to $6,000!

On home equity lines of credit, the fees can be a lot less. Because banks are fighting their competition with brass knuckles for new home equity customers, many will waive their fees and closing costs. You'll see lots of "no-fee" deals in ads. Others will waive their annual fee in the first year and start charging you in the second year. A few will even offer you a cash bonus of $100 or $200 (added to your credit line) to get your account.

A fixed-rate home equity line is rare, but if you find one, there could be extra fees and formulas, such as a $75 "finance charge." Or the fee could vary depending on the amount of your credit line and/or the bank's rate formula that's tied to its prime rate. For example, you might get a loan with no fee if your line is more than $20,000, or, if you borrow less than $20,000, but agree to a rate of the prime plus 2 percent. Or you might pay a $200 fee if you choose to pay the prime rate plus 1.5 percent. It's not much different than the mortgage game: If you get a low rate and cheap fees, they'll take it out of your hide by charging higher points.

Home Equity Scam Operators

Be leery if someone comes knocking at your door and says his company will build you a new room, or put new siding on your house, and all you have to do is take out a home equity loan to pay for it. The Federal Trade Commission has caught a lot of these guys preying on homeowners—particularly the elderly, minorities, and those with low incomes or poor credit.

You could wind up owing tens of thousands of dollars more than what you thought you signed up for, and lose your home. The scam operator may encourage you to "pad" your income on the application to get the loan approved, or may leave blank spaces on the application, which he falsely fills in later. Or he may offer to help you find financing, but request that you first deed your property to him, claiming that it's a temporary step to prevent foreclosure. Once the lender has the deed to your property, he may borrow against it or even sell it. You could wind up on the street!

The FTC has case after case where people lost their homes—or went bankrupt after paying through the nose—to scam lenders who stripped them of their assets. One woman was conned into taking out four successive loans, each one bigger than the other, until she couldn't make her payments and the lender foreclosed on her house. The trick is that these con artists keep pressuring the victim to refinance the loan, over and over again—a process called "flipping." For an important consumer fact sheet on how to avoid these home equity schemes, write to: FTC, Bureau of Consumer Protection, 6th & Pennsylvania Avenue N.W., Washington, D.C. 20580. Or find the FTC on the Internet at www.ftc.gov.

The Least You Need to Know

- Don't borrow what you don't need and can't pay back.
- Always read the fine print in the ads and in your contract and ask if anything isn't absolutely clear to you.

- Don't be dazzled by gimmick rates and freebies when you shop for a loan.

- Don't get tricked by low-ball rates—almost every bank uses this tactic in its advertising.

- Always ask for total costs in *dollars and cents*, not percent.

- Beware of scam operators, especially those on e-mail, who falsify contracts and are out to steal your house from you.

Chapter 17

Protect Your Credit— and Your Privacy— Before It's Too Late!

In This Chapter

- ◆ How your personal identity can be easily ripped off by thieves
- ◆ Why you could lose thousands of dollars—and take years to fix the problem
- ◆ How banks and credit bureaus peddle your private data to anyone who wants it
- ◆ Why the government isn't fully protecting you—yet
- ◆ Why your Social Security number (SSN) is thieves' #1 target
- ◆ Steps to take if you've been ripped off or have become an ID theft victim

The most explosive, hot button issue in the entire personal financial world right now is *privacy*—the right to protect yourself from prying eyes, identity thieves, and companies that want to know your every move. In fact, a

Wall Street Journal poll found that the number one concern of those surveyed was privacy, outranking even terrorism, education, and other burning issues. An AARP poll showed that four out of five consumers opposed corporations internally sharing their customers' data with affiliates. And the Federal Trade Commission reported that 92 percent of households don't trust online companies to keep their personal information confidential.

In 2003 alone, one study estimated that 10 million consumers were victims of identity theft at a cost of nearly $50 billion to those who got ripped off. How can someone swipe your identity? Easily. Anything from stealing your wallet to fishing your last bank statement out of a dumpster.

Identity Theft Is Rampant

The statistics are shocking. The number of Americans whose identities—Social Security numbers, credit cards, drivers' licenses, and bank accounts—have been stolen has soared to the 10 million figure. It's the fastest-growing financial crime in America. The losses to individuals and institutions have been staggering, rising from $442 million in 1995 to nearly $50 billion currently. The typical ID theft victim spends two years trying to remove $18,000 in fraudulent charges from their credit reports. And, those who haven't yet settled their cases have been dealing with the problem for an average of 44 months!

Worse, some families have been taken for many more thousands of dollars. Plus identity theft has even resulted in women being stalked and murdered. One example comes from retired Air Force Lt. Col. John T. Stevens Jr., and his wife, Mary Elizabeth. After a crook swiped their Social Security numbers, they lost their good credit rating, were refused loans, incurred $6,000 in legal bills, and spent three years trying to get their good names back. They discovered they had 33 fraudulent accounts totaling $113,000 on their credit cards. And the battle still isn't over.

Your Money and Your Life

The mother of a 20-year-old New Hampshire woman who was killed by a stalker filed suit against a Florida research company that offers detailed information, pulled from public records, about a person's life, including driving record, bank accounts, bankruptcies, criminal records, civil suits, and property records. The stalker paid $204 to the research firm to obtain the victim's birthday, her Social Security number, her whereabouts, and her place of employment. The woman was murdered outside her employer's office. In California, a Hollywood starlet was murdered after the state sold her driver's license records to a stalker.

Everything Is up for Grabs or for Sale—You Name It

As big financial institutions and insurance companies merge and share each other's information about customers, and as e-commerce technology continues to break down barriers, your privacy is going down the tubes. Credit bureaus sell your confidential financial info to big marketers. Banks peddle it for big commissions. Manufacturers keep tabs on your Internet habits to know what to try to sell you. You might get fingerprinted when you cash somebody else's check at Megabuck Bank. And every time you open a bank account, write a check, apply for a mortgage, or apply for auto, life, or health insurance, your movements are recorded by giant databases that make your life a vulnerable open book, which almost anyone can access.

Some other examples of how your private information may be shared include:

♦ A bank might turn you down for a loan because it found out, through its insurance affiliate that accesses Medical Information Bureau records, that you had a grave illness five years ago.

♦ A bank sells a financial disclosure statement to one of their borrower's employer, who then fires the employee because of his history (but they have to indicate the *reason* for the firing).

♦ A telephone company sells a list of calls to an extortionist who analyzes the pattern of calls, then blackmails the owner of the phone.

♦ A company's database is hacked or stolen and the information sold to individuals or companies for marketing or ID theft purposes.

Those aren't make-believe horror stories, they really happen, and it's up to you— no one else—to protect your personal and financial life. But, it's not easy.

Isn't *Somebody* Doing Something to Protect You?

There's been some movement to guard your privacy, but most of it is coming from state governments, not Uncle Sam. California, for example, prevents any person accepting a credit card payment from writing or recording the cardholder's personal information such as the address, phone number, and Social Security number. But they can ask to see the customer's driver's license or another form of photo ID. Also since 2001 California retailers are no longer allowed to imprint the cardholder's entire card number or expiration date on their retail receipt; only the last four digits of the number.

The attorneys general of 20 states are investigating financial outfits for messing with consumers' privacy. Ten states have proposed tougher privacy laws, and more states will probably do so as well.

Major protection almost came about—but not quite—when, after the federal government passed the Financial Services Modernization Act, a companion bill would have prevented anyone—had the bill passed—from using false or stolen information to get customer information. A byproduct of the legislation also required financial companies to contact their millions of customers, giving them a chance to "opt in" or "opt out" of letting companies peddle consumer data to other organizations. But alas, the mailings were so confusing (on purpose?) that less than 1 percent of consumers responded.

Don't give up hope. As this book is being written, President George W. Bush signed a new federal law creating a two-year prison sentence for anyone found guilty of stealing someone's identity. The sentence jumps to five years if the theft is involved with a terrorist act. Meanwhile, several U.S. senators and Congressmen have proposed laws that would stop companies and individuals from selling SSNs to other parties, and slap criminal and civil penalties on anyone who misuses SSNs.

Your Social Security Number—The Heartbeat of Your Privacy

Nowadays, when you visit a doctor's office or buy something in a store, they're apt to ask you for your Social Security number. Bullfeathers. Tell them no, and if they don't like it, take your business elsewhere.

SSNs were created in 1935 for the sole purpose of tracking a worker's earnings to calculate Social Security benefits. But they've become part of business and government culture everywhere. By law, the only people you *must* give your SSN to are the Internal Revenue Service and other government tax and welfare departments, and state motor vehicle divisions. Under the Federal Privacy Act of 1994, all other government agencies are required to tell you why your SSN is necessary, whether giving your SSN is mandatory or voluntary, and how your SSN will be used. Sure, it's tough to say no when the other guy has you over a barrel, but don't give your SSN to anybody else, period.

Fiscal Facts _____

Social Security numbers are pretty much public information. If an identity thief needs to know someone's SSN, it's easy enough to buy it on the Internet. One website, in fact, will retrieve a person's SSN in one day for $49. SSNs matched with other personal information enables ID thieves to apply for credit cards on the Internet with minimum security from issuers. Shopping on the Internet with such credit cards then becomes duck soup because the transactions are not face-to-face. Then, if the thief builds up a credit history by paying off monthly bills, he or she has the credibility to apply for big ticket items such as loans for cars and real estate property.

Here's a tip: If the outfit insists on an identifier, try giving them just the last four digits of your SSN or suggesting they come up with another identifying number. This problem especially dogs seniors on Medicare, whose ID number on their card is the same as their SSN. Try making a copy of your Medicare card after you first cover up the number, and give out your SSN verbally when you have to.

How to Say "No" Politely

Let's say a department store clerk bugs you for your Social Security number. Here's what to do, advises one privacy expert:

- ◆ Politely explain your position and request the store's cooperation.

- ◆ Talk to someone higher up in the organization.

- ◆ If necessary, threaten to complain to the local or state consumer affairs bureau.

- ◆ Insist they show you the store's corporate policy requiring your SSN.

- ◆ Ask what they need your SSN for and suggest alternatives. What else would it take to satisfy them?

- ◆ Tell them you'll take your business elsewhere.

Watch Your Wallet _____

More than 290 million Americans currently have Social Security numbers. According to the FTC, SSNs are a principal component used by crooks to commit identity theft, the fastest growing financial crime in the country. A September 2003 FTC survey shows the average amount of loss victims reported was $4,800, and they spent almost 30 hours trying to resolve their problems.

Actual losses to individuals and institutions from identity theft tallies $47.6 billion, according to a Federal Trade Commission report on identity theft. More than 75 percent of identity theft crimes involve victims of "true name" fraud. This occurs when someone uses the SSN to open new accounts in the victim's name. Victims spent an average of 175 hours and $808 in out-of-pocket costs (not including lawyer's fees) trying to fix the problem.

Identity Theft Is Everywhere

These are the most common types of ID theft complaints reported by consumers:

- **Credit card fraud.** Forty-seven percent of consumers said somebody opened a credit card account in their name, or unauthorized charges were placed on the card.

- **Unauthorized phone or utility services.** Twenty-two percent reported that the thief had established new telephone, cellular, or other utility service in their name.

- **Bank fraud.** Fifteen percent said that a new bank account had been opened in their name.

- **Fraudulent loans.** Eight percent reported that the ID thief had obtained a personal, business, auto, or real estate loan in their name.

- **Government documents or benefits.** Eight percent said the thief had obtained either of these in their name.

- **Other identity theft.** This includes misuse of the victim's personal information to gain employment or medical services, evade legal problems, open or access Internet accounts, declare bankruptcy, lease residences, and purchase or trade in investments and securities.

- **Multiple types of theft.** About half of all consumers reported that they got stung by more than one of the previous types of ID theft. There's also a 20 percent chance that the thief will write fraudulent checks or make unauthorized withdrawals, and a 10 percent chance they'll get a loan in your name.

Frightened? You should be, but you should also be aware that you can do things to help avoid becoming yet another victim of identity theft. Here are some ways to protect your privacy and your identity:

- Don't give your SSN to anyone over the phone.

- "Opt out" of consumer mailing lists: Call credit card bureaus, magazines, and direct marketing trade organizations and tell them to drop your name from their mailing lists. (To opt out of all three credit bureaus, call 1-888-5OPTOUT.)

- When discarding pay stubs, credit card receipts, and other such documents, cross out the parts that contain your SSN or other identifying information.

- Stop filling out "warranty registration cards." Their sole purpose is to collect personal information about you. Your sales receipt is all you need to ensure that whatever you've purchased is covered by a warranty.

What to Do If You've Already Been Victimized

If you fear that your SSN has already been misused, you can check your Social Security earnings record. Call the Administration's toll-free number at 1-800-772-1213, and ask for a "Request for a Personal Earnings and Benefit Statement" (Form 7004). You also can download an application from the Internet at www.ssa.gov or visit your local Social Security office. If you find too many or too few earnings, or your name or date of birth is incorrect, report the error. The Social Security Administration will fix it.

Suppose the ID Thief Creates a Credit Problem

If your SSN has been misused by someone to get credit, the *Social Security Administration cannot fix your credit record.* You need to contact the institution that approved the credit as well as the following major credit reporting agencies, including the fraud department within each bureau:

- Equifax (1-800-525-6285)

- Experian (1-800-301-7195)

- Trans Union (1-800-680-7289)

When retired Air Force Lt. Col. Stevens and his wife (mentioned earlier in this chapter) testified before Congress on ID theft in 2001, they recounted how they had been victimized by 33 different fraud accounts totaling more than $113,000. Dealing with 15 collection agencies, it took them years—at great cost—to correct their huge problems. But, what they learned enabled them to give expert advice to anyone else falling into a horrible ID theft predicament. The following list contains part of their excellent Congressional testimony in which they told other victims what to do:

- Get copies of your credit report from all three credit bureaus (see Chapter 12 for a number of ways to get your credit reports.

- Inform the bureaus of the fraud accounts. If there are a large number, insist on being assigned one person to work with. This eliminates having to repeat the same information to every different person who happens to answer the phone.

- Don't fall for their "reinvestigation" promise. A reinvestigation consists of asking their customer who opened the account if the information is correct. Of course it is; they accepted the form that opened the account.

- Track down and contact the creditor listed in the credit report. Obtain the name of the individual you can use as your contact. Send them a sworn affidavit that you are not the person who opened the account. Have them submit a statement to the credit bureaus clearing you from fraud on the account. Ask for a copy of the statement.

- Demand a copy of the application that opened the account. You are entitled to it because you are the person being accused of opening the account. Do not send an affidavit until you receive a copy of the application. You can then point out the false information in the application.

- Do not accept a creditor or collection agency offer to settle the account for a reduced amount. If you do, the bad credit is now a permanent part of your credit report for up to seven years. This is a high price to pay to get rid of their nasty letters and phone calls.

- Constantly check your credit reports. Look for any accounts that do not belong to you and immediately challenge them. Pay specific attention to the "inquiry" section. This is a list of creditors checking your records for granting credit or for promotional purposes. This is usually your first clue that someone is trying to open an account in your name.

- Have the credit bureaus put a "fraud alert" in your report. This requires any creditor opening an account in your name to contact you and verify that you are the person making the application.

- Be prepared for a long and frustrating battle. Stand your ground and don't let them intimidate you. Point out that *they* have a problem. Use the application to point out their negligence in not properly verifying the information they accepted to open the account.

To the Steven's list we might add ...

♦ Report the crime to police immediately. Get a copy of the police report.

♦ Notify your bank(s) of the theft.

♦ If you use an ATM card for banking services, get a new card, account number, and password.

♦ Get a new card, account number, and password if you have had checks stolen or bank accounts set up fraudulently, report it to TeleCheck (1-800-710-9898) and Equifax.

♦ Notify the Postal Inspector if you suspect mail theft. Theft of mail is a felony.

♦ Call your telephone, electrical, gas and water utilities. Also contact your long distance company.

♦ Consider seeking legal counsel.

Watch Your Wallet _____

Immediately contact all three credit bureau agencies if you are a victim of identity theft:

♦ Equifax Credit Information Services, Inc.
  1-800-525-6285 (Hearing impaired call 1-800-255-0056)
  PO Box 740241, Atlanta, GA 30374-0241
  www.equifax.com

♦ Experian Information Solutions, Inc.
  1-888- 397-3742/ TDD 1-800-972-0322
  PO Box 9530, Allen, TX 75013
  www.experian.com

♦ TransUnion
  1-800-680-7289/ TDD 1-877-553-7803
  Fraud Victim Assistance Division
  PO Box 6790, Fullerton, CA 92634-6790
  www.tuc.com

The earlier you find out about any identity theft, the less time the thief will have to perpetrate more crimes and do further damage to your credit and good name. That's why it's so important for you to check your credit reports every year.

> **CAUTION**
>
> **Watch Your Wallet** _____
>
> Big banks routinely give out confidential customer account information to callers, using security procedures that authorities say are vulnerable to abuse. In effect, thieves trick clerks into giving them access to individuals' personal information. For one thing, major companies frequently don't require passwords or codes instead of Social Security numbers, mothers' maiden names, and other widely available information to identify callers. Why, despite the fact that the companies have been warned? Because of the expense involved and because bank officials fear their customers will find passwords inconvenient. What kind of protective system does _your_ bank use?

Ask the FTC for Help

If you've been a victim of identity theft, be sure to file a complaint with the Federal Trade Commission (FTC) by contacting the FTC's Identity Theft Hotline at 1-888-877-IDTHEFT (438-4338). The FTC has published a free 21-page booklet, _Identity Theft: When Bad Things Happen to Your Good Name._ For your copy, call the same phone number, or visit www.consumer.gov/idtheft.

Americans only now are beginning to realize the vast threats posed by identity theft and other invasions of their financial privacy. The sooner you learn how to protect your most sensitive personal data, the better. And if your identity is ever stolen, be sure to report it immediately to the right agencies and authorities.

The Least You Need to Know

- Identity theft is robbing millions of people of their personal privacy.
- It could cost you thousands of dollars and ruin your credit for years if someone steals your Social Security number or your bank statement.
- Your bank or financial company can sell your personal financial records to another company, causing you untold grief.
- You should never give out your Social Security number to anyone but the IRS, government agencies, and your state's motor vehicle department.
- There are steps you can take to protect your privacy from thieves and crooks.
- There are things you should do immediately to protect yourself if you become an identity crime victim.

Part 4

Taking Care of You and Your Financial Future

Even if you've been participating in the money world for a long time, and, let's say, getting ready to retire, believe it or not, making a few *new* wise financial moves can set you on the path to real financial freedom.

Financial freedom affords everyone the opportunity to live where you want, pursue the type of jobs that interest you, purchase a home or car, start a family—whatever you dream of.

This section helps you learn how to ensure you, your family and home are protected with the right insurance, offers the latest tax information, and provides detailed information to implement a water-tight retirement plan.

Chapter 18

Getting More from Your Paycheck

In This Chapter

- ◆ Creating an emergency plan if you're fired or let go from your job
- ◆ Knowing one of the best perks you'll ever receive from your boss
- ◆ Making your paycheck work for you

You have the world at your feet. You have a job working for a company that has bequeathed you handsome stock options, a close-to-the-elevator parking space, and a shiny new key to the executive washroom.

Fast forward one year and you find out that the stock options are worthless, your parking space has been sublet to the new CEO, and the new management wants your shiny new key to the executive washroom back.

And then the pink slip arrives.

Today's economy means hard times on the job front, and not just what we saw during the slow economy from 2001 to 2004. No one is immune to cutbacks or outsourcing, and even if you haven't been let go, you may have doubts about your company's future.

What should you do? Arm yourself with a financial emergency plan in case of a layoff and squeeze as much out of your paycheck as possible. This chapter will help you get the most out of your paycheck while protecting your financial future in case of financial calamity.

The Pink Slip Arrives

"You're fired" … two words most people hope never to hear. Unfortunately, no one plans to get fired, which is exactly the problem, as with no game plan in place, people feel frightened and unprepared.

When you are fired or even if you are let go due to company outsourcing, you face a number of key financial decisions. Ideally, you have an emergency nest egg stashed away, which is typically three to six months' worth of living expenses. But even if you don't, there are many ways you can stay afloat.

The Money Line

Before the pink slip arrives, make sure you have an emergency fund. About three to six months' worth of living expenses is the rule. If you work in an industry that's experiencing problems, as airline or technology, you should probably keep a minimum of six months and as much as twelve months if you can. Keep this money in a Money Market fund that has a check-writing feature. This way, as you're adding to your emergency fund, you can take advantage of the higher rates. *Do not keep this money in a checking account.*

First, keep your cool and get into the job market as quickly as you can. Although the job market in 2004 was improving, it still wasn't as strong in years past. And the move toward outsourcing took many good jobs off the market. That said, there are still plenty of employers seeking employees. It just may take longer than you would like to find the right job. And for a while, you may have to settle for a less satisfying job until the economy gets better. The trick is to start job hunting as soon as possible, so that you don't deplete your severance pay or emergency nest egg.

Speaking of severance pay, do not make the common mistake of using your severance check to pay off your mortgage or any other loan balance. You may need the cash to tide you over until you land a new job. Your best bet is a money market fund. If you received a sizable amount, you may want to put part of it into a short-term, high-yielding bank CD (review Chapter 10 for CD shopping information).

Definitely file for unemployment. Don't be shy about this. You and your employer have been funding this government benefit over the years; now you're entitled to make use of it. It will supplement your savings and slow any drain on your emergency fund. If you worked for a company that employed more than 20 people, you are eligible to keep your health insurance at group rates. Under the Consolidated Omnibus Reconciliation Act, or COBRA, this continuation coverage lasts for 18 months, but you must apply within 60 days of being fired or let go.

COBRA is not cheap. You will probably have to pay the monthly premiums that your employer formerly paid, plus an administrative fee. However, it will still be less than if you take out your own individual health insurance policy. A less expensive approach for married people is to join a spouse's health plan, if that's possible. And if you become self-employed, look into membership in the National Association for the Self-Employed. They offer group-rate health insurance.

Whether or not a layoff or getting fired is due to technology or companies sending jobs overseas isn't the point. The point is what *you* should do if it happens to you. You have an overwhelming amount of decisions to make. Keep the following in mind:

- If you have a 401(k) plan through the company, you'll need to decide what to do with it. See Chapter 19 for detailed information, but briefly, you can take the money in lump sum (but unless you roll it over into another IRA you'll pay hefty taxes and penalties), keep the money in the company's 401(k), or roll the money over into an IRA or your new employer's 401(k) plan.

  You may not have as much flexibility with your retirement benefits, unless you're being offered early retirement. You will have to meet with your employee benefits department to determine what is allowed according to their plan. During this meeting, find out how much of your benefits you own, known as being *vested*. You can roll that money into an IRA, or you may have to leave it with the company until you retire. Get the specifics from the benefits department.

- Find out if you have access to outplacement counselors through your company. If so, take them up on it!

- Determine if you are going to receive any type of severance. Two weeks is pretty standard, and employers can pay you in a lump sum or over a period of a few weeks. You can take the lump sum, which could boost the size of your emergency fund. If you know that you'll be employed right away elsewhere, spread out the payments so that the income isn't all taxed in one year. The decision is up to you. If you are going to receive a severance, why not lobby for more? The worst thing that could happen is that they say no.

◆ Negotiate some departing perks that will save you money if you can, such as extension of your health care at their expense, use of an office and phone to help you search for a new job, or a bigger severance package, especially if you've been a loyal employee.

How to Get More Out of Your Paycheck

Don't have time to trek down to your local bank to buy savings bonds? Look no further than your paycheck. Most major companies offer you a chance to purchase Series EE savings bonds through automatic payroll deductions. Although the money is not deducted on a pre-tax basis, these deductions are a great way of breaking the "see-it-buy-it" mentality because the money is deducted automatically from your check. Plus you can use the opportunity as an avenue to stash your "safe" money—money that you can't afford to lose.

You can have the deductions taken out weekly, monthly, or quarterly. Because savings bonds are purchased at a discount from face value (a $100 face value bond has a purchase price of $50), they're a great way to invest your safe money for the future. Over the years, the value of the bond will increase as the interest accrues.

> **The Road to Riches**
>
> If you have at least 10 years until you retire, invest in your 401(k) for growth instead of stockpiling your money into the Money Market Account.

One woman who works for a major brokerage firm in Chicago tells us she has $50 deducted from each paycheck to buy $100 savings bonds each month. "They're for my two-year-old daughter's future," Pam tells us. Good thinking, Pam. In just one year, you'll have invested $600 for $1,200 face value worth of bonds for your daughter's future. (Tip: You can use these as a way to pay for her college education and possibly *not* pay taxes on the interest you'll receive.)

Here's one more tip for getting the most out of your paycheck. Have your check directly deposited. This sounds so simple, but many consumers aren't doing this. They should take advantage of this paperless transition. No bank lines or traffic to wait in. Plus direct deposit guarantees immediate access to your cash at most banks and thrifts. As you learned in Chapter 8 it can take several days for your deposited check to clear. Why wait?

Besides the added convenience, you can make a little extra money off direct deposit with this little strategy: Have your paycheck directly deposited into a Money Market Account to earn the better rate of interest than a savings or checking account. You'll earn interest on payday because your check was directly deposited. When you need money, write a check to yourself and deposit it in your noninterest-bearing checking account to pay the bills.

A Great Employee Benefit

You have access to one of the most convenient and important investment resources—right at your employer's doorstep. It's your employer's *retirement plan*, which is one of the most important asset-building tools available to consumers. Once you participate in your employer's retirement savings program, you avoid one of the biggest mistakes people make: doing nothing.

The younger you start, the better. Your money has more time to grow, and you might have to save less overall. Look at a couple of examples:

> Sylvia gets her first job at age 21. Over the next eight years, she accumulates a bit more than $10,000. Eight years later, she gets married, has two children, and decides to put her career on hold. She stops investing and lets her money ride, earning around 8 percent (compounded monthly) on her $10,000 until she retires at age 65. She has accumulated $176,448.

> Myron doesn't invest a penny until he's about 29 years old. On his twenty-ninth birthday, he decides to stash $70 a month into an investment account that earns the same amount as Sylvia's: 8 percent. He does that for 36 years, all the way to age 65, contributing a total of $30,240. His total accumulation? $174,771.

> Who's better off? They both have relatively the same amount of money by age 65. But Sylvia's initial wad of dough was only $10,000. Myron contributed *three times* that amount—$30,240. Why is this? *Because Sylvia started earlier and had more time for her money to grow.*

Unfortunately, most young Americans don't get an education in how to invest. You can use this book to teach the young adult in your family how to invest even before they get their first paycheck. The sooner they learn how to budget and invest, the further their investments will grow over their lifetime.

Apparently very few parents talk enough to their kids about the importance of investing. Even though Americans have socked away more

The Money Line

If you have a defined benefit plan, check whether the plan is insured by the Pension Benefit Guaranty Corporation. The PBGC guarantees to cover retired workers and the vested portion that current employees are entitled to receive immediately.

than $7 *trillion* into 401(k) plans alone, there is solid evidence that young Americans are not saving enough. Cerulli Associates, a benefits consulting firm in Boston, indicates within the past five years 401(k) balances have dropped nearly 10 percent.

Why the problem? Because many people are living paycheck to paycheck and often can't afford to think about the future. Others don't want money taken out of their check because "they need it *now*." Ya know what? These people who can't afford even a partial deduction now won't be able to afford retirement. Still, others do not contribute because they just don't understand how the dang thing works.

Another culprit is that many people *are* savers, and a company retirement program sends chills down the spines of Americans who couldn't stand the thought of losing money by investing. Saving is something you used to do when you were a kid, often dropping coins into a piggy bank. Sure, you can save today. A prime example is the emergency fund you should save in a *safe* place (such as a money market fund) that will cover three to six months' worth of living expenses.

Contributing to a retirement plan practices the strategy of tax-deferred investing. Stocks, bonds, and mutual funds are purchased within a qualified investment plan, such as a 401(k) and pension plans (which you'll learn more about in this chapter).

By deferring your income taxes, you can increase your investment returns. For example, look at the following table for comparison, assuming a $2,000 per year investment at an average 9 percent return in a tax-deferred versus taxable account.

Advantages of Deferring Taxes

Year	Investment Dollars in a Tax-Deferred Account	Investment Dollars in a Taxable Account
10	$33,150	$28,725
15	$64,200	$51,500
20	$112,000	$83,100
25	$184,700	$125,100
30	$298,000	$184,600

Investing is a different story; you create goals and work toward those goals. True, whenever you invest, there is a potential of risk. If you look at the facts, however, you can see how investing in a company-sponsored program is the best investment deal in America today. For example, here's how much you can save by sheltering your contributions from taxes. If you contribute $2,000 a year in your company's plan and your account earns a modest 6 percent a year for 30 years, you'll have about $168,000, which would be $48,000 *more* than if your $2,000 investment went into a taxable account. And that's not including what you saved on income taxes by investing on a pre-tax basis.

The Fabulous 401(k)

A 401(k) plan, which was dubbed for the section of the tax code it represents, allows you to make contributions on a pre-tax basis. The money is taken out of your check and invested in several different options, all of which you choose. The money grows tax-deferred until you take it out.

The upside of a 401(k) is that you decide which investments you want to put your money in (unlike other company retirement plans, such as a pension). Your investment choices in a 401(k) plan are strictly up to you. Typically, you'll have a choice between a Money Market Account, a general growth or equity stock fund, a fixed-income choice, and an investment in your company's stock. As you'll learn in Chapter 20, any money you contribute is yours, even if you leave the company, and you can roll it over into a tax-deferred IRA when you leave the company. The biggest allure, however, is that you don't pay taxes on the money you contribute.

Many times, your employer matches the money you set aside. For example, some plans will pay 50 percent for every dollar that you contribute; others may even match your contribution 100 percent up to 6 percent of your salary, typically. Meaning, for every dollar you put in, your company matches your contribution by adding a dollar to your retirement account in the plan. Where else can you earn 100 percent on your money like that?

The Money Line

The federal government requires companies to provide only minimal information to workers who take part in a 401(k) plan. Technically, all you're entitled to is a summary of how the plan works, a summary annual report, and an annual statement. If the plan allows you to invest in the company's stock, you are also entitled to receive a prospectus or similar document. Fortunately, many companies provide far more, and you can also do your own research. For example, if a mutual fund is offered in your 401(k), you're free to contact the fund directly and ask for its performance history and other pertinent information.

Dip into Your 401(k)? Sure, but Watch Your Fingers

With your company's 401(k) retirement program, you are allowed to take out a loan in the event of an emergency. The loan must be repaid quarterly and within five years, unless you're using it to buy a house, usually your principal residence. The vacation home in Bermuda is not an exception. If it is your principal residence, you may have up to 30 years to repay, often through payroll deductions. If you borrow from your 401(k), follow these rules:

Fiscal Facts _____

A **403(b) plan** is a pre-tax savings plan offered to employees who work for nonprofit or tax-exempt organizations, such as a school or even a hospital. A 403(b) plan is like a 401(k) because your contributions grow on a tax-deferred basis and the money taken out of your check is in pre-tax dollars. In most 403(b) plans, however, you are allowed to contribute a higher amount than most 401(k) plans. Check with your employee benefits department.

◆ There are hardship rules you will have to follow—and it's usually up to the company to decide—such as uninsured medical costs. If it's to buy the flame red Maserati, forget it.

◆ Try not to leave the company with a loan outstanding. Why? Because the balance will be subtracted before you receive your 401(k) funds. What does this matter? Enter Uncle Sam, who says if you don't pay back the loan within the 60-day grace period, you have to roll the funds over into another qualified plan or an Individual Retirement Account (IRA), or he'll take a chunk out. The IRS considers it an early withdrawal, and will hit you with a 10-percent penalty as well as income tax.

◆ If you take a leave of absence from work, see if you can still make your loan payments. Even though most companies will allow you a grace period of one year, once you return, your loan payments are raised in order to meet the five-year time frame requirement.

Take Advantage of Other Company Plans

Some companies have a traditional pension plan, known as a defined benefit plan, but only 45 percent of large companies offer it, according to a 2003 study by Hewitt Associates. Instead, they're shifting the burden of saving for retirement onto you, the employee, through the 401(k) plan. Make sure you understand all the benefits you are garnering under your company's plan. Most large companies have an employee benefits officer who should be able to explain to you in plain language how their plan works.

A defined benefit plan guarantees that you receive a fixed monthly sum at retirement and for the rest of your life. That's why it's called defined; the benefit you'll receive at retirement is defined in advance. Typically, it is based on the average of the last five years' salary, the number of years of employment, and your age at retirement. You don't make any contributions—the employer makes them each year, so that when you reach retirement age there will be enough money in the plan to pay your lifetime benefits.

If your company offers a defined contribution plan, you'll have more flexibility than a traditional pension plan (defined benefit plan), but not as much as a 401(k). There are two types of defined contribution plans: a money purchase plan and a profit-sharing plan.

So how does a money purchase plan work? You must usually work at your job for at least one year to participate. The maximum annual deductible contribution is 25 percent of your salary or $30,000, whichever is less. The reason it's called a money purchase plan is that the retirement benefits amount to whatever the assets in the account will purchase at the time you retire. The only employer obligation is to make a defined contribution for each worker each year, regardless of profits.

> ### The Road to Riches
>
> If you want to know what your savings bonds are worth today, call 1-800-US-BONDS to find out.

A profit-sharing plan, on the other hand, obligates the company to contribute part of its profits each year, if any, into each worker's account. However, the company can change the rate of contributions, based on profits, or eliminate them in any year. Monthly benefits are whatever the money you have in your account will buy when you retire. You still contribute to this type of account: 15 percent of your salary or $22,500, whichever is less.

Your contributions are made with pre-tax dollars to defined contribution plans, and the money grows tax-deferred, which is a great advantage. Look at the following table to see how much your pre-tax contributions can grow over five years if you save $3,000 a year for five years and your employer matches 50¢ on the dollar. This table also assumes a 10 percent average annual rate of return.

How Pre-Tax Contributions Can Grow

	401(k)	Taxable Account
Amount contributed	$15,000	$15,000
Less your taxes (30%)	$0	$4,500
Invested amount, plus employer's match	$22,500	$10,500
Total amount, assuming 10% average return	$30,220	$12,920

No matter what type of plan is available to you, make sure you ask your employee benefits officer the following two questions:

1. How are my retirement benefits computed?

2. How long will it take until the company's contributions are fully owned by me?

Whether your company offers you a 401(k) or another type of pension plan, it will pay off for your financial future if you participate. Get information from your human resources department about these types of programs so you can save for your retirement!

The Least You Need to Know

◆ If you get fired or laid off, find out whether you can continue your health insurance, how to take possession of the funds in your 401(k) or pension, and if you will get any severance pay.

◆ Take the payroll deduction to invest in savings bonds if your company offers it.

◆ Have your paycheck directly deposited into your bank account to save time and earn an extra day's worth of interest.

◆ Your employer's retirement plan, whether it's a 401(k) or something else, is one of the best investments you can make. If you're not sure how it works, ask your company's benefits specialist.

How Much Do You Really Know About Your 401(k)?

In This Chapter

◆ Why you need a 401(k) now more than ever

◆ Understanding the benefits to a 401(k) plan

◆ Why you should aim for growth in your retirement account

◆ What you can do if you're self-employed or switch jobs

◆ Top 401(k) mistakes—and how to avoid them

Workers who still look at retirement in the traditional sense—retiring at age 65 or earlier with a comfortable nest egg—need a wake-up call. Traditional pension plans offered by employers are on the downswing, according to Hewitt Associates. That means workers who must rely entirely on their 401(k) plans and Social Security to pay all their retirement expenses must plan for retirement much more carefully.

Enter the 401(k), a retirement investment vehicle the U.S. government hopes will cure all future financial retirement ills as Social Security funds continue to dwindle.

The idea is simple. You stash a portion of your salary in a tax-deferred account, and because the money is deducted from your paycheck before taxes are taken out, you pay less to the government each year. A 401(k) is a great tax shelter and an easy way to invest for retirement.

Keep in mind, however, it is not foolproof. This chapter helps pinpoint the benefits available to you by investing in a 401(k) and the pitfalls to avoid.

401(k) Is the Way to Play

More than 20 years ago, there were about 7.5 million participants in about 17,000 401(k) retirement plans with total assets of $94 billion. The average account balance was $12,200.

Today, statistics look sharply higher. Recent data show there were 40 million 401(k) participants with an average account balance of $50,000, and assets have more than doubled to $2 trillion.

What does this mean for you? Plenty. This tax-deferred investment, named for the relevant section in the tax code, is a savings plan that acts as a personal pension fund for employees. With a 401(k), you can defer taxes on a portion of your salary until you retire. Taxes on investment gains are deferred until you withdraw money from the plan. You can begin withdrawing from a tax-deferred investment account without penalty at age $59^1/_2$. Unlike pensions, 401(k) accounts are portable, in that you can "roll over" the account, take it with you, and continue building it at your next employer with no penalty.

> **The Road to Riches**
>
> Hewitt Associates, a global human resources consulting firm, found that retiring at 67—just two years later than the traditional expected retirement age—and contributing an additional 2 percent of savings to a 401(k) plan can provide a significant boost to retirement income.

Because you get to deduct a portion of your earnings—before taxes—and put the money into various investment options, the money that comes out of your paycheck is in *pretax* dollars and it grows tax-deferred until you take it out at retirement. Also you usually can make changes to how you allocate the percentage of money you contribute to each investment option every quarter—some companies offer the chance to do so every month.

Compared with other types of defined contribution plans, such as profit-sharing, 403(b), SEPs (simplified employee plans), and stock ownership plans, the 401(k) far outweighs these plans in terms of asset size.

The Inside Goods

Many 401(k) plans offer a wide range of investment choices, with the most common being money market funds, index-based stock funds, and actively managed growth funds. Corporate bond funds, government securities funds, and balanced stock and bond funds are also typically offered. Company stock is offered and once was the most infrequent type of investment option offered to plan participants, according to the Merrill Lynch Retirement and Financial Planning Survey of Employers.

In fact, a recent study shows employers are making more diversification opportunities available, increasing investment choices from 12 funds in 2001 to 14 in 2003.

Another benefit of the 401(k) is a company match. While it is not a requirement, companies may offer up to 100 percent of every dollar you contribute to your 401(k). Most common matches are 50¢ on the dollar up to 6 percent, for a total of 3 percent of your salary. Typically about one-third of the companies that offer 401(k) plans link their contributions to their profits. There's been a big push to allow employees to contribute as much as possible under the new regulations of the 2001 Economic Growth and Tax Reconciliation Act.

In 2003, more large companies, like those in the Fortune 1000, are offering matching contributions and in some cases increasing the amount of the match. Eliminating a company match is unusual, even during rough economic times.

> **Watch Your Wallet**
>
> Employees who put all their retirement money into their company may experience the same intense financial pain as the employees of Enron and WorldCom. When their companies failed, those employees lost all of their retirement money along with their livelihood as their jobs vanished.

Read the Fine Print

All 401(k) participants receive a summary plan description—but not everyone reads this very important document. For most employees, the summary plan description looks pretty unappetizing. Yet this is one of the most critical pieces of paperwork that you have about your 401(k) plan. Here's why you shouldn't casually toss it aside. It tells you …

- When you are eligible to participate.
- The *vesting schedule* for employer-matching contributions.

♦ The size and timing of employer-matching contributions (if applicable).

♦ How to qualify for, apply for, and receive hardship withdrawals (if applicable).

♦ How to apply for a loan against your 401(k), and interest rate calculations for loans (if applicable).

♦ Withdrawal procedures (at retirement and for rollovers).

♦ Employee contribution rates.

♦ Your rights under the Employee Retirement Income Security Act (ERISA).

♦ Contact information of the plan sponsor and trustee, and the plan identification number (necessary if you want to review filings with the IRS or Department of Labor).

♦ The appeals process if plan rules aren't followed, including the person or firm to be contacted if you file suit against the plan.

Fiscal Facts

When investing in a 401(k), your employer should provide you with a **vesting schedule.** This schedule will provide you with a timeline and what percentage of your employer-matched contributions you are entitled to at what point in your employment. Typically, a period of five years is required to be 100% fully vested.

The document typically runs anywhere from 12 to 20 pages long. This is the document you refer to when you are about to retire or leave your job. It spells out the rules for getting your money. Another reason to keep this document handy is if you die, your beneficiary or relatives will need it to make a claim on your benefits.

If You Leave Your Job ...

What happens if you leave your job and you want to take your money with you? The money you invest is yours, but beware, in order to avoid the tax monster there are rules for moving your money. You must have the transfer made directly from your old plan to your new plan. If you take possession of the money yourself—even if you plan on "rolling it over" into a new plan (whether it's at your new employer or in an IRA)—you will get hit with a 20 percent federal income tax penalty. Wait, there's more. Unless you replace the 20 percent penalty with new funds put into the new plan, it will be treated as a withdrawal and whammo! You'll owe ordinary income taxes on it.

In the old days, you had only two options: either cash out of your 401(k) plan or convert it to an IRA. Here's the lowdown on both, plus some new alternatives:

◆ **Cashing out.** This strategy is considered to be the worst option because of the stiff tax penalties if you are under age 59$\frac{1}{2}$. And one of the enduring problems today has been the tendency of workers to take the money and run when they change jobs. If you have less than $5,000, your old job now has the right to cash you out whether you want them to or not. Try to get your 401(k) plan taken care of before you switch jobs.

Fiscal Facts _____

Despite the various rule changes, including a mandatory 20 percent tax withholding when the money doesn't go into another retirement plan, thousands of Americans each year prefer to take the tax hit and spend the money. That trend may be changing. A 2003 study by Hewitt Associates found that more than half of workers with a 401(k) balance of $30,000 or more rolled over distributed funds into an IRA. After the balance hit $90,000 or more, less than 10% of workers opted to take cash.

◆ **Roll over to an IRA.** You can have your 401(k) transferred into an IRA of your choosing without paying any taxes, penalties, or fees. You can do this yourself by cashing out and mailing a check to your new IRA within 60 days, but withholding taxes apply, and you'll have to wait until tax time to get the money back. It's best to have the companies do it between themselves.

◆ **Staying put.** Ex-employees are allowed to keep their 401(k) plan in whatever the original funds were. They can't contribute new funds, of course, but they can let the old money compound happily. This alternative makes sense if your new employer's plan doesn't look so good.

Watch Your Wallet _____

You are always 100 percent fully vested in your own contributions, but if you leave your employer before five years, in many cases, you will forfeit your employer's match and the earnings on those contributions as well.

◆ **Taking it with you.** You can skip the IRA middleman step and transfer your 401(k) assets from your old employer to your new employer 401(k) program. But before you do this direct transfer, make sure that the new plan is as good as your previous employer's.

A Sure-Fire Investing Program

When you sock away money in your 401(k), it's in pretax dollars. The market growth we saw in the '90s found many plan participants and their friendly 401(k)s sitting on a slight windfall of money for their future.

But for the first time in the 20-year history of the 401(k) retirement program, the average account lost money in the year 2000 even after thousands of dollars of new contributions. Many workers saw the value of their 401(k) plans fall in the early part of this decade, even as they were putting money in. Fortunately, the stock market rebounded in 2003 and average balances jumped 35% that year, exceeding 1999 levels for the first time since 1999, according to a study by Hewitt Associates.

Losses in your retirement portfolio, namely your 401(k), may spur you to second-guess your investment decisions. A 401(k) is not a magical account, and you must buckle down and learn exactly what investment strategies will work best for you.

First, review your 401(k) plan and determine just how diversified your portfolio is. You don't need to worry about a short-term loss if you own good funds in a properly diversified portfolio.

Asset allocation is important because nobody can see the future. Not experts or the government. The rationale behind diversification is that when one type of investment drops, different ones will go up, thereby offsetting each other. This lowers the risk in your portfolio.

How should you allocate your assets? Most experts say that people with at least 20 years before they will retire should aim for a portfolio with 80 percent in stocks. The rest should be in fixed-income investments, such as short-term bond funds.

Those with 10 to 20 years until retirement could ratchet stock holdings down to 70 percent, while those with 5 to 10 years should look at a 60 percent mix.

A Brief Word About a 401(k) vs. an IRA

The name of the game is tax-deferred growth, and both contenders, the 401(k) and IRA, offer this. But, is there one that is better?

It all depends on your tax situation. However, there are several benefits to investing in a 401(k). Even with the new tax laws, you can still contribute more tax-free dollars to your 401(k), depending on your salary and the latest tax law changes. Also many employers will contribute (match) to your 401(k) plan, which is free money to you. So, if you have an employer that pays 20¢ on the dollar, that's like earning a 20 percent *guaranteed* return. Where can you get that these days?

Other benefits to a 401(k) versus an IRA include:

♦ You can invest in a 401(k) with pretax dollars; whether you use a regular IRA, a nondeductible IRA or a Roth IRA, your contributions are done with after-tax earnings.

♦ You can borrow money from your 401(k), but there are rules you must follow, as you'll learn later in this chapter.

♦ The only limitation to participating in your company's 401(k) program is if its investment choices are severely limited, such as it only offers a money market fund and its company stock. At that point, an IRA would definitely make sense.

♦ Remember, you can open an IRA even if you have a 401(k). You just will not be able to take the deduction on your taxes for your IRA contributions but you can still take advantage of tax-deferred growth.

Aim for Growth

Despite the increase of investment options in 401(k) plans, the most frequently found type of investment choice is a money market fund, a vehicle typically used as a "safe haven" during turbulent market conditions.

Here's the paradox. If the goal for investing in a 401(k) is long-term growth, why do most participants choose these overly cautious investments for the long haul?

Call it long-term anxiety. There is a deep-seated apprehension about long-term prospects. Even armed with the belief that their retirements will be financially more difficult than their parents and kicking themselves for not saving for retirement sooner, the typical baby boomer fears outliving the money they have put away, or plan to put away, for retirement.

That's why it does not pay to be too conservative with your retirement strategy. With the majority of 401(k) participants putting 60 percent or more of their contributions into bonds or money market funds, the wake up call on retirement day will require more than earplugs. Sure, stocks are riskier, but over the long run they have far greater growth potential than Money Market funds. Since 1926, there have been 55 years with a positive average annual total return as compared with 23 years of a negative return. According to Harris Investment Management, the average annual return of the S&P 500 is 10.4 percent.

Unless you expect to retire in the next five to seven years, many money managers advise you to put up to 80 percent of your 401(k) money into stock funds.

The bottom line is that ideally your 401(k) plan should have at least half a dozen investment options. Unfortunately, there are still some employers that limit you to three or fewer, although that is changing. If your plan falls short, complain to your Employee Benefits department.

Rules, Rules, Rules

You must leave your contributions in the plan (or roll it over into an IRA if you leave the company, or take it with you to a new employer's plan) until age 59^1/$_2$. However, there are hardship cases when you can withdraw money, such as purchasing a home, emergency medical expenses, or college tuition.

What constitutes a hardship? The withdrawal must be made on account of the participant's (that's you) immediate and heavy financial need—and the withdrawal must be necessary to satisfy such need. Check with your employer to find out exactly what your company's plan will allow.

And as discussed earlier in this chapter, if you leave your job and want to withdraw the money, you must roll it over into a new plan or pay stiff penalties and taxes.

Plans for the Self-Employed

If you're self-employed, you can create your own retirement savings program! Plus, you can contribute much more than the $3,000 IRA maximum. There are Keogh plans, which fall under two types: defined benefit and defined contribution plans. The choice is yours, but make sure you review the paperwork about requirements with a qualified professional, especially if you have employees—then you *must* include contributions for them as well.

The maximum tax deductible contribution to a defined contribution plan is the lesser of $40,000 or 100 percent of compensation as of mid-2004. For defined benefit plans, the maximum tax-deductible contribution is the amount needed to produce the required benefits under the formula. Most recent data show that in 2003, the maximum annual retirement benefit that may be funded may not exceed the lesser of 100 percent of the participant's average compensation for the highest three consecutive tax years as an active participant, or $160,000.

Provided the Keogh Plan is established by the last day of the tax year, you can make tax deductible contributions up to the due date of your tax return.

As a self-employed individual, you also have access to opening up a SEP-IRA, which is a Simplified Employee Pension IRA. A SEP is easier to understand and administer successfully than a Keogh. Sometimes dubbed an "easy-to-manage retirement plan for individuals," a SEP-IRA can be opened and contributions can be made up until the last day of your tax-filing deadline, including extensions.

Avoid These Mistakes

Nobody is perfect when it comes to 401(k) investing. There are a million ways to build a retirement portfolio, and a million ways to screw it up. Don't let a the following mistakes torpedo your best intentions and keep you working long into your golden years:

♦ **Mistake #1: Not contributing enough money to earn a matching contribution in your 401(k).** One of the biggest mistakes is not investing enough money to get the match from your employer. That is almost like walking past a $50 bill you find lying on the sidewalk. A rule of thumb is that you should save 15 percent of your salary to build a comfortable retirement. But, if "life" (mortgage payments, tuition, etc.) gets in the way, try to contribute enough of your salary to get the free match from your employer.

♦ **Mistake #2: Selecting inappropriate funds that don't meet your long-term investment goals.** Start by setting your investing goals, figuring your risk tolerance, and determining your time horizon as a way to avoid being too aggressive or to risk averse. Look for funds that are in the top 30 percent of their categories for one and three years, with a long-time manager at the helm.

♦ **Mistake #3: Forgetting to rebalance your portfolio when necessary.** You want to maintain a balanced, diversified portfolio. Experts say you should rebalance—sell some of your winning shares and put them in a losing fund which will eventually turn around—when they are 5 percent or more away from their target asset allocation for two quarters in a row. The goal is to just keep your objectives on target through this method of asset allocation.

To make sure your retirement years are financially golden, be aggressive about checking your 401(k) plan. Your employer should promptly credit your contributions to your 401(k) account and provide regular accountings of what's happening to your money. Make sure to check your W-2 tax forms against your year-end 401(k) statement to make sure all the money you contributed wound up in the plan.

The Least You Need to Know

◆ A 401(k), named for the relevant tax code, is a type of tax-deferred retirement plan offered by employers to its employees.

◆ Check to see if your employer offers a matching 401(k) program, where for every dollar you contribute they will contribute a percentage up to 100 percent on the dollar.

◆ Remember that you can contribute pre-tax dollars to a 401(k), thereby reducing your tax liability to good ol' Uncle Sam.

◆ Don't be too conservative with your investment options. Unless you're retiring within the next five to seven years, go for the gusto and allocate a large portion of retirement monies to equities, as they tend to perform well over the long haul.

◆ Don't forget that self-employed consumers can create their own retirement plans through Keoghs and SEPs, also known as simplified employee plans.

Chapter 20

Getting the Right Insurance Coverage for Your Needs

In This Chapter

- Understanding why you need to protect yourself
- Learning insurance strategies that will save you a few bucks
- Assessing your life, health, and wealth
- Avoiding insurance you don't need

Many folks believe that paying a lot of money on insurance premiums is like flushing your money down the toilet—that is, until tragedy strikes. Then those expensive insurance premiums seem like the best thing since the invention of the paper clip.

You need to insure your health and protect your wealth. And the more you have to protect, the more you'll spend on insurance. This chapter defines the types of insurance you need. In addition, it will help you get the best buy for your insurance dollars and show you how to shield yourself from unexpected disasters.

Making Sense of Insurance Mumbo-Jumbo

Your insurance needs are determined by which of these categories you fall under: single, married couple with no kids, married couple with kids, or married couple with adult children (empty-nesters). The following list explains the insurance needs for each category:

◆ **Single.** You may want to skip the life insurance depending on how much money you have socked away, but you'll definitely need auto insurance (make sure you get comprehensive coverage if you have an outstanding car loan) and renter's insurance (unless you own your home). Disability insurance is also a good idea; you can usually get this through your employer.

◆ **Married without children.** Look into term life insurance, particularly if one spouse does not work or you own a home. Auto insurance is a must, as is homeowner's or renter's insurance. Get disability insurance through your employer, but look into a supplemental policy if your employer's coverage is not enough.

◆ **Married with children.** When children enter the picture, the necessity for insurance coverage increases ten-fold. For one thing, you definitely need life insurance. Term life insurance is the best bet if you are in a younger age bracket. As you get older, the premiums may rise, so you'll need to reevaluate your situation and perhaps choose another policy. Your car insurance coverage may remain the same, with one addition. If you have children who can drive, see how much a multi-car discount policy would be. You may be able to save as much as 25 percent on your total premiums.

Disability insurance is more important when you have children and your spouse doesn't work. Choose a policy that is guaranteed renewable, and lock into a guaranteed annual premium that cannot be increased and is noncancelable until you turn 65. Add a cost-of-living adjustment clause to your policy for an extra premium. This will raise your disability payments based on an index tied to the Consumer Price Index (CPI).

The Money Line

The Social Security Administration provides assistance to individuals with disabilities. Two types of programs exist: Social Security Disability Insurance and Supplemental Security Income. Both programs are very different in structure, but generally provide disability benefits to individuals who have a disability and meet medical criteria.

Finally, get complete coverage on your homeowner's insurance. Make sure you know what your policy does and does not cover, and purchase additional coverage if necessary.

◆ **Empty nesters.** The kids are gone and you have the house back to yourselves—Hallelujah! All previous insurance needs remain the same, although you may need insurance to cover any debts such as death and funeral expenses, and estate taxes, which are usually cared for by a good life insurance policy.

The Road to Riches

Here are a few ways for seniors to get immediate discounts on insurance coverage:

◆ **Automobile coverage.** Check into senior citizen and multi-car discounts.

◆ **Homeowner's insurance.** Reevaluate your existing policy—you might not need as much coverage anymore.

◆ **Long-term care insurance.** Make sure that there's an inflation-protection rider, that the policy is renewable for life, and that there is a short elimination period, such as 20 to 60 days.

◆ **Life insurance.** Consider purchasing a cash value life insurance policy instead of term insurance, which becomes too expensive as you get older. In a cash value insurance policy, the cash inside the policy builds up and may be used in the future to pay premiums or help pay estate taxes. This isn't true of term insurance.

The rest of this chapter explains the ins and outs of the different types of insurance.

Insuring Home Sweet Home

Home insurance usually boils down to two crucial concerns: protection and price. Although regulated at the state level, home insurance is more of a national product than auto insurance, meaning you will find fewer local variations.

Proper home insurance coverage involves buying the right type of policy and having the proper levels of protection within that policy—including special provisions for jewelry, your computers and televisions, and other particularly valuable possessions. You may also need to supplement this coverage with special protection against natural disasters that are not covered in your basic policy.

No matter where you live, whether you rent or own, you need some sort of insurance to cover your belongings. Homeowners with mortgages are required by their lenders to have home insurance, while renters are not. Many people may think that the policy terms required by their lenders represent "OK" levels of insurance, but this may not be true. Lenders want to make sure their exposure is covered, but that can happen without you being fully protected. Thus, it's important that you calculate your needs as well and make sure they are reflected in your coverage.

If you rent your home, you need to have a renter's insurance policy. Renter's insurance is available through most insurance agents. The form, known as an HO-4 form, covers any damage to your personal property and any structural damage to the building caused by tenants.

The amount you pay on your renter's insurance policy can be on a monthly, semi-annual, or annual basis. No matter what the term, the amount you pay is known as a premium, and the amount of your premium depends on where you live. Do you live in a safe neighborhood or an unsafe one? Is there a 24-hour doorman? Is the apartment unoccupied for more than two hours per day? Another factor is whether you have taken out other insurance policies (such as car insurance) with the insurance agent. If you haven't, your premium will be higher. In 2004, the average annual premium runs up to $200. If you are a condo or co-op owner, you need an HO-6 policy. Similar to a renter's insurance policy, this policy covers risks and damage to your personal property. Building property is covered for 10 percent of contents (such as cabinets and wall fixtures). Make sure you check with your insurance agent about anything that is not covered.

If you own your home, you should already have homeowner's insurance. Mortgage lenders require that you have property insurance before you buy a new home. If you are in the market for a new home and are getting homeowner's insurance for the first time, you should understand the basic forms of homeowner's coverage.

Types of Coverage

If you want to get the right type of coverage for your home, compare the following types of homeowner's insurance. The items that are listed as types of coverage are known as perils, as in "all the things that could go wrong." In the industry, it is known as a standard peril policy. The more coverage you acquire, the higher your insurance premiums will be. It is up to you to decide if you want to pay more in insurance premiums and have more coverage. However, if you try to cut corners on your homeowner's insurance policy to save a few bucks and tragedy strikes, you will be sorry.

- ◆ **HO-1** covers the 11 most common perils: glass breakage, fire or lightning, smoke damage, explosion, riots, damage caused by vehicles, damage caused by aircraft, theft, property loss, vandalism, and weather, such as windstorms, hurricanes, and hail.

◆ **HO-2** covers HO-1 perils plus roof collapse from snow, heavy sleet, or ice; damage from hot or frozen water pipes; heat or air conditioning explosion; damage caused by falling objects; damage caused by electrical surges to appliances (except televisions); and collapse of any part of your home.

Watch Your Wallet

Insure.com reports that since the beginning of the twentieth century, earthquakes have occurred in 39 states. Approximately 90 percent of Americans live in areas considered seismically active. Even so, only a small percentage of people purchase earthquake insurance. Even in California, where earthquake fears are a daily fact of life, only 17 percent of homeowners and 20 to 25 percent of people in all types of housing have earthquake insurance according to the California Earthquake Authority (CEA). Earthquake insurance is not covered by typical homeowners insurance and needs to be purchased as a separate policy.

◆ **HO-3** is a special form that covers HO-1 and HO-2 and other risks to an older home, except floods, wars, and earthquakes. You do pay a premium for having replacement cost.

◆ **HO-4** is a renter's insurance policy. It covers only property from 17 listed perils.' Depending on the insurance company you choose to purchase a policy from, your premiums will vary along with the types of perils each policy covers.

◆ **HO-5** includes replacement cost, and personal property and is covered for 75 percent of the home—as opposed to HO-3, where 70 percent is covered. To qualify for this type of coverage, your home must have been built after 1950 and must be in decent condition. It's required that you have a smoke detector, a dead bolt lock, and a hand-held fire extinguisher. If you don't have these items, you *cannot* get an HO-5 policy. You will pay more in premiums for this type of policy, but it does provide the most extensive coverage (including HO-1 and HO-2 disasters). Not many of these policies are sold today.

The Money Line

Although your home and its contents are at risk from fire, theft, windstorms, and other perils, the land your home sits on is not. Don't include the value of the land in deciding how much homeowner's insurance you need to buy.

◆ **HO-6** policies, as previously described, are for condo and co-op owners only.

- **HO-7** policies cover dwelling and personal property from 11 perils. This type of insurance policy differs from HO-1 in that it covers repairs or actual cash values, not rebuilding costs. This is for homes where some historic or architectural aspects make the home's replacement cost significantly higher than its market value.

The Money Line

Only about one-quarter of the homes in areas most vulnerable are insured against flood loss, according to the Federal Insurance Administration (FIA). Flood insurance is relatively inexpensive. Recent statistics indicate the annual premiums average $353, with the average amount of insurance purchased approximately $125,000.

Depending on your insurance needs and the type of policy you select, it is also imperative that you ask your insurance agent what is *not* covered so you can determine if additional coverage may be needed. For example, the HO-3 policy does not cover flood damage, but you can purchase separate flood insurance. However, you do have to qualify for this insurance by meeting the federal zoning standards, so again check with your insurance agent to determine if you even need this type of coverage. The National Flood Insurance Program "backs" this type of insurance, but be aware that flood coverage is limited. It does not provide coverage for valuables stored below the ground level in your basement—except for major appliances, such as a freezer or washer and dryer.

How to Save Money on Homeowner's Insurance

There's no escaping it: You must have homeowners insurance to buy a house. What you can escape are the extra costs that most folks end up paying because they haven't shopped around. Here are a few financial secrets that will help trim the fat:

- **Raise your deductible amounts.** If you're willing to accept a higher deductible, you can save almost 15 percent on your premiums.

- **Take protective measures.** Installing a burglar alarm, dead bolts, or a smoke detector, purchasing a hand-held fire extinguisher, and/or having a nonsmoking household protects your home and lowers your premiums.

- **Get replacement cost insurance.** Most insurance policies plan to give you the actual cash value of your personal property in the event of loss or damage. Folks, it's not worth it. If you buy a $3,800 leather couch today, five years from now it will be worth only $1,800 (because it's used). If you have a fire when that couch is five years old, the insurance company will pay you $1,800. Just try to find the same type of couch for $1,800. It's not likely. However, if you have replacement cost insurance, the insurance company is required to pay you whatever it costs to purchase a new replacement item.

◆ **Purchase your homeowner's insurance from the same insurance company that insures your automobile.** Purchasing both policies in a type of package agreement from the same agent or company may qualify you for a discount.

◆ **Pay your homeowner's insurance annually.** Although most insurance policies have annual, semi-annual, and monthly terms, you will save a few dollars if you pay it on an annual basis. For example, a renter's insurance policy with a $200 per year annual premium may cost you $110 on a semi-annual basis. This comes out to be an extra $20 out of your pocket.

◆ **Make a home video of your property and all of its contents.** By doing so, you ensure—and insure—that your claims will be paid. Just remember to keep the video in a safe deposit box in case of damage to the home. And update your information annually, especially if you've added valuables to your home such as art or a home entertainment system.

◆ **Familiarize yourself with the additional coverage and exceptions noted on your policy.** For example, if your policy allows you to have additional coverage on credit card losses, don't take it. Why? Because most standard credit card companies limit you to a $50 loss per card. That's just wasting money. Read the fine print!

Understanding Car Coverage

The liability involved when you are in a car accident is phenomenal, which is why automobile insurance costs so much. You need to know what is required in your state and what's worth paying for. Comparing the differences between the two can save you a few dollars. The following sections cover the types of coverage available and give you some money saving strategies.

Types of Coverage

Liability coverage is required in almost every state and is split into two parts: bodily injury

Fiscal Facts

Insurance types usually refer to liability coverage limits as a series of three numbers. For example, your agent might say that your policy carries liability limits of 20/40/10. That stands for $20,000 in bodily injury coverage per person, $40,000 in bodily injury coverage per accident, and $10,000 in property damage coverage per accident.

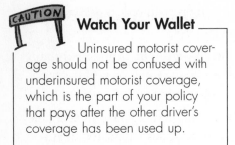

Watch Your Wallet

Uninsured motorist coverage should not be confused with underinsured motorist coverage, which is the part of your policy that pays after the other driver's coverage has been used up.

liability and property damage liability. Bodily injury liability provides insurance against lawsuits. Most states require a minimum of $25,000 per person and $50,000 per accident. If you want to protect your assets in the event of a lawsuit, you'll need as much as $300,000 worth of coverage. Property damage liability covers damage done by your car to other people's cars and property. The standard minimum for this is $10,000.

If you're a victim of a hit-and-run accident, you'll need uninsured motorist coverage. Uninsured motorist coverage allows you to collect lost wages and payments for any medical expenses that result from an accident with an uninsured motorist. Do *not* skip over this type of insurance, especially because an increasingly high number of drivers have dropped their insurance coverage because of high premiums. And you should especially include this if you don't already have a comprehensive medical plan and long-term disability insurance.

You must also have comprehensive coverage if you have an outstanding car loan (which many of us do). Comprehensive coverage covers theft and damage to the car from riots, fire, flood, falling trees, and theft.

Collision coverage, which pays for damage to your car if you're in an accident or replaces a vehicle that is a total loss, is optional unless you have a loan on your car. this type of coverage is usually required by the lender if you do have a loan.

Medical payments coverage and personal injury protection (PIP) covers medical, hospital, and funeral bills that result from an automobile accident—no matter who is at fault. PIP goes one step further and covers any lost wages. If you have a good medical plan and/or disability insurance policy, you may want to pass on these types of coverages, because they can be expensive.

Additional Features

Several supplemental types of coverage are available, either as separate premium items or included in augmented policies.

- ◆ Rental reimbursement, a common add-on, covers vehicle rentals required because your car is damaged or stolen.

- ◆ Coverage for towing and labor charges in case of a breakdown is also common. If you are a Triple AAA auto club member, you may not need this supplemental coverage since Triple AAA offers these features.

◆ Auto replacement coverage guarantees your car will be completely repaired or replaced, even if these costs exceed its depreciated value.

How to Save Some Moolah

When you apply for automobile insurance, you always want to look for the best rate possible, but that's not always so easy. Insurers take into account certain considerations when they give you quotes on auto insurance. Keep these financial tidbits in mind to help cut costs on auto insurance:

◆ **Do some comparison shopping.** You don't always have to go to your friendly insurance agent down the street. In fact, if you do your homework, you'll find that the price of similar auto coverage can vary as much as 80 percent from insurer to insurer. Check with the largest national insurers, which could potentially save you a few bucks if you buy directly from them.

◆ **Drive safely and defensively.** This tip is just common sense, but the fewer traffic violations and accidents you have under your belt, the lower your premiums will be. Maintain a good driving record!

◆ **Don't buy the latest "fad" or "hot" car.** In 2003, the top-choice vehicle targeted by thieves was the Saturn CL. Insurance premiums on this automobile as well as the Acura Integra may be higher in some states as a result of their popularity among auto thieves.

◆ **Buy a car that will handle well if you are ever in an accident.** Ask the car sales rep how much of the car is damaged during an accident and whether or not it holds up well in an accident. For example, if you buy a car that falls apart in a fender bender, your insurance premiums will be much higher than if you buy a car that is a bit more resilient in an accident. In addition, find out how expensive any repairs may be. The more expensive it is to repair, the higher your premiums will be. You can check the safety of a particular model at the website of the Insurance Institute for highway safety, www.heysafety.org.

Watch Your Wallet

Protect your wallet—and your car—by seeing which vehicles thieves target most in your state. Log onto www.cccis.com, an insurance research and data service, for more information.

◆ **Raise your deductible and pay premiums annually.** Carrying a higher deductible will decrease your insurance premiums. For example, increasing your deductible from $200 to $500 on collision coverage could reduce your premium by as much as 30 percent—potentially saving you hundreds of dollars. Choose the highest deductible you can afford, then set aside that amount in a savings account so you'll have the funds available if needed.

Knowing the Do's and Don'ts of Buying Life Insurance

Life insurance is a bugaboo in mainstream America because not many people understand it. However, it's really quite simple. Most folks buy life insurance to provide benefits for their survivors in case they die before "their time."

As you do for car insurance, you pay premiums when you buy life insurance. Your annual premiums are based on your age, your health, how much money your insurance company can earn by investing the money you give them (your premiums) until you die, and the expenses the insurance company incurs for mailings and commissions for its agents. Whew!

What makes life insurance a difficult concept to grasp is choosing which kind will best suit your personal needs. The most common reason to purchase life insurance is to support your family members who depend on your income in the event that you die prematurely. Life insurance can also prove helpful by providing immediate cash to pay estate taxes when you die or to repay business loans (if you are an owner of a business and you die prematurely).

Although life insurance can be confusing, figuring out the differences in insurance policies doesn't require a secret decoder ring. You just need to find out if you need life insurance and, if so, how much you need.

Do you need life insurance? The rule of thumb is that if you're young and single and have no one else depending on your income, you don't need it. Even if you're married, if both of you are working, you probably don't need life insurance. But, if there are family members who depend upon your income, you definitely do.

How much insurance you need depends on how old you are and how well your family can live without your income. Rough rules of thumb suggest an amount equal to six to eight times your earnings.

Consider the following factors:

- ◆ Take into account your family's immediate need for cash to cover death-related expenses. This would cover uninsured medical costs, funeral expenses, debts, taxes, and estate-settlement fees. The National Funeral Directors Association indicate this amount averages at least $7,500.

- Tack on 6 to 12 months of your family's lost net income because of your death (to take immediate economic pressure off of your family).

- Calculate your family's expenses on an annual basis. (you learned how to do this on a monthly basis in Chapter 2) What percent of these expenses are covered by your income? The mortgage still has to be paid and Junior's college tuition bill is still due. Also how much will these expenses grow over the next five to eight years?

- Contact the Social Security Administration at 1-800-772-1213 to see if your spouse and children are entitled to survivors' benefits. If your family is eligible, have them determine what percentage of your current income the benefits cover. Why? Because if the survivors' benefits replace 30 percent of your income, you would have to purchase 30 percent less in life insurance benefits. Got it?

Without any mind-bending calculations, here's a basic rule of thumb for purchasing life insurance, according to a Citibank report. After the death of its principal income producer, a family requires 75 percent of its former after-tax income to maintain its standard of living. It must have at least 60 percent to get along at all. If you want to figure out your after-tax income without the help of a CPA, simply multiply your gross income by 60 percent if you earn a high income, 70 percent if you earn a moderate living, and 80 percent if you have a low income. Otherwise, if you want to simply figure out a rough estimate, just make it five to eight times your current wages. It comes out to about the same amount as Citibank's calculation.

Finally, you need to decide what kind of life insurance you need. Yuck! Because this could be the American public's most-despised question, we're going to make it easy on you and help you save a few bucks along the way. There are two very basic types of life insurance coverage: term insurance and permanent insurance.

Term life insurance policies provide life insurance protection for a specific period of time or term. If you die during the coverage period, the beneficiary named in your policy receives the policy death benefit. If you don't die during the term, your beneficiary receives nothing.

Permanent insurance policies provide insurance protection for your entire life as long as the policy remains in force. In addition to insurance protection provided, this type of policy also builds internal cash values, often described as a savings account within the policy. These policies are often known as cash value insurance.

Whichever type of life insurance you decide to buy, keep the following things in mind:

◆ **Check out the insurance company's financial stability.** Even though term insurance policies always get paid—even if the insurance company goes belly up—those of you who are weak-kneed when it comes to your money should check on the health of the insurance company. Contact Weiss Research at 1-800-289-9222 for more information. Another source is A. M. Best (www. ambest.com) The National Association of Insurance Commissioners (NAIC also provides ratings online. Log onto www.naic.org. These services will provide you with the financial strength of the insurance company and give you an explanation of how it grades each company. Of course, you want the highest rated companies possible, with grades of A++ and A+.

◆ **Buy your life insurance from a fee-only financial planner or a "direct-purchase."** You can save up to 40—sometimes 50-percent—on an insurance agent's commissions if you go to a discount insurance broker. Better yet, if you purchase a policy directly from an insurance company, you can avoid the middleman altogether. Whichever type of life insurance you're purchasing, contact USAA at 1-800-365-8722 or www.usaa.com for more information. Ameritas also provides low-cost cash value insurance policies to the public. Contact them toll-free at 1-800-745-6665 or on the web at www.ameritas.com. Internet users can log onto various websites such as InsWeb.com (www.insweb.com), and nsBuyer (www.insbuyer.com). In addition, if you're not sure about your policy, contact the National Insurance Consumer Organization (NICO) for information about how they can evaluate your proposed insurance policy (typically, the performance per $1,000 of coverage). Write to them at 121 N. Payne Street, Alexandria, VA 22314.

◆ **Consider life insurance as an option to pay estate taxes if you build up a sizeable net worth.** As you see in Chapter 21 which discusses estate planning, life insurance can help alleviate the sting for wealthy people who owe Uncle Sam a lot in estate taxes. Make sure you review your situation with an estate-planning attorney (not your insurance agent) to figure out what options are available to you.

Term Insurance 101

Term insurance is usually the least expensive form of insurance coverage and is very affordable when you're young. As you get older, your risk of dying increases, so the cost of term insurance goes up. This risk is known as the mortality rate.

As with most other insurance coverage, you pay premiums annually, semiannually, or quarterly for term insurance. For this premium, you receive a predetermined amount of life insurance protection. If you are the insured spouse and you die during the term you are insured, your beneficiaries will collect. If not, all of the premiums are gone, since there is no cash buildup in the policy, as there is in other types of life insurance policies that promote savings features (and hefty commissions). You will probably be required to take a physical examination to qualify for term insurance.

Term insurance is very inexpensive, which is why it's a popular life insurance policy. However, it only provides for death protection—there's no build-up of the money you pay in premiums.

When you buy term insurance, you can buy it with level (same) premiums for one year, called annual renewable term (ART), and renewable until age 90. This means that while the rates can increase each year, you do not need a physical exam to renew your policy; it is renewable until age 90, but not guaranteed. Other term policies and specified time periods are typically five, 10, 15, or 20 years. At the end of these time periods, the term insurance is renewable at sharply higher premium levels because you are older and statistically more likely to die during this time period.

> **The Road to Riches**
>
> Young women who are non-smokers tend to pay the least amount in premiums for term insurance. Because the cost of term insurance does not depend solely on age (where the younger you are, the lower your premiums are) and women live longer than men, women will pay less—especially if they don't light up.

Some people refer to term insurance as "renting coverage" because the only way your insurance policy pays out is if you die during this period. The payouts are offered in a lump sum payment or a steady stream of payments to your beneficiaries.

Make sure your policy offers a guaranteed renewability feature, so you don't have to take a medical test to continue coverage for another term, especially as you get older. Also if you have an annual renewable term policy, you can convert it to a whole-life policy—without a medical exam. This is called guaranteed conversion, and allows you to convert from rising premium term insurance to a fixed-premium whole life (cash value policy, which you'll learn about later in this chapter) policy. Here's a tip: If you think you may do this sometime down the road, make sure your term insurance policy is convertible into a whole life policy without another medical examination. There's an additional cost for this provision, but as you get older you'll end up saving more in premiums by doing so and avoiding the medical examination.

Here are some things to keep in mind when looking at a term insurance policy:

♦ **Make sure the illustrations that your insurance agent gives you show the rates you will pay and the maximum guaranteed rate they can require you**

to pay. There is a state law that regulates the maximum guarantees. But remember, policy illustrations are not guarantees—even if they're in black and white. Term premiums are subject to change based on mortality and the insurance company's finances.

♦ **Compare a level premium term policy to an annual renewable term (which increases after each term).** You know that premiums on ordinary ART policies increase in cost every year, right? Well, some companies offer a form of level premium term, in which they project that the annual premium will remain the same for 5, 10, or 20 years. At the end of the specified time period, your policy may kick back into a policy that has increasing premiums every year, or remain level for five years and then kick back into increasing premiums. Ask your agent if the premiums are projected or guaranteed. Insurance companies are not obligated to meet projected premiums—even if they are in the illustrations they give you.

♦ **Don't always settle for a short-term level premium policy.** Why? Because the premiums may skyrocket after the short-term is over. Again, because this is the life insurance industry, it depends on the policy. Make sure the agent explains all details in black and white.

♦ **Choose a guaranteed annual renewable term to avoid medical exams.** This ensures that you do not have to have a new medical exam every year to renew your term policy. Avoid those policies, which are known as reentry term.

If you would like quotes on term insurance, contact one of the following quote services. There is no obligation to purchase term insurance, but make sure they can handle the transaction in your state if you do buy a policy.

♦ **TermQuote** (1-800-444-8376 and www.termquote.com) maintains a database of 70 companies and will search to find the lowest cost term insurance policy based on your specifications, your age, and health condition.

♦ **SelectQuote** (1-800-983-8688 and www.selectquote.com) tracks term insurance prices nationwide.

♦ **INSurance INFOrmation** (1-800-472-5800) provides only advice—they do not sell insurance—but will find the lowest cost term insurance policy for you and can even reevaluate your existing policy.

♦ **Insurance Quote Services** (1-800-972-1104) sends a free booklet, *Simple Guide to Insurance Savings,* in addition to providing a quote service on low-cost term insurance. They will do a simple analysis on your life insurance needs based on your criteria and personal situation.

Cash Value Insurance

Sometimes known as permanent insurance, cash value insurance generally covers longer-term needs because term insurance becomes too expensive as you get older. But beware: Cash value insurance only makes sense for a few people and generates a lot of commissions for the insurance agent (unless you buy low-load or no-load insurance).

Cash value insurance combines life insurance and a savings "account." Most of the money you pay in premiums goes toward life insurance, and a few bucks are deposited into this "account" that is supposed to grow in value over time. Sounds like a winner, huh?

Wrong. The biggest hit your account takes in the early years you're building it is the commission that your insurance agent earns, which is shown to you in the illustration he or she shows you. What most folks don't know is that the commission is built right into the premium you pay for the insurance.

Watch Your Wallet

It may take years until the true return (what the insurance company promised you) on your account is equal to what it's supposed to be. To find out how much and what portion of your premium is going into your account, ask your insurance agent to show you the surrender value on the piece of paper (usually a ledger) he has. If the amount in the first few years is ZILCH, that's what your little account is getting.

All of the cash value insurance policies offer a tax-deferred savings feature to the insurance protection component of the policy. It is merely a death benefit plus an investment fund.

Interestingly enough, both term and cash value policies come in two varieties: participating and nonparticipating. Why all this gobbledygook? It seems confusing, but pay attention and you'll know more about how to make life insurance work for you than anyone you know!

Participating insurance entitles you to receive dividends (kind of like stock dividends) from the policy. These dividends are considered a refund of the portion of the premium that the insurance company did not pay in death benefits or administrative expenses over the previous year. This means that if the insurance company is collecting all of these premiums and no one died or administrative costs for the year were low, all the policyholders would get a "refund" in the form of dividends.

So what do you do with these dividends? You can take them as cash, and, of course, pay taxes to the IRS because the dividends are considered income; you can reinvest your dividends and *reduce* the future premiums you have to pay; or, you can buy additional "paid-up" (more) insurance. The choice is yours.

Nonparticipating policies pay no dividends, so there's nothing to reinvest. Instead, your premiums are fixed when you buy a policy at a set amount. True, these premiums on a nonparticipating policy will be less than those on a participating policy, but non-participating policies *do not* offer the perks of reinvesting your dividends for future growth or whatever you choose to do with the money.

Be careful: Some insurance company illustrations show that dividends from a paid-up policy can cover the premiums for a new policy when they *don't*. Instead, the new policies will really borrow against the death benefit (like a loan) in order to pay the premiums. Watch out for the fine print!

Because cash value insurance policies are not straightforward (it would make life too easy if they were), here's a rundown of the terms you can expect to hear about from an insurance agent:

♦ **Whole Life.** Your premium stays the same every year, and your death benefit is fixed. Because the amount of the premium is much more than what you would need to pay death benefits in the early years, the extra money is "deposited" into your "account" (inside the policy), which earns interest and grows tax-deferred. You can choose from two types of whole life policies. In the first, you pay the same level premiums into your old age—where you can borrow against the policy to get some extra cash in your retirement years. In the second, you pay premiums for a fixed number of years only; after that, the cash value in your "account" pays for the premiums. This is known as vanishing premiums. But be careful. If you don't have enough cash value built up to pay for those future premiums, your policy will be the thing that vanishes! And then you're stuck with kicking in more money. Whole life premiums are often invested in long-term bonds and mortgages.

♦ **Universal Life.** Unlike a standard whole life insurance policy, universal life offers you flexibility because it allows you the decision of changing the premium payments or the amount of the death benefit, as long as certain minimum requirements are met. (Sometimes, if you don't meet the minimum requirements or you violate the rules, your tax liability may skyrocket if you borrow or withdraw the money.) *You* decide how to design your policy. You can pay hefty premiums, build up a lot of tax-deferred cash value in your account, and then later change your mind that you want your cash value to pay for your premiums.

Or, you can opt for lower death benefits and a larger cash buildup or a smaller cash buildup and higher death benefits. It's up to you. You can even take a cash withdrawal and lower the death benefit. There's no interest expense if you do this, but even if you pay back the withdrawal, this permanently lowers the death benefit. Typically, there's enough cash value earnings to cover the cost of the insurance. Universal life premiums are invested in and reflect the current short-term rates available in the money market.

◆ **Variable Life.** Even though the annual premiums are fixed, the cash value of your account doesn't earn a fixed rate of return. The growth of your account in the policy depends on what investment choices you make. Generally, the investment choices are mutual funds managed by the insurance company. You have the option of shifting your money around. Note that the death benefit also rises and falls based on the performance, but it will never drop below the original amount of insurance coverage you specified on your contract.

◆ **Single-Premium Life.** The person who would benefit from this type of policy is someone who is older, has a lump sum of cash to invest on a tax-deferred basis that meets with IRS guidelines, and wants insurance benefits for his or her beneficiaries. These policies can earn a fixed rate of interest (like those in a whole life or universal life), or you can choose your own investment (as in a variable life policy).

Whatever you do, don't look upon a cash value insurance policy as retirement savings or your first means to accumulate growth on a tax-deferred basis. Even if your insurance agent tells you that your cash value account is compounding on a tax-deferred basis, that shouldn't be the reason to buy a cash value policy. If you're seeking tax-deferred growth, you should be participating in a company's 401(k) or an individual retirement account.

Insuring Your Paycheck

Have you ever thought about what would happen if you were suddenly unable to perform the work that provides your income? You should. According to the Health Insurance Association of America, if you are between the ages of 35 and 65, your chances of dying are equal to your chances of being unable to work for three months or more because of a disability through illness or injury. It is stressful enough trying to deal with an injury or illness that you don't want to have to worry about whether or not you're going to receive your salary while you're off work.

The Money Line _____

- One year of disability can wipe out 10 years' worth of savings.
- Forty-three percent of all foreclosures result from a disability in the family.
- Only 47 percent of the labor force is covered by disability insurance.

Your earning power is the most valuable asset that you will ever own—not your home, your car, or even your antique furniture. If you own your home, you probably have homeowner's insurance in case of loss or damage, and automobile insurance protects you and your family in case of a car accident. So why not insure your paycheck, too?

If you're like most folks, you probably have some type of access to a company-sponsored disability plan. Under the plan, most companies extend a form of paid sick leave or actual disability payments in case you are unable to work for a long time period. According to these plans, in order for you to receive benefits, many companies require you to be totally disabled. Other companies have both short-term and long-term disability plans. Ask your employer what provisions the company provides for both short- and long-term disability. The industry standard is 26 weeks for short-term disability, and you must qualify for most long-term disability plans. On average, an employer will pay the premiums for its employees' short-term disability insurance policy. For a long-term disability policy, it is standard for the employer and the employee to split the cost of the premium.

If you are paying part of the premium on disability insurance and your employer is paying the remainder, the benefits you receive are taxable equal to the amount of the premium your employer pays. For example, let's say your annual premium on your disability insurance policy is $1,200. You pay a third of your annual premium ($400), and your employer pays the other two-thirds ($800). If you were to become disabled and start collecting benefits, the portion of the premium that your employer paid would be considered taxable income. You would owe ordinary income taxes on your monthly benefits check.

Make sure you find out as much as you can about your company's disability plan. One woman we know did her homework before she went in for surgery. She was able to take a short-term disability leave for eight weeks and received 60 percent of her salary while recuperating at home. Many folks who don't do their homework go back to work a lot sooner without recovering fully and risk injuring themselves further.

If your company does not sponsor a plan, you can purchase your own individual policy. However, you have to have a job to receive disability insurance—no ifs, ands, or buts. But, only you can determine which type of disability policy is best. Your goal should be to maximize your coverage without paying for any unnecessary benefits.

Annual individual policy premiums range anywhere from $800 to $1,800, sometimes a lot more, depending on the bells and whistles you add to the policy. You will need enough coverage to provide between 60 and 70 percent of your gross earned income. Sit down and figure out what your living expenses would be if you were disabled for three to six months or more. Keep in mind you'll have to cover the mortgage or rent, automobile expenses, food, clothing, and utilities. Plus, you will incur additional expenses: medicine, doctor visits, and possibly nursing care.

Also keep these other factors in mind if you're considering buying disability insurance:

- ◆ **Realize that you will pay a higher premium for disability insurance if you have a risky job.** The cost of disability insurance is determined by your job and the amount of income you want. If you are in a hazardous occupation class (for example, if you are a firefighter, carpenter, or construction worker), you might not be able to receive long-term disability at any cost, unless it's through a company or a union.

- ◆ **Stay in good health and maintain a good credit report.** You will be required to take a medical exam to qualify for disability insurance. Plus the insurance company looks into your credit history. If you have a poor credit history or have recently filed for bankruptcy, an insurance company might not cover you.

- ◆ **Start your policy as soon as you can.** Why? The younger you are, the less your annual premiums will be.

- ◆ **Set a long elimination period.** This is the period of time before the benefits start. What you can do is match your emergency fund to this time period. Your premiums may be reduced by nearly 10 percent.

- ◆ **Avoid policies that pay only if you are totally disabled.** Instead, look for a policy that covers the *own occupation*. This guarantees that you will receive the full guaranteed disability payment, no matter what other work you do, as long as you are not able to return to your original occupation.

- ◆ **Make sure your policy is noncancelable as long as you keep paying the premiums.** Also make sure it has a guaranteed annual premium that can never be increased. Also crucial is a waiver of premiums clause, which states that you don't have to pay any more premiums once you become disabled.

◆ **Shop around.** Want the best price? Get quotes from three different insurance agents. Then contact USAA Life Insurance Company (which sells directly to consumers) at 1-800-365-8722 and compare prices. You can also get disability insurance quotes online at InsWeb at www.insweb.com.

◆ **See what Social Security has to offer.** Through Social Security you will receive disability income if you are completely disabled for five months and the disability is expected to last for at least one year or your lifetime.

Identifying Some Insurance Products You Don't Need

You want to cover your life, health, and wealth, right? That's why you're reading this chapter: to protect yourself and your loved ones. Unfortunately, many companies are jumping on the insurance bandwagon to take advantage of consumers, making them think they need these superfluous policies. Not so. Here's a list of what to avoid:

◆ **Credit life and credit disability policies.** Sold by credit card companies, such as VISA and MasterCard, these policies will pay a small monthly income in case of liability or a small benefit in case you die with an outstanding loan. Skip this coverage and purchase disability insurance instead.

◆ **Extended warranties.** Never purchase an extended warranty on anything— a television, VCR, or even an automobile. If something breaks down, it's likely that it would cost less to pay for it out of your own pocket.

◆ **Flight insurance.** This type of insurance is based on fears and misconceptions. Instead of protecting yourself with flight insurance, in case you die while flying, choose a good life insurance policy that protects you wherever you are—even if you're at 31,000 feet.

◆ **Life insurance for your children.** Touted on late-night television, this form of insurance boasts inexpensive monthly premiums to provide coverage for your children. It's not necessary at all, and it can be quite expensive. Besides, what parents would spend the benefits from a life insurance policy on their children if something terrible happened?

◆ **Mechanical breakdown insurance.** If you currently own a new car or have a leased vehicle that is still under warranty, this type of insurance is not necessary.

A good insurance policy can protect you from financial difficulties and provide assurances that your loved ones will be taken care of in the event of a premature passing.

Even events such as the birth of a child can impact your insurance needs. Whatever the circumstances, make sure you deal with a reputable insurance company. Remember: The policy is only as good as the company that wrote it.

The Least You Need to Know

◆ Renter's insurance is inexpensive and can help you replace your belongings in case of fire, theft, or other disaster.

◆ Homeowner's insurance is required by mortgage lenders.

◆ You can save money on your car insurance premiums by being a safe driver, driving a reliable car, and shopping around.

◆ There are two types of life insurance: term and cash-value. Term insurance is a better deal unless you're older or wealthy.

◆ Long-term disabilities that leave you unable to work can result in financial disaster.

Chapter 21

Tackling Your Taxes

In This Chapter

◆ Learning the basics on the latest tax law changes

◆ Avoiding the most common tax mistakes

◆ Knowing strategies to keep tax liabilities to a (legal) minimum

◆ Finding a good tax pro

When it comes to taxes, Americans are faced with ever-changing tax laws. These days, being smart about your taxes is more than just using a black pen instead of a pencil on your tax return, although the Internal Revenue Service says that's the biggest mistake taxpayers make when filing their returns.

New tax laws—such as the Economic Growth and Tax Relief Reconciliation Act of 2001 and the Jobs & Growth Tax Relief Reconciliation Act of 2003—are just some examples of the latest changes. Both bring about immeasurable changes and deductions not seen in 20 years.

We don't expect you to leisurely read the U.S. tax code or sit on the edge of your seat until a new law is enacted. If you want to make sure you're doing all that you can to keep the money you work so hard for, you can learn how to avoid common problems people make when it comes to tax planning and how to find the right tax professional for your situation in this chapter.

The Latest Tax Hoopla Defined

Your investment and retirement planning strategies, marital status, and, if you're self-employed, business decisions affect your tax situation, also. So do the latest tax law changes.

For example, the Jobs & Growth Tax Relief Reconciliation Act of 2003 may actually have more of an effect on you than the Economic Growth and Tax Relief Reconciliation Act of 2001, which was hailed as the biggest tax reduction in the last 20 years. It's important to keep in mind the changes that 2001 Act brings about and that many provisions take effect in distant future years. As you know from past tax law changes, such as the Taxpayer Relief Act of 1997 and the IRS Restructuring and Reform Act of 1998, it's a sure bet that between now and 2010 there will be more tax law changes enacted, some making these provisions better and quite possibly some making them worse.

Keeping in mind there are two national elections before the year 2010, many of the provisions of this law may be changed before their enactment dates. Due to budgetary provisions, this entire Act is actually repealed in the year 2011, unless Congress further acts to extend some provisions. Therefore, this becomes a very confusing tax law change.

The Latest, Latest Changes (and Stay Tuned for More)

With enactment of the 2003 act, tax brackets changed again. There are still six brackets, and only the bottom two—15 percent and 10 percent are still the same. The new top four brackets dropped and are now: 35 percent, 33 percent, 28 percent and 25 percent. Higher wage-earners will in essence keep more of their income. Without action by Congress, though, the earlier tax rates will return after 2010 with a maximum rate of 39.6 percent and the bottom 10 percent rate will be dropped.

The 2003 law provided relief to married people filing jointly who claim a standard tax deduction. They will be able to deduct $9,500, the same amount that two people filing separately could in the past. Likewise, the law expanded the 15 percent tax bracket so that the upper limit for a married couple was twice that of a single person in the same bracket. As a result of these changes, many married couples should see their tax bill drop, but only in 2004 unless Congress extends the break.

There were other changes as well. The 2003 law increased the deduction for each qualifying child to $1,000 from $600. The credit phases out as income rises and will be dropped after 2004 unless Congress takes action. The law also raises the exemption amount in the Alternative Minimum Tax (AMT, as it's commonly known) to $40,350 from $37,750 for unmarried individuals. The AMT minimum raises the amount for married couples to $58,000 from $49,000 and for married people filing separately, half those same amounts.

For individuals who invest in securities, the 2003 law brings much relief. The top tax rate on dividends has been slashed to 15% from 38.6%. The maximum tax rates on capital gains for securities held more than one year dropped 5 percentage points to 5 percent for those in the 10 percent and 15 percent tax brackets and to 10 percent for those in the higher brackets. Again, unless Congress votes in an extension, the rates will return to higher levels in 2009.

The 2003 law did not change the publicized provision of the 2001 law deals—the repeal of the estate tax. However, you must keep in mind that since this repeal takes effect in 2010, and we still have two more presidential and congressional elections before then. For specific questions as it relates to your estate tax planning matters, consult your tax adviser.

The Most Common Tax Mistakes

Tax planning doesn't just concern the wealthy. The money you save in taxes creates more investment dollars that can be put to work for you and your family if you start your tax planning now. Plus, preparing for April's tax season ahead of the typical last-minute schedule will help you get your records in order for when you really need them.

The Money Line _____

According to the General Accounting Office, the government agency that audits the IRS, about half of the 10 million correction notices the IRS issues each year are "incorrect, unresponsive, unclear or incomplete" as they relate to notices reported by banks and brokerage firms regarding interest and dividend payments. If you get an incorrect notice, you can contest it or contact your local problem resolution office.

All returns are examined for mathematical errors. Mistakes in arithmetic or in transferring figures from one schedule to another result in an immediate correction notice. If the error leads to a tax deficiency, you automatically receive a bill for that amount.

If you overpaid, the excess is applied to future taxes, credited, or refunded at your request. You can't appeal such corrections, but you can ask in writing that they be reviewed if you think the IRS made a mistake. Check the figures on the IRS correction notice. They have been known to make their own mistakes. Arithmetic mistakes alone rarely lead to a full audit.

Here are additional common mistakes made by taxpayers:

Mistake 1: Failing to keep good records. Getting organized is imperative. At some point, most people have the motivation to sort out their tax records, but they seem to drop the ball several months later. If you are one of those consumers whose sock drawer is stuffed with unopened envelopes holding your mutual fund statements and past IRS tax returns, kick the habit. It's time to clean house.

Solution: You have several options for maintaining good records, including tax software programs for your computer and your basic file folder for file statements. Tax preparation software packages for your computer can save you time and money. You just have to answer a few questions, and the software program plugs the information into the appropriate tax form. In addition, most tax-software packages print and file your returns automatically.

Mistake 2: Not withholding the right amount of taxes. Estimated tax payment and underpayment penalty rules have eased somewhat for Americans, but that does not give you the green light to ignore the rules. On the other hand, if you're anticipating a tax refund, all that means is that you've overpaid the government. You could have put that "extra" money to work for you in an investment instead of loaning it to Uncle Sam.

Solution: If you make estimated tax payments (as do many self-employed individuals or people who earn a whopping taxable income from investments outside a tax-deferred account), you should constantly monitor your tax-paying situation. The best way is to get Form 1040-ES, "Estimated Tax for Individuals," from the Internal Revenue Service by calling 1-800-TAX-FORM. Your goal should be to not overpay but not underpay; try to get as close to the mark as possible.

Mistake 3: Getting help when it's too late. This mistake is so common it's not even funny. It's like trying to prevent a cavity that has already made its way into your molar—there's no way to do it. Because many of your personal finance and investment decisions will affect your tax plan, get preventive help before it's too late.

Solution: Once you assess your personal financial picture and investment game plan, you'll need to monitor it consistently, especially as you build your wealth and accumulate a higher net worth. In the section "How to Find a Tax Pro" later in this chapter, you'll read which types of tax pros can help you, no matter what your circumstances are.

Mistake 4: Not contributing to a tax-deferred investment program. Up to certain limits, Individual Retirement Accounts (IRAs), 401(k)s, and other popular tax-deferred retirement plans allow you to reduce your taxable income by the amount of your contribution. Even if you only receive a partial or no tax deduction, investing your money in a mutual fund within your IRA takes advantage of the power of tax-deferred compounding.

Solution: Take advantage of the magic of tax-deferred compounding. If for 30 years you invest $3,000 a year in a mutual fund in your IRA instead of in a taxable account, assuming a 9 percent annual return, you will have accumulated almost $650,000 in your IRA. In contrast, you would have accumulated only $422,000 in a taxable account in the same amount of time. The capital gains and dividend distributions made would be tax-deferred for the entire 30 years. So just do it!

Mistake 5: Not replacing personal debt with mortgage debt to the extent possible. It's a smart tax planning strategy if you do this, especially because interest expense on mortgage loans is 100 percent tax-deductible. Interest expense on personal debt, such as credit cards or personal loans, is *not* tax deductible at all.

Solution: If possible, and where applicable, you may wish to consider a home equity loan to pay off your personal debt. The interest on a home equity loan is 100 percent tax deductible, and you can get rid of your personal debt, too! Check out Chapter 16 for more on home equity loans.

Mistake 6: Forgetting to check last year's income tax return for important items. For example, if you have $10,000 worth of gains and $10,000 worth of losses in one tax year, you can net the losses against the gains, and not have any taxable income from your investments. However, if your ordinary income (from your wages or salary) is $30,000 and you had $10,000 worth of losses (and no gains), you could only apply a total of $3,000 to your ordinary income to reduce your taxable income.

Solution: Carry forward the remaining loss amount on next year's return. Under current IRS rules, the remaining amount over $3,000 (in $3,000 increments) can be applied to the *following year's* tax bill.

Mistake 7: Not taking a profit because you're afraid to have a capital gain.
When you buy low and sell high, you earn a profit, which is a capital gain.
And, depending on your income tax bracket, you are subject to pay capital gains.

Solution: Don't shy away from taking a gain. Of course, review the tax implications a capital gain will have on your investment portfolio—and tax return—with your tax professional. After all, why are you investing in the first place?
To lose money? We hope not.

Mistake 8: Not properly tracking your investment basis. A basis is the original value of your investments. If you have mutual funds, for example, each year those funds will report to you the dividends and capital gains you earned. These dividends and gains will be taxable to you in the year reported. When you sell these funds, your gain will be the difference between what you receive on the sale of your "basis" (technically your amount realized less your initial investment basis).

Solution: Look for opportunities to reduce the taxable portion of your gain.
Your accountant will tell you that the basis actually increases once any initial financial gains you've reinvested are taxed. If you reinvested taxable gains from these funds, those gains (all of the dividends and capital gains reported) are added to your basis to reduce your gain (or increase your loss). For example, if you bought a fund for $1,000 and reinvested $100 in dividends and $25 in capital gains, your basis is now $1,125. If you sell the fund for $1,300, you only have to recognize $175 gain on that sale.

Mistake 9: Choosing the wrong filing status. Usually newly married couples have this problem—not knowing which filing status to choose. They have two options: married filing jointly and married filing singly.

Solution: Follow the advice of the IRS, at least in this instance. The agency confused newlyweds (and other married folks) to complete returns based on both situations and, based on the bottom-line outcome (whether you owe a little, a lot, or expect a refund), make your decision then. Nine times out of ten you'll "save" more in taxes by filing jointly.

Mistake 10: Anticipating a large refund. If you regularly look forward to receiving a huge income tax refund, know this: You're having too much in taxes withheld from your paycheck and, in effect, giving an interest-free loan to the IRS.

Solution: Change the number of allowances you claim on a W-4 form will increase your take-home pay.

Mistake 11: Forgetting to attach the right copy to your tax returns. Sounds silly, but it happens.

Solution: Attach all the "Copy Bs" of your W-2 forms to your return in order to avoid future correspondence with the IRS. And above all, make copies of all your returns and correspondence—just in case!

Mistake 12: Losing track of your receipts. In the real world, you either have proof of your deductions or you lose them. Always keep your receipts and checks if you want to deduct them.

Solution: Keep deductible receipts and checks for at least three years from the due date of the year filed, or the actual date filed, if later. Unless the IRS can prove fraud, the statute of limitations to disallow deductions is three years. Once this three-year period has elapsed, the IRS is prohibited from even questioning these deductions. Receipts for expenses that may be deducted in later years, such as improvements to your home, should be kept for three years after the return on which they are claimed.

Investments and Taxes

Whenever you invest your moolah, you have tax consequences to consider. For example, when you buy low and sell high, you earn a profit, which is a *capital gain*. And depending on your income tax bracket, if it's a sizeable gain, it can really make a difference in your bottom-line return figures.

The government did Americans a favor seven years ago in the Taxpayer Relief Act of 1997 and an even bigger favor with the 2003 tax act. As a result, assets sold after being held more than one year will be taxed at no more than 15 percent. That's a far cry from the 28 percent rate in the mid-1990s. So how can you determine if you should invest your money in an investment vehicle that stresses capital gains or income (usually in the form of interest payments or dividends that are taxed at your income tax rate)? The decision depends on your investment objective, but also creates different tax consequences.

Fiscal Facts

Capital gains are profit, expressed as the difference in purchase price and selling price, when the difference is positive.

Here's an example. Let's say you are in a higher tax bracket and invest more of your money in taxable bond funds. You get a pretty steady income stream through interest payments. These interest payments are taxed at *your* income tax rate. If you are taking out any cash distributions, that is a taxable event and subject to your tax bracket.

On the other hand, if you are investing in an investment that stresses capital gains (profit), it's a different story. For example, if you are investing in growth funds (no dividend income, rather long-term appreciation), any capital gains you realize are taxed at a maximum rate of 15 percent—a rate much less than taxable income brackets for high-income individuals.

The general rule of thumb is not to necessarily base your investment decisions solely on tax implications. If that were the case, many investors would never sell their investments! Your investment strategy is more important than a tax strategy. If you think market prices are dropping, you should take your profits and pay your taxes. A capital gain is always better than a capital loss!

Two of the Biggest Tax Blunders Ever

When folks hear "tax-free" or "tax-exempt," they jump for joy. The allure of tax-free investing is appealing, but it's not for everybody.

Many times, investors put their money in tax-exempt investments, such as municipal bonds, for the wrong reasons. Investors jump at the chance to boast of receiving tax-free income. But many of these municipal-bond funds tend to have lower yields than comparable taxable mutual funds for investors in lower tax brackets. If you are in a higher tax bracket, investing in municipal-bond funds is worth checking out because the income distributions you receive are exempt from federal tax. (Remember that the capital gains payouts are taxed.)

The best way to determine whether a fund's tax-free yield is competitive with the yield of a similar taxable fund is to find your taxable equivalent yield. If you want to calculate your taxable equivalent yield, take your marginal tax rate (your tax bracket) and subtract it from 100. For example, if you are in the 28 percent tax bracket, subtract 28 from 100 to get your denominator, which is 72. Therefore, if you were deciding whether to invest in a tax-exempt or a taxable fund, you would take 5.25 percent (the tax-exempt municipal bond return rate) and divide it by 72 to get your taxable equivalent yield, which is 7.29 percent. That means to benefit from investing in a taxable bond fund you would have to earn at least 7.29 percent on a taxable bond fund to end up with the same amount (after taxes) you would receive if you had invested in a tax-exempt bond fund.

The following table, "Tax-Free or Not Tax-Free?" does the math for you so you can easily determine whether a municipal-bond fund is a worthwhile investment for you. Compare the taxable equivalent yield for municipal bonds listed under your tax bracket with the rates listed for Treasuries and corporate bond funds to see which provides the highest yield. As you can see in the table, the lower the tax bracket, the less incentive there is to invest in tax-exempt mutual funds.

Tax-Free or Not Tax-Free?

Investment	Return	Your Tax Bracket			
		35%	28%	15%	10%
Municipal-Bond Fund	5.25%	8.08%	7.29%	6.18%	5.83%
Treasury-Only Bond Fund	6.00%	9.23%	8.33%	7.06%	6.67%
Corporate-Bond Fund	7.50%	7.50%	7.50%	7.50%	7.50%

Another blunder is when folks forget to swap or exchange investments to take a tax-loss and offset any other capital gains. If you sell an investment for a profit, you must pay capital gains tax on that profit. Depending on your level of income, you are taxed on the gain at 15 percent, which is the maximum tax rate on capital gains.

If you sell an investment at a loss, you can get a tax benefit, too. For example, if you have exchange privileges with your mutual fund family, consider using it in the event you are going to take a loss. Why? First, if you exchange shares of one mutual fund for shares of another mutual fund, it is considered a sale and a new purchase. If the sale of the first mutual fund constitutes a loss, you can use that amount to offset any other capital gains you have realized. This is considered a tax swap. Although your investment position is the same, you've saved on taxes. If you want to repurchase the shares in the same fund, you must wait 31 days before doing so according to IRS rules, in order to take the tax loss on the initial sale. If you don't wait the 31 days, it is known as a "wash sale," and you don't get to claim the loss. All capital gains and losses are reported on Schedule D of your tax return.

> ### The Road to Riches
>
> You can deduct up to $3,000 in losses from capital gains, thereby reducing your capital gains taxes. If you have no gains to offset your losses, you can deduct up to $3,000 from your ordinary income. Any additional amount can be carried forward to future years.

How to Find a Tax Pro

Congress keeps talking about simplifying the tax code, yet it doesn't seem to get any easier. If you don't understand the tax system, you probably pay more in taxes than necessary. A good tax professional will cut through the muck and identify tax-reduction strategies that will help reduce your tax bill, possibly increase your deductions, and decrease the likelihood of an audit (which can be triggered by any mistakes you make).

Hiring a professional isn't cheap, but you can save a few bucks if you know what to look for. Keep the following tips in mind before you hire anybody:

- **Don't hire the first tax adviser you find.** You don't buy the first house you look at, so apply the same theory here. You will be telling this person the most intimate financial details of your life. Make sure you interview at least five tax professionals face-to-face before you make your final decision. If the person is a true professional, he or she should spend quality time with you, ask a lot of questions, and above all, listen to you.

- **Ask the tax adviser about his or her credentials.** A continuing crackdown on unscrupulous tax preparers in the past five years has created stricter guidelines for tax preparers who file electronically. This effort screened out preparers with criminal records and severe financial problems who were claiming false refunds on clients' electronic returns. Preparers with access to IRS computers must be at least 21 years old and be a U.S. citizen or permanent resident alien. Credentials for all other types of tax preparers are listed in the appropriate section below.

Watch Your Wallet

Just because a CPA specializes in accounting issues doesn't mean he or she files tax returns. Make sure you find out if the CPA does before you shell out any dough.

- **Understand how the adviser gets paid.** There are flat fees, hourly fees, and fees based on a percentage of your return. The method of compensation is important because it can sway an adviser to recommend one course of action over another. By knowing the adviser's motivation, you can guard against any self-serving advice.

Get the Lowdown on CPAs

You will need a CPA if your tax situation is complex. For example, if you are self-employed, run a small business, or have a high salary and claim many deductions, a CPA can not only help you prepare your return but help you plan your taxes throughout the year. He or she looks at your entire financial picture and how each of your financial decisions (whether it's unloading a poor-performing stock or buying real estate for income) will impact your tax situation over the long haul. In addition, she can save you thousands of dollars in taxes by helping you conduct your financial affairs in a way that minimizes the government's tax bite.

Follow these guidelines when using a CPA:

♦ **Get a letter of engagement from the CPA.** This will list in detail what the CPA will do for you and what she will charge. Because a CPA charges more than any other tax preparer, the letter should state whether you are charged on an hourly basis or as a flat fee per return. You should also get an estimate of the time the CPA will spend on your return. If the CPA works on an hourly basis, ask her to guess how long it will take to do your tax preparations and complete your returns. However, if your CPA gives you a flat fee, see what other types of services are included in this fee, such as tax planning advice or whether she will attend an audit.

♦ **Don't simply dump your box of receipts and tell the CPA, "It's up to you to figure this all out."** One way to minimize their fees is to provide accurate records. You'll end up paying bucks deluxe if you're disorganized.

♦ **Find out how many tax returns the CPA works on each year.** If it's fewer than 300, consider him a candidate. If he prepares any more than that, he's probably sacrificing quality. Also see what percentage of your CPA's clients had to file extensions last year. If it's more than 20 percent, the CPA is probably swimming in (and behind on) paperwork.

♦ **Find a CPA in your area by contacting the AICPA (American Institute for Certified Public Accountants).** This is the professional organization for CPAs, and you can reach it at 1-800-862-4272.

Try an Enrolled Agent

Enrolled agents are the biggest secret in the world of tax preparation. They are tax experts who worked for the IRS at least five years as auditors or who have passed a strict two-day test of federal tax law. If you don't mind that an enrolled agent doesn't have "CPA" listed after his name on the letterhead, an enrolled agent can be just as good—for much less money. Enrolled agents are experts in all areas of tax preparation; some even specialize in a few areas of the law. Make sure you determine an agent's specialty before you hire him. The best way to find an enrolled agent near you is to contact the National Association of Enrolled Agents (NAEA) at 1-800-424-4339 or on the web at www.naea.org. They will send you a list of three agents in your area.

Learn the Truth About Tax Attorneys

Tax attorneys know the ins and outs of federal tax law, but they do not prepare tax returns. Their role is to offer tax advice to your CPA or enrolled agent if you are in a complicated legal tax jam.

Hire a tax attorney if—and only if—you find yourself in a major legal jam resolving tax issues, such as a serious tax dispute with the IRS that can only be resolved in Tax Court. You may also need a tax attorney when you are working on the details of your estate plan and how it will affect your tax situation. Keep in mind, however, that these professionals are expensive! You will pay a price for their legal advice. Tax attorneys charge as much as several hundred dollars per hour, sometimes more if they represent you in court. Their fees may be deductible, but it's not guaranteed.

If a legal problem arises and your CPA cannot recommend a competent tax attorney, call the American Bar Association at 312-988-5000 or find one listed in the *Martindale-Hubbell Law Directory*, which lists lawyers by state and specialty.

Watch Your Wallet

> You do not want to be troubled by a nagging concern that your CFP is recommending products because of the commissions they generate instead of for their appropriateness of your situation. Make sure you get a written estimate of any fees you must pay, and make sure he or she is certified by the IRS to help you with your tax returns.

Know When to Use a Certified Financial Planner: A Jack-of-All-Trades

Imagine someone who knows your entire financial picture *and* can prepare your tax return. Sound like a financial dream come true? A certified financial planner (CFP) can create a budget for you, help you build an investment portfolio, and assist you with retirement and estate planning and tax preparation. Since CFPs must be licensed by the International Boards of Standards and Practices for Certified Financial Planners (IBCFP), look for their accreditation. There are a lot of financial planners out there masquerading as professionals; unless they have the acronym, don't deal with them.

Watch Your Wallet

> Fees for instant refunds are costly because they're based on an interest rate on this short-term "loan" that can run as high as 20 to 30 percent on an annual basis.

CFPs do *not* have the same credentials as a CPA. People who choose CFPs to help with their tax preparation often do so because they know their whole financial picture.

CFPs are compensated in one of three ways: on a commission-only, fee-only, or commission and fee basis. The least expensive of the three for you (if you plan to maintain a working relationship with this person) is fee-only. For tax preparation, the most common form of payment will be fee-only. Fee-only planners do not get a dime for any type of investment recommendations they make, which is one of the reasons this condition works out best for most folks. When you find a fee-only planner, he or she should give you a no-cost, no-frills initial consultation to assess your financial condition. Based on this information, the CFP will give you an estimated fee that is set in advance. Typical rates average $75 an hour, depending on the complexities involved.

To find a qualified CFP in your area, contact the Institute of Certified Financial Planners (ICFP) at 1-800-282-7526 or search for a qualified CFP in your area on the web at http://www.cfp.net/default.asp.

Using H&R Block and the Like

Places like Jackson Hewitt Associates process millions of tax returns each year and file electronically, which speeds up your refund if you are expecting one. In addition, some chains offer an instant refund, which is actually a loan that is paid back when your refund arrives from the IRS.

If you don't have a complicated tax situation, check out a national tax preparation chain. They are convenient, and they help you on a first-come, first-serve basis. However, keep in mind that you probably won't establish a long-term relationship with your tax preparer as you would with other tax professionals. The best way to find a national chain near you is to look in the Yellow Pages or online. H&R Block offers online tax filing for $19.95 to $99.95, depending on whether you prepare and file your return or they organize and prepare it for you.

Going It Alone

Even if you have a CPA do your taxes, you should know *every* single detail that goes into your income tax return! If you prepare your own tax return, you know the ins and outs and can monitor your tax situation. Just make sure you keep up with any major changes in federal tax laws.

If you do go it alone, the IRS can actually help you. Although the IRS won't fill out your return, it will help you do so free of charge. All IRS offices hold tax preparation clinics, distribute free IRS publications, and answer tax questions over the phone. To contact them, call 1-800-829-1040. There are some free books and publications that can help you, such as Publication 17, *Your Federal Income Tax*, which is published by the IRS to help with individual tax-return preparation.

If you get organized, learn the ins-and-outs of the tax code, and allow yourself plenty of time to prepare the return, you'll be surprised how much less stressful tax-time can be!

The Least You Need to Know

◆ The key to having a less stressful tax time is to keep your tax-related documents organized. Tax-preparation software can help you do this.

◆ Investing in IRAs and 401(k)s is a great way to reduce your tax liability.

◆ Before you invest in stocks, bonds, or mutual funds, make sure you assess what effect those investments will have on your tax situation.

◆ Tax attorneys and CPAs are only necessary if your tax situation is complex. Less expensive sources of help include enrolled agents, certified financial planners, and tax preparation chains such as H & R Block.

◆ The cheapest way to handle your taxes is to do them yourself.

22

Retiring R-I-C-H!

In This Chapter

- Why it pays off to start socking away today
- How to button down a plan that really works
- How to decipher the smorgasbord of retirement accounts available
- How to maximize your money if you're already retired
- How the latest tax law changes affect your retirement—for the better

The savings rate of American consumers has shriveled to almost nothing, putting it at the lowest level since the Great Depression, according to the Commerce Department.

What have you got to say about it? How much money are you saving for your future?

The amount of money you have earmarked for your retirement probably will be insufficient in relation to your needs. But there's something you can do about it today.

Let's hop on the retirement plan bandwagon and create a financially sound future for you and your heirs. This chapter explains what you can do for retirement starting today, some common mistakes you should avoid, and the different types of investment products and accounts that will get you from here to there.

Why It Pays to Sock Money Away

How many of you had a piggy bank during your childhood? That plump porcelain pig that held all your loose change was the only method of saving you knew about. You knew you were supposed to save for a rainy day, but not many people understood *why* they were supposed to do it.

That rainy day is closer than you think. So why save for it now? The earlier you start saving for retirement, the less you'll need to save to have enough money to live well. Many people live an average 15 to 20 years in retirement, yet only save enough money for about half of that.

Income during retirement is based on three building blocks: Social Security, pension plans, and investment assets. And the only one you really can control is the third.

Investment assets for your retirement include income from 401(k)s, Individual Retirement Accounts (IRAs), and other retirement plans. They also include any assets you have, including investment accounts, home equity (if you plan to sell your house without buying another one), inheritances that you know you'll receive, and all other liquid assets.

If you're counting on Social Security, forget it. Given the funding problems in the Social Security system, benefits are projected to provide only 21 percent of your current income. If you earn $26,000 a year, expect to receive an average estimated monthly benefit check of $455.

Why We Avoid Thinking About Tomorrow

The statistics on how we relate to saving money are not encouraging. So if you need some motivation, consider this: It takes $480,000 in savings earning 6 percent after taxes to yield $30,000 in annual income for 20 years, adjusted each year for inflation. The sooner you start, the faster your nest egg will grow.

A Big Six accounting firm survey shows that unless we save a great deal more than we currently do, three out of four Americans over the age of 20 will have less than half the money they need to retire and maintain their pre-retirement standard of living.

In fact, on average Americans would have to reduce their expenses by 60 percent—or get a job flipping burgers—in order to make it through their twilight years without running out of money.

If your after-tax expenses currently run $50,000 a year and you retire today, you would have to cut your spending by at least $30,000 if you want your money to last as long as you do. And that huge cut in your budget assumes that you have the good sense to die on the day you spend your last penny. If you survive longer than the actuaries estimate, you'll outlive your money.

That is not a good problem to have.

Perhaps a future inheritance is something you are counting on for your retirement. Your parents may well be in good financial shape, thanks to being part of that lucky post-war generation of unparalleled affluence. Even middle-income people may well have estates of $1 million or more. But you need to be aware that inflation, longevity, and the rising cost of long-term medical care can eat away at the value of your inheritance, which you may not get until you're in or near retirement.

Retirement may seem like a long time away, but tomorrow always comes, you know. It's hard to get yourself motivated to save for retirement because it generally requires spending less money now. You can always pay a financial planner to help you get organized, but in the end you have to motivate yourself to change and follow the planner's advice.

Know that if you delay any longer, you're going to have to come up with more money down the road for the same end result. Keep reading to learn how you can start saving today.

Understand the Power of Saving

Read these motivating facts:

- A 25-year-old woman who saves $100 a month until she retires will have six times more money when she retires than if she were to begin saving $100 a month at age 45.

- A 50-year-old woman who contributes $500 a month to a retirement plan will never catch up with the 30-year-old woman who has been socking away $100 a month.

- If you save $3,000 a year at 6 percent for 30 years in a regular savings account, you'll have close to $185,000 after paying taxes. However, if you shelter your $3,000 each year in your IRA at 6 percent, your savings increases to over $250,000 because of the tax-deferred feature.

Let's get started.

Stop Making Excuses

If you don't take advantage of saving your money from taxes, then you *really* don't have money to save! Sure, you may be saving for a child's college education or saving your money to buy a home, but that money is typically in taxable accounts. So you're paying "extra" taxes by keeping your money in those accounts. Of course, you must continue to save for those financial goals, but *your financial goal of retirement is important, too*. Scholarships, Pell grants, and student loans are available for your children, but Social Security won't provide for you the way a scholarship can provide for your child. You can save for retirement if you reduce some of your current living expenses or find additional ways to increase your income.

> ### The Road to Riches
>
> Perhaps you don't have access to a company-sponsored program. No matter what the excuse (because that's what they really are), you can still save for retirement.
>
> Don't think that you don't have enough money to save or even that it's too late to do so. It's never too late. It's better to have something when you reach retirement than nothing at all. You won't have anyone to blame but yourself. And you will have daily opportunities to do so when you have to deny yourself things that you want or need.

Just because you contribute to a retirement plan doesn't mean that you'll never have access to your money until you're older, either. Although the IRS will hit you with a penalty if you withdraw your money before age 59½, you can access your money, depending on the circumstances. For example, if you contribute to a 401(k), some companies will allow you to borrow against your cash balance, but that's up to the company. There are also hardship withdrawals you can take—not for a whirlwind vacation, but for when you're in a financial pinch (as a result of a medical emergency, for example).

Finally, don't count on your cash value life insurance policy to take advantage of tax-deferred growth. True, cash value life insurance policies provide tax-deferred growth, but there's no tax deduction. And you don't "benefit"—your heirs do when you die and the policy kicks in. You can borrow against your life insurance policy, but if you die with the loan outstanding, your intended heirs will receive less than you planned.

Turn These Must-Do's into Can-Do's!

Part of your everyday money management should include planning for retirement. You don't need to go overboard and deny yourself day-to-day necessities (like food, shelter, and basic clothing needs) because you fear you'll wind up impoverished if you eat today. That's not the point. But if you have the benefit of time when it comes to evaluating your retirement plan, take advantage of it.

The earlier you begin to plan for your golden years, the less money you'll have to save to live well in the future. Why is this? Because the sooner you begin, the more your money has time to compound.

Experts say that if you have more than a 10-year time frame, invest your retirement money for the long term. Younger people can take advantage of the potential growth that some investments offer, especially equities. Obviously, you don't want to gamble your retirement savings when you get close to retirement, but if you have time on your side, take advantage of more aggressive investments that offer higher degrees of potential growth.

Don't be *too* conservative in your retirement savings. This tip is aimed especially at the younger generation saving for retirement. Too often, younger people make the mistake of being conservative in their retirement-savings strategies. The biggest mistake is when they invest their 401(k) money in a Money Market fund as their long-term retirement choice. Even with Money Market fund rates hovering around 4 percent, this is still a bad move especially when rates usually do not keep up with inflation. Even if you are close to retirement, don't forget that you will probably live for a long time as a retiree, so your funds will still need to grow.

Take advantage of *every* opportunity to shelter your retirement money from current income taxes. These opportunities, which are discussed in detail later on in this chapter, are different types of investment products that offer a tax-deferred feature. You can shelter your money from current income taxes through an individual retirement account, a company-sponsored retirement plan, or an annuity.

Even if you have a retirement program at work, open and contribute to an IRA to take advantage of tax-deferred growth. Depending on your income level, if you are covered by a company-sponsored plan, you may not receive a tax deduction on your IRA contributions. Are you *not* going to open an IRA because you don't receive a tax deduction? You still get the tax-deferred growth, just not the perk from Uncle Sam.

Retirement Accounts Explained in Simple English

Individual retirement accounts were set up for you to make an annual contribution of up to $3,000 or 100 percent of earned income that year, whichever is less, up until the year you reach age 70½. In other words, your contributions must come from a salary, wages, or self-employment income. Even alimony counts.

The Road to Riches

A $3,000 IRA contribution works out to $57.69 per week. If you begin at age 21 and contribute until you're 71, at an average annual growth rate of 10.6 percent, today's 21-year-old contributing $3,000 to an IRA every year will build up a next egg of $4.8 million. If you start at age 40, the same investment would grow to just under $680,000 by the time you reach age 71.

Fiscal Facts

More than 41 percent of U.S. households owned Individual Retirement Accounts as of the beginning of 2004, up from less than 40 percent in 2001. Roth IRAs accounted for almost all of the increase.

What if you're a nonworking spouse? If you are part of a couple with one spouse working and the other not working, the working spouse may contribute an extra $250 (for a total of $3,250). However, the contributions must go into separate accounts—one bearing the name of the working spouse and one bearing the name of the nonworking spouse. The account held by the nonworking spouse is called a spousal IRA. Spouses who work part-time and have no company benefits can open up their own IRAs. The same rules apply.

Ironically, an IRA causes a lot of confusion, as the most common question people ask is, "Should I invest my money in a mutual fund *or* in an IRA?" The truth is that you should invest your money in a mutual fund *inside* an IRA. An IRA is an account that shelters your contributions from current income taxes. The contribution you make should be made by your tax-filing due date.

So Who Is This Roth Guy Anyway?

Similar to the traditional IRA, the Roth IRA shares the upside in the strategy of tax-deferred growth, but not the tax deductions, depending on your taxable situation.

The great thing about the Roth IRA is that it gives you access to tax-free money upon retirement. Most workers are eligible for a Roth IRA. If you are single or head of the household and your gross income is $110,000 a year or less, you can opt for a Roth. If you are married and file a joint tax return and have a gross income of $160,000 or less, you are also eligible. Even if both you and your spouse have pension plans or 401(k)s, you can still contribute up to $3,000 each into a Roth.

Another valuable benefit of the Roth IRA is that you do not have to begin making withdrawals at any age. A regular IRA requires you to start taking withdrawals at the age of 70½.

Whereas the traditional IRA is a tax-deductible contribution of up to $3,000 of earned income, the Roth IRA is not. Monies that go into a Roth IRA are made with an after-tax contribution of up to $3,000 per year. You don't get the deduction, but you do get another wonderful benefit: When you take the money out at retirement, the entire amount—including any capital gains, dividends or interest—is not taxed. You can contribute to both an IRA and a Roth IRA within the same year simply by dividing up your contribution, but the paperwork involved in having two accounts may not be worth it.

Here is a bullet-point basic to help you understand the Roth IRA:

♦ Most of the rules that apply to traditional IRAs, such as the types of investments you can have within the account (no commodities, for one), also apply to Roth IRAs.

♦ You can contribute to a Roth IRA even if you are over age 70½ and even if you participate in a 401(k) plan or other employer plan. But, you or your spouse must have taxable compensation income, and your modified AGI (adjusted gross income) must not exceed certain limits: $110,000 on a single return or $160,000 on a joint return. Nonworking spouses can put up to $3,000 in a Roth IRA if the couple qualifies with income of less than $160,000 on a joint return.

♦ You're not eligible to make annual contributions to a Roth IRA unless you have taxable earned income (from wages, for example); however, one caveat is that alimony income is included as taxable earned income.

♦ First-time homebuyers, who hold their Roth IRAs for at least five years, can withdraw a limited amount of earnings tax-free even before the age of 59½.

For more information on Roth IRAs, check with your tax adviser or financial professional.

They're for Your Benefit

The range of retirement plan alternatives is broad, but most plans fall into one of two major categories:

1. Defined contribution plans provide an individual account for each participant (that's you), and for benefits based solely on the amount contributed to the participant's account. These include—but are not limited to—money-purchase plans (which are a type of pension plan where companies make a minimum contribution to the plan each year), profit-sharing plans, and 401(k) plans.

2. Defined benefit plans are retirement plans other than an individual account plan (like a defined contribution plan). Retirement benefits must be definitely set. For example, a plan that entitles you to a monthly pension for life equal to 25 percent of your current monthly compensation is a defined benefit plan.

Pension and IRA Changes

Starting in 2002, IRA contributions increased in a stepped up basis as a result of the Economic Growth and Tax Relief Reconciliation Act of 2001. The following table details the increases:

IRA Contribution Maximums, By Year

Tax Years	Maximum Deductible IRA
2002–2004	$3,000
2005–2007	$4,000
2008 and later	$5,000

After 2008, the limit will be adjusted annually for inflation. For individuals 50 and older, extra contributions are allowed as a catch-up provision, i.e., $3,500 for years 2002 to 2004; $4,500 for 2005; $5,000 for years 2006 to 2007; and $6,000 for years 2008 and later.

Roth IRAs are included in the previous increases.

Annual defined benefit and defined contribution limits increased after 2001. The defined contribution dollar limit rose to $40,000 and is being adjusted annually. The annual compensation taken into account for these qualified plans also increased after 2001 to $200,000. In 2002, the maximum annual deferral for 401(k) plans was $11,000 and is being increased by $1,000 each year until reaching $15,000 in 2006.

These liberalized rules allow you to contribute more for your retirement. Social Security changes were not part of the package; therefore, the liberalization of these retirement rules are an indication that the government wants you to take care of your own retirement.

Another Way to Save for Retirement

Socking away $3,000 or more a year into a retirement program is great. But, for those of you who have more money to invest, and want to take advantage of tax-deferred growth, you may want to think about an annuity.

What exactly is an annuity? You already know what CDs and mutual funds are, right? Well, an annuity is an insurance company product with fixed-rate CDs and no-load mutual funds in it, which are mutual funds that do not carry any sales charges on them.

It's like creating an IRA that you can contribute an unlimited amount of money to. Plus you are not obligated to take out the money by age 70^1/$_2$, as you are required to do with an IRA. However, unlike an IRA, you cannot deduct your contribution on your income tax returns, but you can still take advantage of their tax-deferred feature. The money you invest in an annuity is made with *after-tax* dollars.

Once you put your money in, you must leave it there until you turn 59^1/$_2$. If you dip into the money, watch out! You'll get nicked with a 10 percent federal tax penalty on any interest earnings to date—but not your principal. Plus the insurance company hits you with surrender charges—sometimes as high as 7 percent in the first year, although they do gradually decline 1 percent each year, until they vanish.

The Money Line

There's one great advantage to a variable annuity that goes beyond the tax-deferred compounding: a guaranteed death benefit. This means the insurance company guarantees that when you die, your beneficiaries will receive *at least* as much as you invested in the original annuity or the current account value, whichever is greater. Make sure whoever sells you your contract explains how this works.

They come in two different types: an immediate annuity and a tax-deferred annuity. With an immediate annuity, you give a lump sum of money to the insurance company. Based on your age, life expectancy, and current interest rates, the insurance company calculates how much they'll send you each month—no matter how long you live—and invest it accordingly to provide for these specific dollar amounts.

To set up a tax-deferred annuity, typically, you give the insurance company a lump sum of money to invest, and it grows on a tax-deferred basis over a number of years. The beauty of a tax-deferred annuity is that you don't pay any taxes on the earning or profits that are built up in the annuity until you take the money out. If you want, you can add money to your tax-deferred annuity in various amounts over time. This is known as a flexible-premium deferred annuity.

Within a tax-deferred annuity, you have two options: a guaranteed-rate or a variable annuity. Guaranteed rate is just like it sounds: It pays a fixed interest rate that is guaranteed for a period of 1 to 10 years. (It's up to you.) A variable annuity, though, allows you to choose among a wide range of mutual funds, such as stock, bond, or money market funds. Obviously, because these types of investment products don't guarantee a rate of return, your return in a variable annuity can fluctuate.

Most often, if you have more than a 10-year time horizon, and want to take advantage of tax-deferred growth, a variable annuity is a great place to begin. But, there are some questions you should ask the insurance agent before you invest your cash.

◆ **Find out what the total expense, including all fees, would be for maintaining this account.** Even though there are no up-front sales commissions or loads that are charged (remember, these are no-load funds and do not have any sales charges on them), there are still expenses involved. Find out what the surrender charges are, management fees (no-load funds have them, although they vary), and mortality fees, which take into account your projected life span.

◆ **Have the agent explain what funds are available within the annuity.** Just as you do when you are mutual fund shopping, check out what types of funds are available and the performance history of each. Within each variable annuity is a pool of mutual funds. Make sure they're well-established funds that you have heard of from your research.

◆ **Determine up-front if you can add more money to the annuity.** If it's possible, find out how much the minimum amounts are and if the additional money you invest will also extend the period of surrender charges. You don't want that to happen. Additionally, find out if the annuity will allow an automatic investment program similar to an automatic investment plan set up by a fund company. This way, you can have your monthly investment electronically transferred from your bank account to your annuity. Discipline, discipline, discipline!

What to Do Now That You're Retired

For the past thirty-some-odd years, you've spent a lot of time doing your homework—and contributing as much as possible to retirement accounts. After all, you want your retirement lifestyle to be comfortable, right? Right! But there are some rules you still have to follow *during* your retirement to keep the money growing, so it can keep on flowing.

◆ Continue to have your money grow and compound tax-deferred as long as possible.

◆ Be flexible with your funds so you can cushion yourself against any changing market conditions.

◆ Monitor the changing tax laws and how they affect your distributions.

◆ Keep a small portion of your retirement assets in growth investments (depending on your risk tolerance).

Your retirement income is probably based on how much you decide to receive in distributions (the money you eventually take out from your retirement plan) and when. You must begin taking distributions from your IRA by April 1 of the year *after* you reach age 70½. It's okay if you start taking distributions before you reach 70½, but not before 59½, if you want to avoid the penalties imposed by the IRS. There are no limitations on how much or how little you can take out.

Once you turn 70½, it's a whole new ballgame. The first important question is one that only you can answer, and the answer will be different for everyone.

Do you want to take the least possible amount out of your IRA leaving the balance to grow tax-deferred? Or are you dependent on your IRA for living expenses and just trying to stretch out the withdrawals to cover your life expectancy?

Taking minimum withdrawals is the choice you should make if you have enough other assets—outside your IRA—to use for retirement expenses. You'll want to use that IRA money last, letting it grow as long as possible and leaving the balance for your surviving spouse.

On the other hand, many of you are counting on that IRA money to provide the bulk of your living expenses in your retirement. You'll want to take as much money out as possible every month, without running out of cash at the end of your life. That requires a different sort of calculation.

There are two great unknowns as you make this decision about withdrawal options. The first is, of course, you don't know when you'll die; and, if you're married, you don't know which spouse will die first.

The second unknown is how your investments will fare within your remaining IRA.

IRS rules dictate that you must take out enough money in distributions each year to use up your IRA account over your life expectancy.

So how does the IRS know how long you're going to live? It's based on IRS mortality tables; your IRA *custodian* (the firm or company where your IRA is held) can help you calculate the amount.

You should have other retirement savings that you have put aside if you outlive your IRA and the IRS' mortality table. If you want to make your money last longer, have your annual distributions based on the joint life expectancy of *both* you and your spouse. If your spouse is much younger than you are, that would extend the payments over a longer period of time. If you are not married at the time, your calculation can be based on the life expectancy of you and your beneficiary (although there is a 10-year maximum age difference allowed).

The Early Bird Gets ...

Imagine being 65 years old and living on $22,000, with almost a third coming from Social Security benefits. Many of you might spout off, "Oh, that's not going to happen to me!" yet it's a very real statistic for the 13 million seniors who live on that type of fixed income. So ask yourself: Can you live on that?

It's no secret: Rumors of the depletion of the Social Security fund in 20 years are nothing new. But, government funding could change. Whether Social Security is here or not, don't consider benefits to be your only means of paying for your living expenses.

As you work and pay FICA taxes, you earn Social Security credits. The number of credits needed for retirement benefits depends on your date of birth. If you were born January 2, 1929, or later, you need a total of 40 credits.

To learn the secrets of the Social Security system and make the most of your benefits, be informed, but don't let Social Security be the end to your means. The following sections describe tips that will help you get the most out of your Social Security benefits when the time comes.

Secret #1: No Matter How Old You Are, Get an Idea of What Your Retirement Benefits Are Now

Call the Social Security Administration at 1-800-772-1213, and ask for an *Earnings and Benefit Estimate Statement*. The SSA will send you a form asking you how much you earned last year, your estimated earnings for this year, the age you plan to retire, and your estimated future annual earnings.

Based on this information, you'll get a complete earnings history, along with estimates of your benefits for retirement at age 62, 65, or 70. It includes estimates of disability or survivor's benefits and lists the total Social Security taxes you have already paid.

Secret #2: Verify Your Social Security Record Every Three Years

Make sure all the taxes you have paid are credited to your account. Errors identified early are easier to correct. If you happen to run across an error, have your past tax returns and pay stubs available for proof.

Secret #3: Delay Retirement and You'll Increase Your Social Security Benefits

Age 65 is considered to be full-retirement age for receiving full benefits, but only for people born before 1938. The date moves out with each year. For example, the retirement age for people born in 1960 and later is now 67 years. Benefits are reduced if you retire sooner and collect them; they are increased if you delay retirement. You can start collecting benefits at age 62. It may pay to wait if you ...

♦ Have sufficient financial resources and do not need Social Security benefits to meet living expenses.

♦ Earn so much from your income that it triggers a tax on your Social Security benefits.

♦ Earn so much from your income that you will lose benefits due to an earnings limit.

You may be better off using your savings or investments for living expenses. By spending your savings, you'll have less interest income to push benefits into the taxable range. Plus waiting to collect Social Security will mean bigger benefit checks in the future.

Whatever your situation, understanding the quirks and rules involved in applying for Social Security benefits will only make the system work for you. After all, you'll be working for it for quite a long time, right?

Count on You!

Average-wage earners can expect Social Security benefits to replace only 38 percent of their monthly income, according to the Social Security Administration. (Maximum-wage earners can expect benefits to replace 28 percent of their income.) So where can you get the remaining 62 percent if you're an average-wage earner?

Don't count on bonuses, commissions, stock options, severance pay, or even vacation pay. These all chalk up to income that will count toward the Social Security earnings limit, which can eventually reduce your Social Security benefits. That's why the following income sources are so important—they don't count toward the earnings limit:

♦ Pensions and retirement funds

♦ Investments (unless you are in the brokerage business)

◆ Individual Retirement Accounts (IRAs and Roth IRAs)

◆ Annuities and some tax-exempt trust funds

◆ Rental properties

◆ Gifts or inheritances and lottery winnings

◆ Money received from a reverse mortgage plan

So even if you've built up a sizeable IRA and take distributions from it as a source of income, you don't have to fret about not getting your full Social Security benefits.

A Final Word

Geez, why all these calculations and numbers in the retirement world? It doesn't have to be intimidating. No matter if you're single, married, divorced, or widowed, you should do something to prepare for retirement. Much of your fear will quickly disappear once you realize how easy it is to make your savings grow for retirement. The name of the game is to take one buck and turn it into two (then four, then sixteen, etc.) for a financially healthy tomorrow.

The Least You Need to Know

◆ Company pensions and Social Security won't cover all your financial needs for retirement.

◆ Be fully prepared for retirement and start a retirement savings plan *now*.

◆ It's never too early to take advantage of company retirement plans such as 401(k).

◆ If you don't have access to a company retirement plan, or if you are looking for tax-deferred growth, consider opening up an IRA.

◆ Regardless of age, get an idea of what your retirement benefits are now.

Glossary

11th District Cost of Funds   Adjustable-rate mortgage index based on the average yield on deposits at thrifts in Federal Home Loan Bank's 11th District, which is based in San Francisco. Index is used by lenders nationwide.

12b-1 fees   Also known as 12b-1 plans, charges that cover marketing and promotional costs of mutual funds. Fees range from $1/4$ percent to 1 percent of the fund's total assets each year.

1-Year Treasury Constant Maturity   Adjustable-rate mortgage index based on a number calculated by the Federal Reserve. Index is used by lenders nationwide.

401(k)   Employer-sponsored retirement plan named for the relevant section in the tax code. It allows employees to make payroll contributions on a pre-tax basis, with some employers matching contributions. Money is invested in options of employee's choosing within the plan.

403(b) plan   A 401(k) for employees of nonprofit or tax-exempt organizations, such as schools and hospitals.

adjustable-rate mortgage (ARM)   Home loan whose rate changes periodically based on a published index, often with annual and life-of-loan rate limits. ARMs often have low introductory rates.

annual credit card fee   Dollar amount a card issuer charges for the right to have the card for one year. The fee can be waived under certain conditions, such as carrying a balance.

annual percentage rate (APR)   Complex mathematical formula that includes the interest rate and certain loan charges in determining the true cost of borrowing money.

annual percentage yield (APY)   Annualized return on bank deposits. The actual amount paid in interest depends on how often the yield changes, the account balance and, in the case of CDs, the term.

annuity   An investment sold by insurance companies that consists of fixed-rate CDs and no-load mutual funds. Accountholders contribute an unlimited amount of money and earn interest and dividends on a tax-deferred basis.

ATM card   Bank-issued card that allows you to withdraw cash from a checking or savings account using an automated teller machine. Many banks charge fees for using an ATM machine owned by another bank or financial network.

average daily balance   Formula for calculating the balance of a deposit or loan account. The dollar figure is used several ways, such as calculating credit-card interest, interest earned, and whether fees should be applied for dropping below the minimum checking, savings and other deposit accounts.

back-end load funds   Mutual funds that charge a penalty if you withdraw your money before a certain time. The penalty decreases and is eventually eliminated over time.

bankruptcy   Process through federal courts for relieving debts. Chapter 7 discharges all debts, except some taxes and maybe alimony payments, and Chapter 13 allows people with steady income to pay off bills over a 36 to 60-month period.

basic checking   No-frills checking account with low or no minimum balance to avoid fees, no interest earned and no extras such as overdraft protection.

biweekly mortgage   Home loan in which borrower makes the equivalent of half the monthly payment every two weeks for a total of 26 payments each year. Payment method is touted as a faster way to pay off a mortgage and thus save money, but expect to pay an upfront fee of $300 and an administration fee with each payment.

blue-chip stock   Stock issued by a well-known and financially secure corporation that pays steady dividends in good and bad times.

bond   An IOU issued by a corporation or government entity that pays back principal and interest over time. The yield on a bond depends on a number of factors including the creditworthiness of the issuer and the term of the bond.

bounced-check charge   Also known as a non-sufficient funds (NSF) charge, the amount a bank charges when there is not enough money to cover payment of a check. This charge has become a source of big profits for many banks.

capital gain   Profit on the sale of a stock or other asset calculated by subtracting the purchase price from the selling price. When calculated for tax purposes, expenses that can affect the gain are figured in.

ARM caps   The maximum number of percentage points the rate on an adjustable-rate mortgage can rise or fall on a periodic basis and in total. On a one-year ARM, for example, the caps are usually 2 percent annually and 6 percent over the life of loan.

cash advance   Cash withdrawal made using a credit card. The interest rate is usually higher than that on card purchases.

cash-value life insurance   Combination of life insurance and savings account in one policy. Most of the premium goes toward life insurance and a few bucks are deposited into an account that is supposed to grow in value over time.

certificate of deposit (CD)   Time deposit at a bank that pays interest over a term as short as seven days and as long as 10 years. Except in certain circumstances, a penalty is charged for withdrawing the principal before the term ends.

checking account   Liquid bank account on which holders write checks and sometimes earn interest. At a credit union, the account is called a share draft account.

closed-end mutual fund   Mutual fund that has a fixed number of shares, and therefore, its share price rises and falls based on demand, not the value of the fund's investments. Most mutual funds are open end and thus add shares with each investor purchase.

closing costs   Charges associated with funding a mortgage include points, recording fees, documentary stamps, mortgage insurance, document preparation and inspections. Some of the charges are factored into the annual percentage rate.

commodity   A bulk good such as grain, oil, and gold that's traded on an exchange market or for cash. The most popular exchange is in Chicago.

Community Home Buyer's Program   A Fannie Mae-sponsored program for helping homebuyers. Traditionally, the program requires 5 percent down payment with 2 percent coming as a gift from family or friends, but there are also 100 percent loan programs.

Consumer Confidence Index   Measure of consumer sentiment about the current and future state of the economy reported monthly by the Conference Board.

Consumer Price Index   A periodic figure issued by the U.S. Department of Labor that measures changes in the cost of living on a scale. The stock market closely watches this measure of inflation.

convertible bond   A corporate debt that allows the bondholder to convert some or the entire amount owed into company stock.

corporate bond   An IOU from the company that repays the amount borrowed plus interest over a stated period of time.

coupon rate   Bond rate that is either fixed for a period of time or floats with a predetermined index.

credit and debt counseling   Practice of helping consumers manage the level and payment of their debts. Because the quality of counseling varies widely, consumers should investigate the background of a credit counseling firm before signing up for its services.

credit history   Record maintained by a credit rating agency of a consumer's debts, payment history and other information. Lenders use the data to determine whether or not to extend credit to a borrower.

credit life and credit disability policies Sold by credit card companies, such as Visa and MasterCard, those policies pay a small monthly income in case of disability or a small benefit in case of death to pay toward a loan balance. Consumers get better benefits from disability or life insurance.

credit-life insurance High-cost coverage that pays off debts in the event the policy-holder dies. Insurance experts point out that of every $1 people spend on this protection, only 40 cents is paid out in claims. Most people don't need the insurance, as life insurance policies or other assets already cover debts.

credit limit The maximum dollar amount that can be borrowed against a credit line. Some credit card issuers charge a penalty for exceeding that amount.

credit report Record produced by credit rating agencies for potential lenders. Consumers should check their report for inaccuracies at least once a year.

credit union Not-for-profit financial institution owned and controlled by people called members who share a common bond such as work, faith, family or geography.

currency risk The risk that the exchange rate will change for the worse between the date that money is converted to another currency and the date the money is converted back.

current market value The dollar value of an investment if it were sold today versus what it was purchased for or its value for accounting purposes.

cyclical stock A stock whose price follows economic cycles. For example, share prices of companies in the leisure travel industry tend to rise during periods of prosperity and fall during recessions.

debit card A bank-issued card that looks and works like a credit card, but deducts the amount purchased from a checking account. Most debit cards also work as ATM cards.

debt consolidation loan Although this loan reduces the number of debt payments to one check, it's rarely a good deal. About 80 percent of the time, you'll only wind up more deeply in debt.

defined benefit plan Retirement plan that guarantees you will receive a fixed monthly sum at retirement for the rest of your life.

defined contribution plan Company-sponsored retirement plan based on what the assets in the plan will purchase at the time you retire.

disability insurance Coverage that pays a percentage of income lost due to an injury or some other cause that prevents you from working part or full time.

discount rate The interest rate that the Federal Reserve charges banks to borrow money. The figure is widely watched as an indicator of interest rate trends and is used to set business and consumer loan rates.

dividend A corporation's profit payment on each share of its stock. The dividend can fluctuate, though some companies make a practice of paying the same amount.

dividend reinvestment program (DRIP)   Corporate-sponsored plan by which shareholders use their dividends to buy more company stock at no commission.

dollar-cost averaging   An investment strategy in which you make fixed, regular investments in a stock or mutual fund regardless of whether the market is rising or falling.

Dow Jones Industrial Average (DJIA)   Daily average of closing stock prices of 50 large companies trading on the New York Stock Exchange. Index is widely watched as an indicator of stock market trends.

down payment   The amount you must pay to secure financing for the remainder of the purchase of a car, home or other possession. The figure is usually expressed as a percentage of the purchase price.

ex-dividend date   For stocks, the four days before the record date that investors who purchase the stock for regular-way—three-day—settlement are no longer entitled to receive the dividend. During this period, stocks usually trade at a slight discount.

expense ratios   Typically expressed as a percentage of total investment, what shareholders pay toward mutual fund operating expenses.

extended warranty   Private warranty that covers damages and other problems with goods after a manufacturer's warranty expires. Usually a poor value except for protection on items that are easily damaged and expensive to fix, such as a laptop computer.

face value   The listed dollar amount of a stock, bond or other equity. The current or market value may be much different.

Federal Deposit Insurance Corporation (FDIC)   Federal agency responsible for protecting deposits at U.S. banks. Insurance is limited to $100,000 per person at each institution, but additional coverage is available through combinations of account ownership.

federal funds rate   Rate charged by banks to borrow money from each other. This figure is widely watched to determine interest rate trends and is used to set business and consumer loan rates.

Federal Housing Administration (FHA)   Agency that guarantees payments on mortgages under several different programs. The dollar amount is capped based on home price and varies by region of the country.

Federal Reserve   Independent federal agency whose board sets U.S. monetary policy and a variety of interest rates including the discount rate and federal funds rate. The Fed, as it is known, also writes some banking rules.

Federal Trade Commission   Agency responsible for monitoring business practices and protecting consumers against fraud and other abuse.

fee disclosure statement   Document that lists all fees and the reasons why they're imposed on a bank account.

fixed-rate credit card   A card whose annual percentage rate does not change. However, the card issuer can, with 15 or more days' notice, alter the rate from time to time. An alternative is a variable-rate card.

fixed-rate mortgage   Home loan in which the rate and, therefore in most cases, the payment does not change. An alternative is an adjustable-rate mortgage.

front-end installment loan   Loan in which the monthly interest charge is based on the original amount owed, not the current balance or some other formula that reduces the amount of interest with each payment.

gold, platinum, and titanium credit cards   Upscale credit cards that require a higher income and stronger credit history and provide perks such as emergency roadside service, buyer protection plans and travel services. Some cards pay bonuses in terms of airline miles or case for each dollar charged.

grace period   The number of days you have to pay off all new purchases charged to a credit card without a finance charge. The number of days varies by card issuer and may be eliminated in certain circumstances.

growth stock   Stock of a company that has maintained faster-than-average gains in earnings and profits over the last few years and whose outlook, while not certain, suggests that the trend will continue. Some mutual funds invest partly or completely in growth stocks.

home equity line of credit (HELOC)   A form of a second mortgage that works more like a credit card in that you can borrow money, pay it back and borrow again without getting a new loan each time.

home equity loan   A fresher name for a second mortgage. You borrow a set amount and pay it off over a set time period.

I-Bond   U.S. savings bond whose rate is indexed to the Consumer Price Index and is sold in denominations as low as $50.

identity theft   Increasing danger to all Americans of having their Social Security numbers and other private information stolen and used by criminals and used to create fake identities. Victims can be robbed of their savings or falsely saddled with responsibility for credit card purchases.

income stock   Stock that pays a high dividend relative to its share price. Mutual funds purchase these stocks for investors looking more for income than appreciation.

initial public offering   First sale of a company's stock to the general public. Offerings carry large risk, as the stock's performance is unknown.

interest-bearing checking account   Checking account that pays interest and usually has a higher minimum balance and other requirements to avoid fees.

Individual Retirement Account (IRA)   Retirement account for working and non-working people that allows contributions of earned income to grow on a tax-deferred basis until age $70^{1}/_{2}$.

junk bond   Corporate bond that offers a higher yield usually because there's a higher risk related to repayment of principal or source of income to pay interest.

Keogh account   Retirement account for self-employed people that has defined benefit and defined contribution plans.

leading economic indicators   Issued monthly, a widely watched index of 10 economic indicators that together predict economic activity six to nine months in advance.

level-premium term insurance   Life insurance policy in which the issuer projects that the annual premium will remain the same for 5, 10, or 20 years.

liabilities   Everything you owe at a given time including auto loans, student loans and mortgage, even outstanding bills such as those on credit cards.

London InterBank Offered Rate (LIBOR)   Rate that international banks charge to borrow money from each other. This widely watched, volatile rate is used an index on business and consumer loans.

lifeline accounts   Designed for low-income folks such a senior citizens, this account has monthly fees up to $6, low or no minimum deposit and allows a small number of checks per month with no fee.

liquid account   A bank account from which you can withdraw money at any time without a penalty.

load fund   Mutual fund that charges a sales commission.

management fee   Money paid to the portfolio manager of a mutual fund. Typical management fee expenses run about $1/2$ percent.

market risk   The danger of gaining or losing money on investments due to the ups and downs of the financial markets.

maturity date   Day when your principal is due to be returned to you. This date can apply to a bond, CD or other fixed-term investment.

Money Market Account (MMA)   Bank account that usually pays higher yield than a checking account, but limits you to three checks a month to parties other than yourself. MMAs often have higher minimums to open and avoid a below-balance charge than checking accounts.

Money Market mutual fund (MMF)   Similar to a MMA, a mutual fund with check-writing privileges.

mortgage broker   A company that brings home lenders and individuals together. A broker is not the same as a mortgage banker, which is connected with a financial institution and can fund a loan.

mortgage company   An organization that specializes only in mortgages. It can be affiliated with a bank.

municipal bond   A debt obligation issued by a town or city. It often has the lowest interest rates of all bonds because the interest payments are exempt from federal taxes.

mutual fund   Pool of money collected from investors that is invested by professionals in stocks and bonds. Investors own shares in the fund, which has a specific investment goal such as income or appreciation.

NASDAQ Composite Index   Measure of the value of all stocks traded on NASDAQ. The index is commonly used to track technology stocks.

National Credit Union Administration (NCUA)   Federal agency that insures deposits at federal and state-chartered credit unions much the same way that the FDIC insures bank deposits

no-load fund   Mutual fund that does not charge shareholders a sales commission. However, the fund may have costs such as management fees or advertising expenses.

odd lot   A term used in buying or selling stock in which the number of company shares does not equal a multiple of 100. Stockbrokers usually charge higher fees to buy or sell odd lots. Share orders divisible by 100 are known as round lots.

overdraft protection   A bank service that covers payment on a check when there is not enough money in the account. The bank loans money to you at interest and may also charge fees for the service.

over-limit fee   Charge for exceeding the maximum balance you can carry on a credit card.

principal, interest, taxes, and insurance (PITI)   The four main elements of a monthly mortgage payment. The principal and interest are applied to the mortgage and the taxes and insurance are deposited in separate accounts and used to pay those costs on a periodic basis.

prime rate   Traditionally, the rate banks charge their best business customers. The rate is also an index for consumer loans, in particular HELOCs.

Private Mortgage Insurance (PMI)   A policy that lenders require if homebuyers make a down payment of less than 20 percent. PMI normally adds between $20 and $100 to the monthly payment and the insurance guarantees loan repayment if the borrower defaults. Under federal law, borrowers can apply to have PMI dropped once their equity in the home exceeds 20 percent of the property's value.

profit-earnings ratio   The value of stock derived by dividing the price by its earnings per share. The figure is often used to determine whether stock is overvalued.

profit-sharing plan   Employer plan in which the company deposits part of its profits each year into each worker's account. The company can change the rate of contributions, based on profits, or eliminate them in any year.

reverse mortgage   The opposite of a regular mortgage, it pays money to a homeowner based on a loan guaranteed by the house. The borrower must be 62 years or older and the home must be almost free of other debts, and without any tax liens.

rollover IRA   An individual retirement account created when a worker leaves a job and deposits the assets of a former employer's 401(k). A rollover IRA avoids taxes, penalties, or fees and helps with tax records by keeping funds from the employer plan separate from those in a personal IRA.

Roth IRA   Similar to a traditional IRA with two distinctions. First, there's no tax deduction for making a contribution. Second, withdrawals at retirement are tax free.

Rule of 78   A complicated formula for calculating the interest component of monthly loan payments. Percentages vary by state law, but generally most of the early payments go toward interest.

Standard & Poor's 500   An index of 500 stock prices widely watched to determine trends in the stock market. Some mutual funds tailor their portfolio to the index.

savings account   A bank account that pays interest and has no check-writing privileges. Some accounts do have ATM cards.

secured credit card   Designed for folks with a poor or no credit history, a card opened by depositing funds in a savings account. The money is used as a payment guarantee.

Simplified Employee Pension IRA (SEP-IRA)   A form of IRA for self-employed people that's easier to understand and administer than a Keogh.

Series EE savings bond   A popular type of U.S. savings bond whose purchase price is 50 percent of the face value amount and whose rate changes on May 1 and November 1 of each year.

simple interest loan   Loan whose interest payments are based on the remaining balance.

single-premium life insurance   Coverage purchased by making one payment. Policy best benefits a person who is older and has a lump sum to invest on a tax-deferred basis that meets federal tax guidelines.

small cap stock   Stock of a company whose market capitalization (stock price times number of shares) is $250 million to $1 billion. Small cap mutual funds are popular with investors looking for fast growth and who can tolerate high market risk.

Social Security   A contributory social insurance program that provides benefits to millions of Americans. Workers contribute to the system during their careers and earn entitlement to family benefits upon retirement, disability, or death.

sub-prime loan   Loan offered to people with poor or no credit. The rate is usually much higher than that for borrowers with good credit histories.

term life insurance   Life insurance protection for a specific period of time or term.

treasury-only money fund   A mutual fund that invests only in short-term U.S. Treasuries, and whose interest is exempt from state and local income taxes. In contrast, a government-only money fund invests both in Treasuries and obligations of federal agencies.

Treasury STRIPs   An increasingly popular way to invest for appreciation, these Treasury securities are sold at a deep discount to their face value because they pay no interest and mature at full value.

U.S. agency bond   Bond issued by a government agency, but unlike a Treasury is not backed by the full faith and credit of the U.S. government.

U.S. savings bond   A debt obligation that's popular with small savers. Savings bonds can be purchased for as little as $50. There are both Series EE and Series HH bonds. You can exchange EE bonds purchased before January 2003 for HH Bonds and earn tax-exempt interest on them.

U.S. treasury   A debt obligation issued by the federal government. There are bills, notes and bonds that can be as long as 30 years. Because repayment is guaranteed, some safety-oriented money market funds invest only in treasuries.

universal life insurance   A policy with the flexibility to change the premium payment or the amount of the death benefit as long as certain minimum requirements are met.

variable life insurance   A policy whose annual premiums are fixed and the cash value of the account doesn't earn a fixed rate of return. The account's growth depends on the return on investments chosen by the policyholder.

variable-rate credit card   Card whose rate changes on a periodic basis with a broadly published index. Variable-rate cards usually have lower rates than fixed-rate cards.

vesting schedule   The timetable on a 401(k) plan that determines how much and what percentage of employer matched contributions an employee is entitled to. Typically, a period of five years is required to be fully vested.

Veteran's Administration loan   Usually called a VA loan, this type of mortgage is federally insured or guaranteed, has no down payment and has some of the same features as an FHA loan. Borrowers must have current or previous military service to be eligible.

whole life insurance   Policy in which the premium and death benefit are fixed. Because in the early years the premium is greater than what's needed to pay the death benefit, the surplus funds are invested on a tax-deferred basis.

yield to maturity (YTM)   Measure of the total return you can expect if you hold a bond until maturity.

zero-coupon bond   U.S. Treasury bond issued with no coupon rate. Investors buy those bonds at a deep discount from their face value.

Index